Best Hikes Near
PORTLAND

HELP US KEEP THIS GUIDE UP TO DATE

Every effort has been made by the author and editors to make this guide as accurate and useful as possible. However, many things can change after a guide is published—trails are rerouted, regulations change, techniques evolve, facilities come under new management, and so on.

We would appreciate your comments concerning your experiences with this guide and how you feel it could be improved and kept up to date. While we may not be able to respond to all comments and suggestions, we'll take them to heart, and we'll also make certain to share them with the author. Please send your comments and suggestions to the following address:

The Globe Pequot Press
Reader Response/Editorial Department
P.O. Box 480
Guilford, CT 06437

Or you may e-mail us at: editorial@globepequot.com

Thanks for your input, and happy trails!

Best Hikes Near PORTLAND

FRED BARSTAD

FALCONGUIDES®

GUILFORD, CONNECTICUT
HELENA, MONTANA

AN IMPRINT OF THE GLOBE PEQUOT PRESS

FALCONGUIDES®

Interior photos by Fred Barstad

Art on page iii © Shutterstock

Text design by Sheryl P. Kober

Maps by Tim Kissel, Trailhead Graphics Inc. © Morris Book Publishing, LLC

Library of Congress Cataloging-in-Publication Data is available on file.

ISBN 978-0-7627-4604-0

Printed in China

10 9 8 7 6 5 4 3 2 1

Contents

Overview

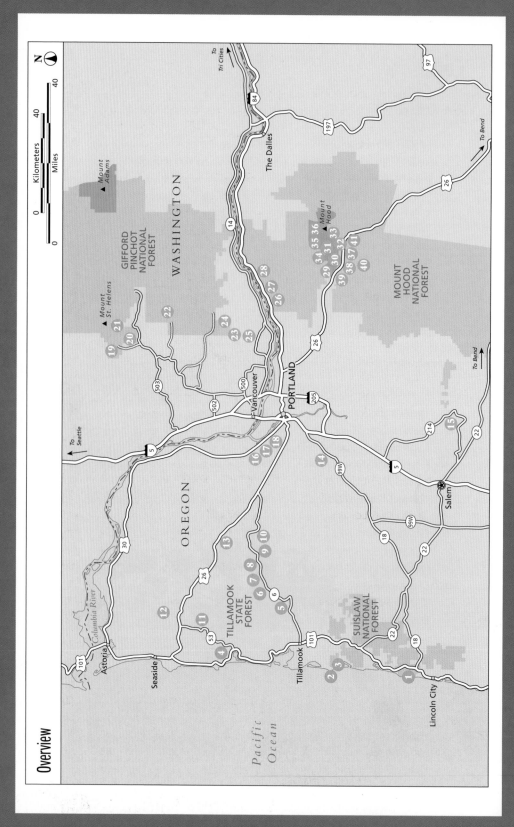

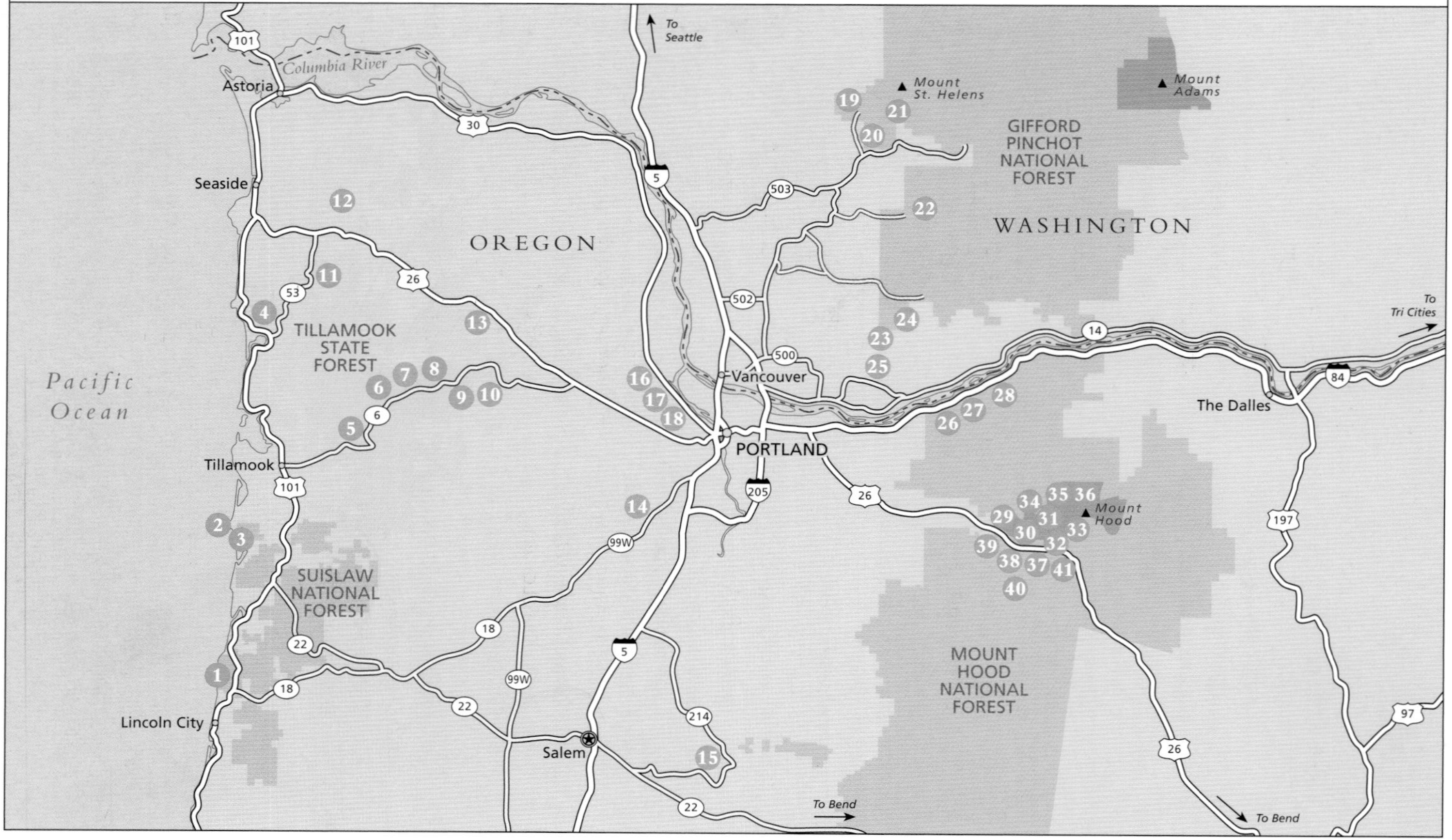

0 Kilometers 40
0 Miles 40
N
To Seattle
To Tri Cities
To Bend
To Bend
Columbia River
Pacific Ocean
OREGON
WASHINGTON
GIFFORD PINCHOT NATIONAL FOREST
MOUNT HOOD NATIONAL FOREST
TILLAMOOK STATE FOREST
SUISLAW NATIONAL FOREST
Mount St. Helens
Mount Adams
Mount Hood
Astoria
Seaside
Tillamook
Lincoln City
Salem
PORTLAND
Vancouver
The Dalles
101
30
5
503
502
500
14
84
197
97
26
205
99W
18
22
214
53
6
1 2 3 4 5 6 7 8 9 10 11 12 13 14 15 16 17 18 19 20 21 22 23 24 25 26 27 28 29 30 31 32 33 34 35 36 37 38 39 40 41

Acknowledgments

I would like to thank Dave Kaufman, Karla Evans, and Marq Box for hiking with me on these trails. Thanks to Randy Peterson, ODF Recreation project manager for the eastern part of Tillamook State Forest; Larry Sprouse, ODF Support Unit Forester for the Astoria District Clatsop State Forest; and Mary Ellen Fitzgerald, R6 USFS coordinator, for reviewing portions of the text. Thanks to Marie Deuell for information on Forest Park. Thanks also to the Forest Service employees at the Zigzag Ranger Station and Mount St. Helens National Volcanic Monument Headquarters for furnishing road and trail information. Most of all, thanks to my wife, Sue Barstad, for hiking and camping with me and editing the raw text.

Introduction

Whether you wish to hike to an isolated Pacific Ocean beach, tromp through the lush rain forest to the rugged peaks of the Coast Range, climb into the subalpine country on the western slopes of Mount Hood, or ascend to the summit of an active volcano, hikes within an hour's drive (or slightly more) of the greater Portland metropolitan area offer it all.

> **An isolated beach, lush rain forest, rugged peak, subalpine country, the summit of an active volcano—Greater Portland has it all!**

The coastal and most of the Coast Range hikes, as well as the hikes within the Willamette Valley, are generally snow-free year-round. Although you may need rain gear in the winter and spring, these walks can be very pleasant at all times of the year.

At higher elevations the trips into the Cascade Range are generally snow-free from mid-June through October. Several of these hikes lead you into superb subalpine territory, with fantastic views of the fire peaks of the High Cascades. The highest and probably the most strenuous of these hikes takes you to the summit of Mount St. Helens.

Besides the out-of-town hikes, Forest Park, within the city, has more than 50 miles of trails available to hikers. Slightly farther from downtown, the spectacular Columbia River Gorge, with its dark basalt cliffs and magnificent waterfalls, is laced with forest trails just waiting for the hiker's boots.

Geography and Climate

Within an hour's drive of Portland, a wide range of geographic features can be found. At the western edge of this region are the Pacific Ocean beaches and in a few spots, mostly near the mouths of major rivers, a coastal plain. Very close to the beaches and in some cases all the way to the breakers, forming exposed headlands, is the Coast Range, which has even heavier rainfall than the coast itself. East of the Coast Range the low and fertile Willamette Valley, still fairly damp but much drier than the Coast Range, stretches south from Portland. Farther east the Cascade Range wrings out most of the remaining moisture from the Pacific storms. The Cascade Range is much higher than the Coast Range and in places has up to 150 inches of annual rainfall, of which a good part falls as snow. Except for the highest parts of the Cascade Range, the entire region enjoys a mild marine climate.

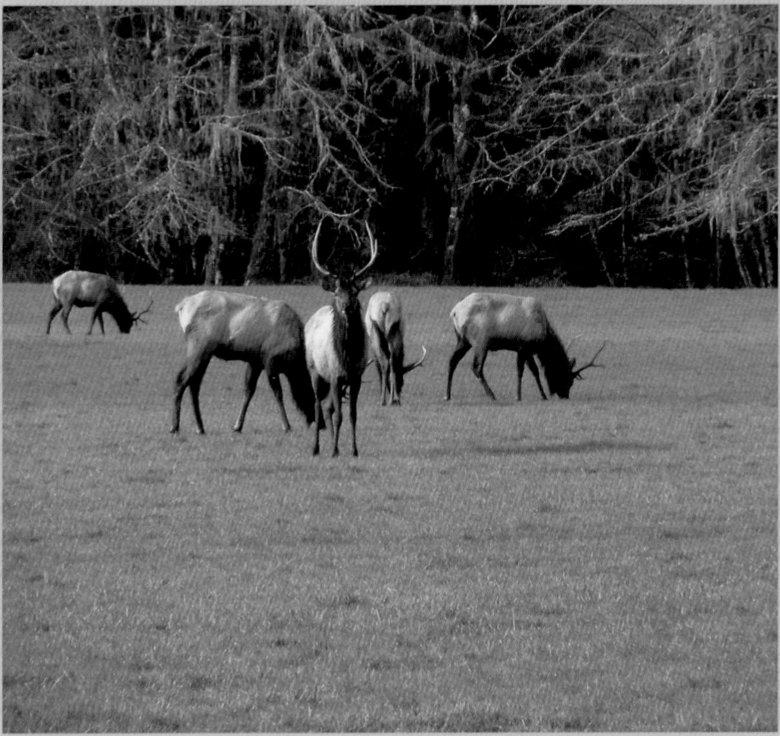

Roosevelt elk

Large Wildlife

The most common large animal in this area is the black-tailed deer (*Odocoileus hemionus columbianus*). You can expect to see them on any of the hikes described in this book, even in Forest Park, within the city of Portland.

Roosevelt elk (*Cervus elaphus roosevelti*) are the largest animals in the region. A large bull may reach half a ton in weight. The Coast Range and the area south of Mount St. Helens is prime range for these majestic animals. They are also found in smaller numbers around Mount Hood.

Black bears and cougars are possible on nearly all the hikes described in this guide, but they are shy and seldom seen.

Hazards and Being Prepared

There are a few simple things you can do that will improve your chances of staying healthy while you are on your hikes. One of the most important things to do is to be careful of your drinking-water supply. All surface water should be filtered, chemically treated, or boiled before drinking, washing utensils, or brushing your teeth with it.

Check the weather report before heading into the mountains. Inform friends or relatives of your itinerary and when you plan to return. If you are planning a long or difficult hike, be sure to get into shape ahead of time. This will make your trip much more pleasant as well as safer. Of all the safety tips, the most important is to take your brain with you when you go into the wilderness. Without it, no tips will help, and with it, almost any obstacle can be avoided or overcome. Think about what you are doing, be safe, and have a great time in the outdoors!

Encounters with Stock and Mountain Bikers

Meeting stock traffic is a common occurrence on a few of the trails in this region. So it's a good idea to know how to pass stock with the least possible disturbance or danger. If you come into contact with stock, try to get as far off the trail as possible. Equestrians prefer that you stand on the downhill side of the trail, but there is some question as to whether this is the safest place for a hiker. If possible, I like to get well off the trail on the uphill side. It is often a good idea to talk quietly to the horses and their riders, as this seems to calm many horses. If you have a dog with you, be sure to keep it restrained and quiet. Dogs cause many horse wrecks.

Mountain bikers use some of the trails covered in this book. It is the responsibility of bikers to yield to other users, but in some rare cases they may not see a hiker quickly enough to prevent a collision. Bikes are quiet, so the hiker should keep a careful watch for their approach.

Read the "Canine compatibility and other trail users" section at the beginning of each hike description to find out if the trail you are going to hike is open to these other users.

Forest Roads

Most of the roads leading to the trailheads described in this book are either paved or made of a reasonably good gravel surface. Rough roads requiring a high-clearance vehicle are noted in the "Finding the trailhead" section at the beginning of each hike description.

Some of the paved roads are only one lane, with turnouts. Be very careful on these roads. Because of their smooth paved surfaces, many drivers drive much too fast on them. Brush grows up to the edges of some of these roads, and sometimes this brush hangs out over part of the lane, severely limiting your sight distance.

Wilderness Regulations

The maximum size of a group traveling together in the Mount Hood or the Salmon-Huckleberry Wilderness is twelve. This includes any combination of stock and people.

Motorized vehicles and equipment are prohibited in the wilderness, as are all wheeled vehicles including bicycles, wagons, and carts. The exception to this rule is that wheelchairs are permitted if they are that person's only means of transportation. Landing of aircraft or air drops, hang gliders, and parasails are also not allowed.

Zero-Impact Hiking

Enjoy and respect this beautiful landscape. We all should do everything we can to keep it clean, beautiful, and healthy.

While you are hiking or doing anything else outdoors, remember to practice the zero-impact principles:

- Leave with everything you brought in.
- Leave no sign of your visit.
- Leave the landscape as you found it.

You'll find some Green Tips specific to the Portland area throughout this book. For information about the Leave No Trace Center for Outdoor Ethics, go to www.lnt.org.

Northwest Forest Pass and Wilderness Permits

A Northwest Forest Pass is required to park at many of the trailheads. These passes are available at any national forest office and many retail outlets. If a Northwest Forest Pass is required, it is so noted at the beginning of each hike description. A wilderness permit is necessary to enter the Mount Hood Wilderness and the Salmon River Trail in the Salmon-Huckleberry Wilderness. Wilderness permits are self-issuing and can be obtained on the trail near the wilderness boundary.

How to Use This Guide

Trail Mileage

The author personally hiked these trails, many of them in both directions. The mileage was very difficult to gauge exactly. Mileage from Forest Service signs and maps were taken into account whenever possible. Times were kept while hiking. Mileages were calculated using the approximate speed at which the author hikes over various types of trails. The mileage printed in each hike description was figured by combining these means and in some cases by pacing off the distance.

Difficulty Ratings

The trails in this book are rated easy, moderate, or strenuous based on the roughness of the trail, elevation change, and difficulty of following the route. Trail length and hiking time were not taken into account when measuring difficulty.

The trails that are rated "easy" will generally have gentle grades and are easy to follow; however, there may be short sections that are rocky or eroded. Anyone in reasonable condition can hike easy trails given enough time.

Trails rated as "moderate" will climb or descend more steeply than easy trails. They may climb 500 or 600 feet per mile and have fairly long sections that are rough or eroded. Some route-finding skills may be required to follow these trails. If route finding is required for a particular hike, the hike description will so state. A person in good physical condition can hike these trails with no problem. However, people in poor condition and small children may find them grueling.

Trails rated as "strenuous" are best left to expert backpackers and mountaineers. These trails may climb or descend 1,000 feet or more per mile and be very rough. Short sections of these trails may be very vague or nonexistent, so route-finding skills are a requirement for safe travel. In some cases there may be considerable exposure; falling from the trail or route can cause serious injury or even death. Many of these trails are not usable by parties with stock.

Maps

Take a good topo map with you on your hikes. Topo maps that cover the area are listed at the beginning of each hike description.

Trail Finder

Hike No.	Ocean Views			Along Streams			Peaks and Ridgetops			Lakes			Old-Growth Forests			Backpacking			Waterfalls		
Level	E	M	S	E	M	S	E	M	S	E	M	S	E	M	S	E	M	S	E	M	S
1		●						●													
2		●						●						●							
3		●																			
4			●																		
5				●																	
6					●												●				
7			●						●												
8						●			●									●			
9																			●		
10																					
11										●			●								
12		●						●													
13										●											
14																					

E = Easy; M = Moderate; S = Strenuous

Trail Finder

Hike No.	Ocean Views			Along Streams			Peaks and Ridgetops			Lakes			Old-Growth Forests			Backpacking			Waterfalls		
Level	E	M	S	E	M	S	E	M	S	E	M	S	E	M	S	E	M	S	E	M	S
15				●															●		
16																					
17																					
18																					
19					●			●			●						●				
20																					
21									●												
22				●												●			●		
23								●													
24								●													
25								●													
26					●			●						●						●	
27					●									●			●			●	
28					●									●			●			●	

E = Easy; M = Moderate; S = Strenuous

Trail Finder

Hike No.	Ocean Views			Along Streams			Peaks and Ridgetops			Lakes			Old-Growth Forests			Backpacking			Waterfalls		
Level	E	M	S	E	M	S	E	M	S	E	M	S	E	M	S	E	M	S	E	M	S
29								●									●				
30								●													
31								●			●						●				
32														●			●				
33											●						●				
34								●									●				
35				●															●		
36															●			●			●
37							●														
38									●									●			
39																					
40				●									●			●			●		
41								●			●										

E = Easy; M = Moderate; S = Strenuous

Map Legend

Roads

- 80 Freeway/Interstate Highway
- 101 U.S. Highway
- 1 State Highway
- 1431 Other Road
- Unpaved Road
- Towns & Cities

Trails

- Selected Route
- Trail or Fire Road
- Paved Trail or Bike Path
- Direction of Travel

Water Features

- Body of Water
- River or Creek
- Waterfall

Land Management

- State Parks & Forests
- National Parks & Forests
- Mount Hood National Forest
- Experimental Forest

Map Symbols

- 20 Trailhead
- Bridge
- Building/Point of Interest
- Campground
- Gate
- Mountain/Peak
- P Parking
- Pass
- Picnic Area
- Restroom
- Scenic View
- ? Visitor Center/Information
- N True North (Magnetic North is approximately 15.5° East)

Coastal and Coast Range Region

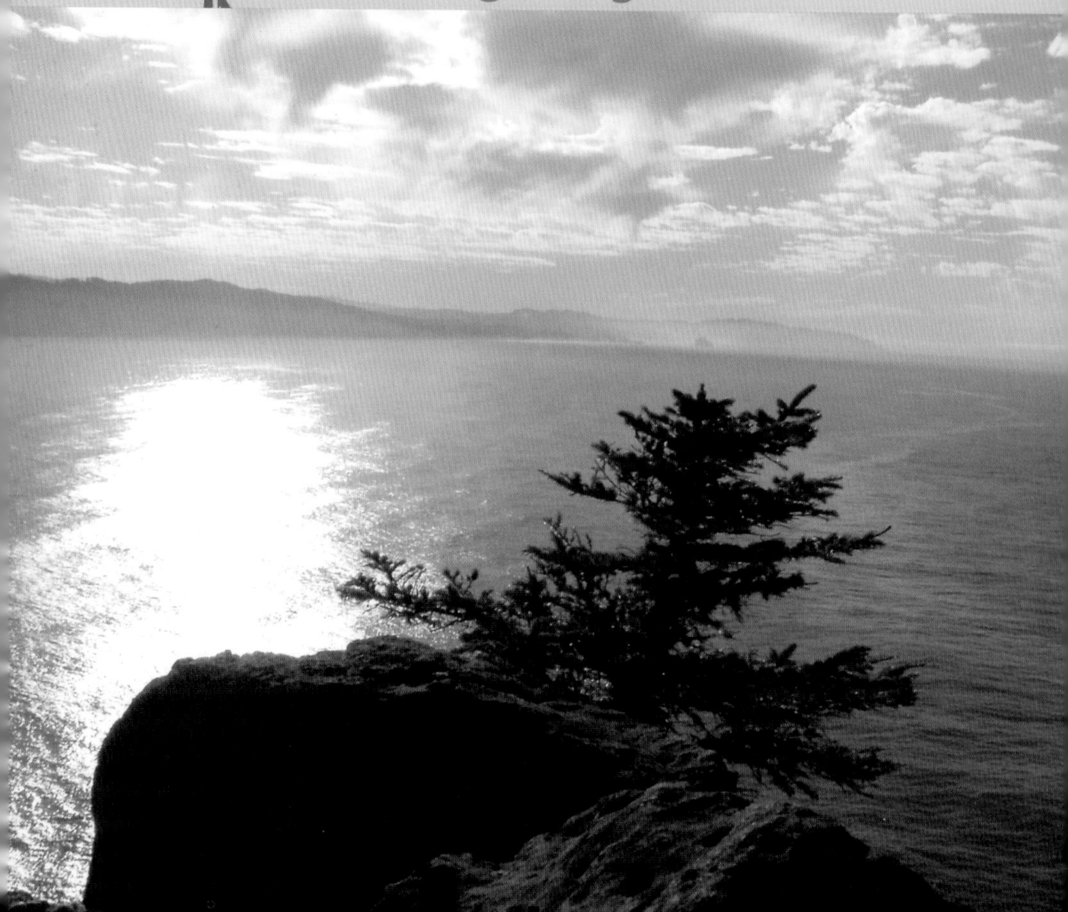

Looking south from Cascade Head

This region west and southwest of the Portland area features hikes on coastal headlands and in the lush canyons and rugged peaks of the northern Oregon Coast Range. The region is accessed by U.S. Highways 101 and 26 and Oregon Routes 18 and 6. Hikes 1, 2, and 4 take you to viewpoints high above the breakers. Hike 3 leads to a semi-secluded beach. On Hikes 7, 8, and 12, you climb to the summits of very rugged peaks, where you can take in views from the Pacific Ocean to the snow-clad peaks of the Cascade Mountains. Hikes 11 and 13 lead to lakes nestled in the forested mountains, and Hikes 5 and 6 follow the beautiful Wilson River. Hike 9 leads to a charming waterfall while Hike 10 partially follows a historic wagon road. With the exception of the hikes to the peaks, most of these routes can be hiked almost year-round.

From wild surf to rugged peaks to a charming waterfall, coastal hikes will feed your soul.

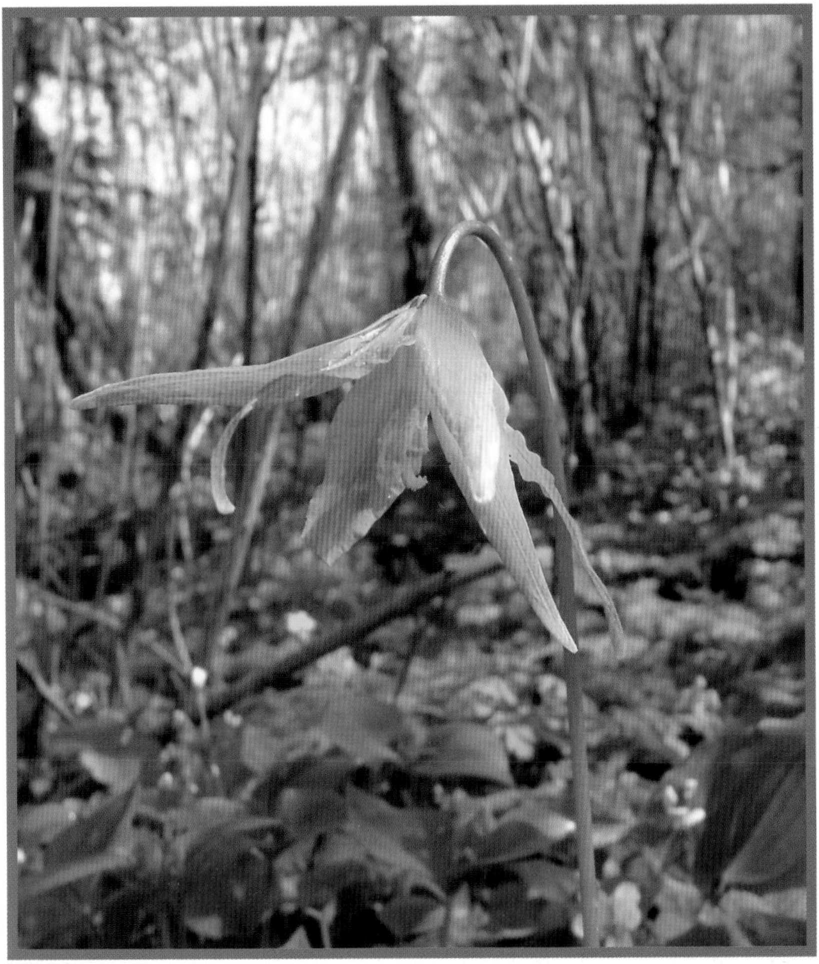

Pink fawn lily

1

The Nature Conservancy's Cascade Head Trail

Hike through the moss-hung forest to the pristine open headlands of Cascade Head. Then stop for a break or lunch at the Upper Viewpoint, and enjoy the eye-popping view from more than 1,200 feet above the crashing Pacific surf. After the break, stroll through a vigorous second-growth forest of Sitka spruce and red alder, to the trailhead on Road 1861, before returning to the Knight County Park Trailhead.

Start: Knight County Park Trailhead
Distance/type of hike: 7-mile out-and-back day hike with a shuttle option at certain times of the year
Approximate hiking time: 3.5 hours
Difficulty: Moderate to strenuous, due to steep grades and some erosion of the trail surface
Best season: Year-round
Canine compatibility and other trail users: This is a hikers-only trail. No dogs, stock, bikes, or camping are allowed.
Fees and permits: None, but a donation box is available along the trail if you wish to contribute.
Maps: The one in this book is probably all you will need for this hike. The USDA Forest Service Cascade Head Experimental Forest and Scenic Research Area pamphlet has a map that shows the area but not the trails. There is also a map on the reader board at the Knight County Park Trailhead. The National Geographic Oregon topo on CD-ROM Disk 2 covers the area and shows these trails fairly accurately. Also DeLorme's *Oregon Atlas and Gazetteer,* p. 58, D1.
Trail contacts: The Nature Conservancy, www.nature.org. Pacific Northwest Research Station, PO Box 3890, Portland, OR 97208; (503) 326-5641

Green Tip:
Keep your dog on a leash unless you are certain it can follow your voice and sight commands. Even then, keep the leash handy and your dog in sight. Do not let it approach other people and their pets unless invited to do so.

Special considerations: Please stay on the trail and do not enter the closed areas. These areas have been closed to protect the fragile environment and especially to protect the endangered Oregon silverspot butterfly. The first 0.6 mile of this trail passes through a maze of land ownerships—please stay on the trail and avoid conflicts.

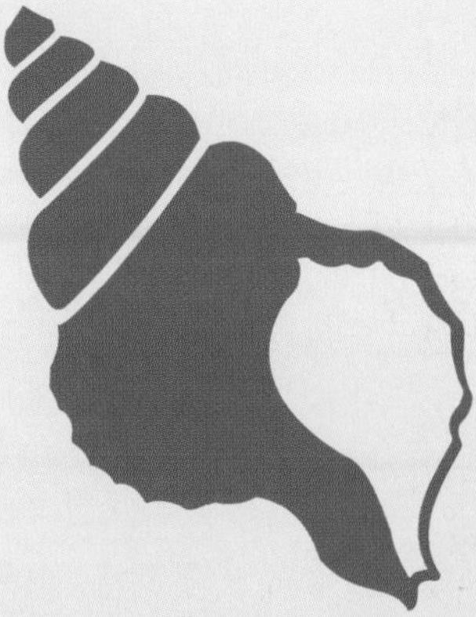

Finding the trailhead:
From southwest Portland drive Oregon Routes 99 W and 18 to McMinnville (about 30 miles). These highways run nearly parallel for a few miles near McMinnville. You can take either one, but it is generally faster to follow OR 18. From McMinnville, take OR 18 for 48 miles southwest to the junction with US 101. Turn right (north) onto US 101 and go 1.2 miles to the junction with Three Rocks Road. Turn left on Three Rocks Road and drive 2.3 miles to Knight County Park and the trailhead at the north end of the parking lot. There are adequate parking, restrooms, and a boat launch at Knight County Park.

THE HIKE

For the first 0.4 mile, this route passes through lands owned by several private landowners. Please stay on the trail at all times and respect their property rights. The USDA Forest Service, Siuslaw National Forest, and The Nature Conservancy own the rest of the land along the trail. To protect plant communities and endangered species, much of the land owned by The Nature Conservancy is also closed to public entry. The main trail is open but side paths are not. The entire area is part of the Cascade Head Experimental Forest and Scenic Research Area.

From this nearly sea-level start, The Nature Conservancy's Cascade Head Trail parallels Three Rocks Road northeasterly for a short distance, through the alder trees and sword ferns. The trail soon crosses Three Rocks Road, then begins to climb as it parallels Savage Road. Soon the track becomes a boardwalk for a few yards. Below and to the right flows a sluggish stream. The course soon crosses a small wooden bridge as you traverse the moss-hung forest. After following another short board-

1

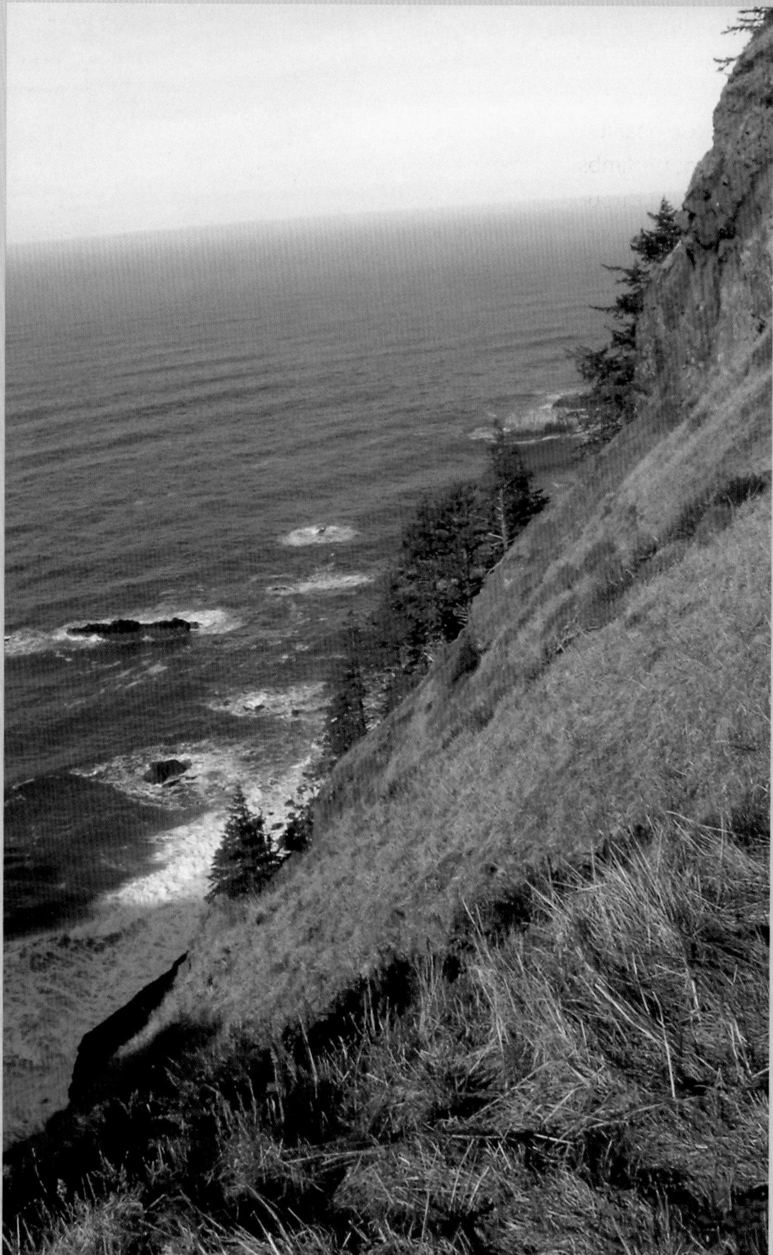

Steep slope on Cascade Head

walk, the tread climbs moderately, makes a switchback, and then crosses Savage Road. The track then descends slightly along Savage Road before recrossing it to reach the old Cascade Head Trailhead. The old trailhead is approximately 0.4 mile from Knight County Park. Parking is no longer allowed at the old trailhead or along Savage Road near it.

The route climbs to the north, leaving the old trailhead. Steps ease the way as you ascend through the forest of Sitka spruce and red alder. After crossing a couple of short boardwalks, the course crosses a bridge, then climbs moderately for a quarter mile to another bridge. Just past this bridge there are a couple of water tanks to the left of the trail and a few yards farther along a sign to let you know that you are leaving the national forest. Did you even know that you were in the national forest in this maze of land ownerships?

Soon the route passes through an area of dense brush, then descends a few steps to a bridge over Teal Creek. A plaque on the bridge commemorates Doctors Russ Maynard and Carl Petterson, who loved Cascade Head and built this bridge in 1976. Once across the bridge the route climbs a series of wooden steps.

A little less than 0.2 mile after crossing the bridge, the track reenters the Siuslaw National Forest. A quarter mile farther along after crossing a couple more small wooden bridges, the course leaves the national forest again and enters The Nature Conservancy's Cascade Head Preserve. As you enter the preserve, there is a box next to the trail, where you can leave a donation if you like. There is also a trail register box and a reader board. Dogs, horses, bikes, motor vehicles, camping, and hunting are prohibited in the preserve.

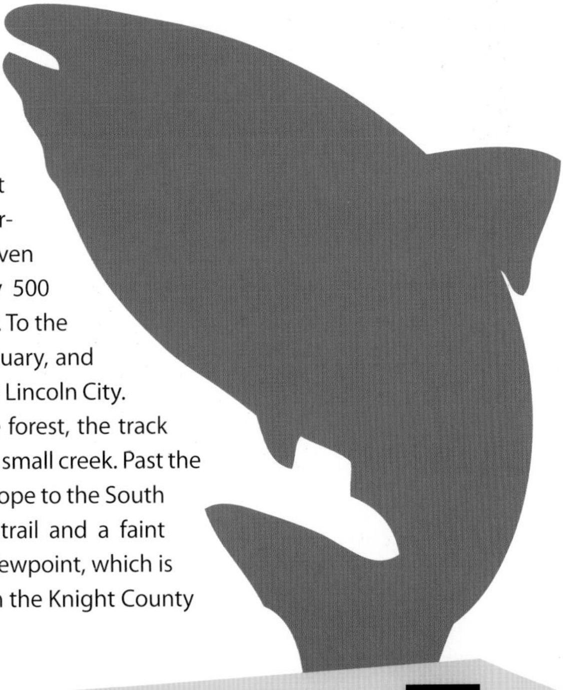

Shortly after entering the preserve, the route leaves the forest to traverse the south-facing, grass-covered slopes, called prairie headlands. Without the timber, the view becomes marvelous. You can see, hear, and even smell the ocean, which is nearly 500 feet below, to the south and west. To the southeast is the Salmon River Estuary, and far to the south along the beach is Lincoln City. About 0.25 mile after leaving the forest, the track crosses an alder-filled draw with a small creek. Past the draw the route climbs the open slope to the South Viewpoint. A switchback in the trail and a faint path to the left mark the South Viewpoint, which is at 520 feet elevation, 2 miles from the Knight County

The Nature Conservancy's Cascade Head Trail

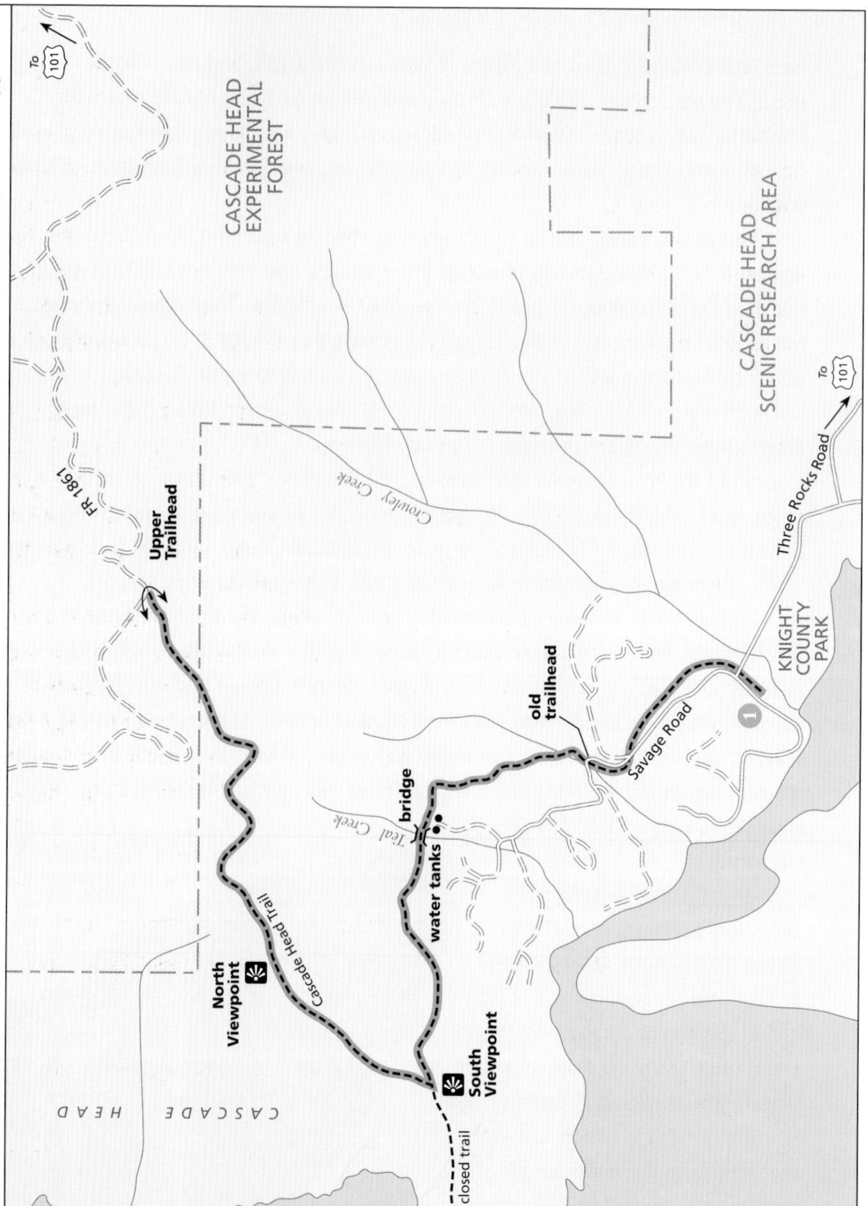

Park Trailhead. The path to the left is no longer open to the public—please stay on the main trail.

Make the switchback to the right and begin the steepest part of this hike. In the next 0.5 mile, the route climbs nearly 700 feet, making eight switchbacks along the way. Stay on the trail. As you near the top, there are some dangerous and unstable cliffs to the left. Signs mark this area. The North Viewpoint is reached at 1,217 feet elevation, 2.5 miles from the trailhead. This is the spot to stop, next to the benchmark, and eat lunch while you take in the best view on this hike. The only problem is that it is often breezy here. If it's cool and windy, put on your windbreaker before you feel the need for it. It's much easier to stay warm than to get warm.

Leaving the North Viewpoint the route descends slightly to the northeast, along the open rounded ridgetop. In 0.1 mile the trail moves to a north-facing slope and enters a dense second-growth Sitka spruce forest. A few huge rotting stumps attest to the size of the forest that once stood here. In the woods the route follows a long abandoned roadbed. Soon some red alder appears between the Sitka spruce trees, and sword ferns cover much of the forest floor.

A little less than 0.3 mile after entering the woods, the course reaches a saddle where there is a reader board, donation box, and trail register. The trail passes beneath a wooden gateway arch 0.3 mile from the saddle. Here you reenter the Siuslaw National Forest. Another 0.3 mile of hiking brings the hiker to the Road 1861 Trailhead. Road 1861 is closed to motor vehicles from January 1 to July 15. Return the way you came, unless it's between July 15 and December 31, in which case you can see the options below for an alternate way to exit.

MILES AND DIRECTIONS

0.0 Begin at the Knight County Park Trailhead. GPS 45 02.518N 123 59.531W.

0.4 Arrive at the Old Trailhead.

2.5 Stop for lunch at the North (Upper) Viewpoint and benchmark. GPS 45 03.415N 124 00.216W.

3.5 Arrive at the Upper Trailhead on Road 1861. This is the turnaround point. GPS 45 03.641N 123 59.298W.

7.0 Return to the Knight County Park Trailhead. GPS 45 02.518N 123 59.531W.

Options: From July 15 to December 31, if you want to take a car to the Road 1861 Trailhead from the Knight County Park Trailhead, first drive back to US 101. Turn left (north) and drive 2.6 miles on US 101 to the junction with Road 1861. Turn left on Road 1861 and follow it to the trailhead, which will be on the left side of the road.

2

Cape Lookout Cape Trail

The narrow and rugged ridge of Cape Lookout stretches 1.8 miles into the Pacific Ocean. The top of the cape is mostly timbered but the sides are steep to vertical cliffs that drop hundreds of feet into the wild Pacific surf. Along the hike to the end of the cape, many viewpoints offer vistas of the ocean and its beaches. About 0.5 mile west of the trailhead, a short distance to the right (north) of the trail is the site of a 1943 plane crash.

Start: Cape Lookout Trailhead
Distance/type of hike: 4.8-mile out-and-back day hike
Approximate hiking time: 2.5 hours
Difficulty: Moderate. The grade of the trail is generally easy but there are a few places where the trail surface is rough and/or muddy.
Best season: Year-round
Canine compatibility and other trail users: Restrained dogs are allowed, stock and mountain bikes are not.
Fees and permits: None
Maps: *Cape Lookout State Park Hiking Trails,* available at the campground entrance; National Geographic Oregon topo on CD-ROM Disk 2; DeLorme's's *Oregon Atlas and Gazetteer,* p. 58, B1
Trail contacts: Cape Lookout State Park, 13000 Whiskey Creek Road, Tillamook, OR 97141; (503) 842-4981
Special considerations: Much of the year the trail can be very muddy in places, making good hiking boots with lug soles essential for comfort and safety. Keep back from the cliffs and especially keep children back—in places one misstep could end in tragedy.

Finding the trailhead:
From the Portland metro area, drive west on U.S. Highway 26 to the junction with Oregon Route 6. Leave the freeway and head west on OR 6 over the Coast Range to Tillamook. Head west from Tillamook on Highway 131 for 4.9 miles, then turn left on the Three Capes Scenic Drive (signed to Cape Lookout). Follow Three Capes Scenic Drive south for 8 miles, then turn right into the trailhead parking area, which is at

approximately 800 feet elevation. There is adequate parking at the trailhead. The trailhead is 2.7 miles south of the entrance for the Cape Lookout State Park Campground.

THE HIKE

Two trails leave from the Cape Lookout Trailhead. The North Trail leads 2.3 miles north to the Cape Lookout State Park Campground. The well-maintained Cape Trail described here heads west traversing a south-facing slope, through a dense but open forest of mostly Sitka spruce. In a short distance the junction with the South Trail is reached. To the left the South Trail descends to the beach, then follows it on south to Sand Lake. Hike straight ahead at the junction, staying on the Cape Trail. The route contours along the slope for almost 0.3 mile before reaching

Trail through the salal

the ridgeline of the cape, beneath the twisted and contorted Sitka spruce and western hemlock trees. A little farther along, the course bears off the right (north) side of the ridge and descends gently. Soon the track again regains the ridgeline, allowing for an ocean view to the south.

In another 0.1 mile, after passing a benchmark, the tread crosses back to the right side of the ridge. Then the trace descends, passing some rather large Sitka spruce trees. Soon you will follow a series of boardwalks, easing the passage over wet areas, and then the route rounds a ridgeline and makes a couple of switchbacks as it descends to a couple more boardwalks, in a saddle on the ridgeline. By now you have dropped to about 430 feet elevation. Leaving the saddle, the course bears right of the ridgeline and climbs slightly. In about 0.1 mile the track makes a couple more switchbacks and regains the ridge. The trail climbs, gaining about 150 feet of elevation from the saddle to the point where it levels out near the ridgetop. The ocean comes back into view to the right and soon the tread passes the 1½-mile mark next to a short boardwalk.

Green Tip:

Consider the packaging of any products you bring with you. It's best to properly dispose of packaging at home before you hike. If you're on the trail, pack it out with you.

The trail is soon back on the left (south) side of the ridge again, where it cuts a route through low-growing Sitka spruce and western hemlock trees. Between these gnarled and contorted wind-whacked trees, salal bushes fill the voids in the vegetation. The tight growth bridges over the top of the trail in places, forming a tunnel. In other places the route is just a trench through the dense shrubbery. You must climb or step over the tree roots that cross the trail in several spots.

The route soon begins to descend gently again, making a switchback and crossing three short boardwalks. Then just to the left of the ridgeline, the course skirts the top of 400-foot-plus cliffs that drop directly into the surf. The tread crosses and recrosses the now narrower ridgeline several more times, climbing slightly. Then you descend gently to the viewpoint at the very end of Cape Lookout.

This is the place to take a break, eat a snack, or have lunch. The view to the south along the coastline is fantastic from this nearly 400-foot-high vantage point. To the west and south, a cable guardrail offers some protection from possibly slipping off the cliffs. To the north and east, a dense stand of salal brush and spruce trees block the view behind the bench. During certain times of the year, this can be a great whale-watching point.

Return by retracing your steps to the Cape Lookout Trailhead.

Cape Lookout Cape Trail

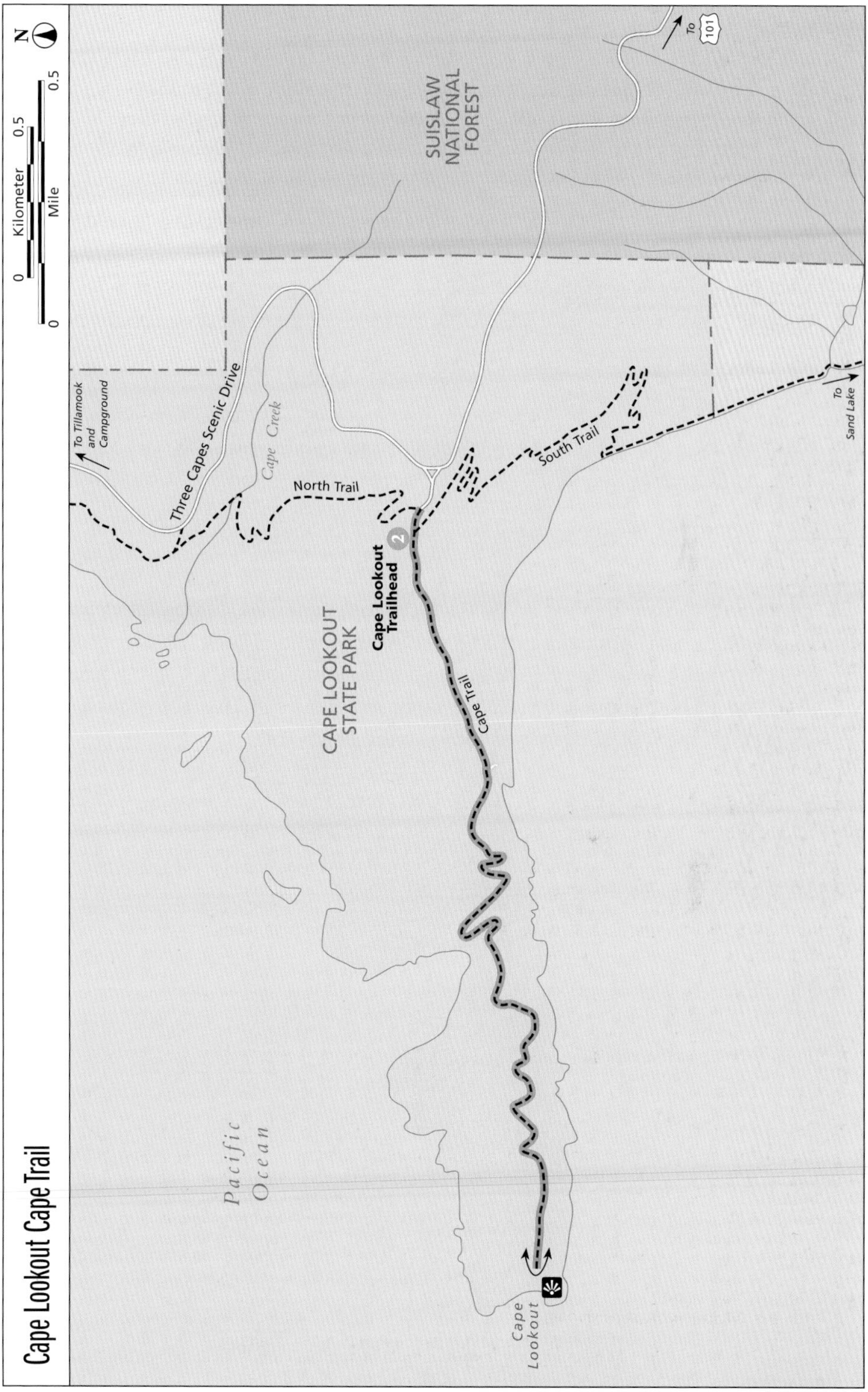

2

Gray whales migrate past Cape Lookout on their way north to their feeding grounds in the polar seas in the spring, and in the fall as they head south to the warm waters along the coast of Baja California to give birth.

MILES AND DIRECTIONS

0.0 Begin at the Cape Lookout Trailhead. GPS 45 20.477N 123 58.471W. Head west on the Cape Trail.

2.4 Arrive at the Cape Lookout Viewpoint and turn around. GPS 45 20.262N 124 00.407W.

4.8 Return to the Cape Lookout Trailhead. GPS 45 20.477N 123 58.471W.

Options: If you are camped at the Cape Lookout State Park Campground, you may want to hike from there to the viewpoint at the end of Cape Lookout. From the campground, hike south for 2.3 miles on the North Trail to the Cape Lookout Trailhead, gaining about 800 feet of elevation along the way. Then turn right and follow the Cape Trail, as described above, to the viewpoint.

3

Cape Lookout South Trail

Descend the South Trail from Cape Lookout Trailhead to a somewhat secluded beach 800 feet below. This hike offers tremendous views of the steep and rugged south face of Cape Lookout. The entire hike is through dense coastal forest.

Start: Cape Lookout Trailhead
Distance/type of hike: 3.6-mile out-and-back day hike
Approximate hiking time: 2 hours
Difficulty: Moderate. Although the trail surface is good, you must climb continuously on the return trip.
Best season: Year-round
Canine compatibility and other trail users: Restrained dogs are allowed, stock and mountain bikes are not.
Fees and permits: None
Maps: *Cape Lookout State Park Hiking Trails,* available at the campground entrance; National Geographic Oregon topo on CD-ROM Disk 2; DeLorme's *Oregon Atlas and Gazetteer,* p. 58, B1
Trail contacts: Cape Lookout State Park, 13000 Whiskey Creek Road, Tillamook, OR 97141; (503) 842-4981
Special considerations: This is a downhill hike from the trailhead to the beach, and you must hike uphill on the return. Be sure everyone in the group is up for the 800-foot return climb. Be very careful of the surf—there are no lifeguards to protect you here.

Finding the trailhead:
From the Portland metro area, drive west on U.S. Highway 26 to the junction with Oregon Route 6. Leave the freeway and drive west on OR 6 to Tillamook. Head west from Tillamook on Oregon Route 131. In 4.9 miles turn left on the Three Capes Scenic Drive (signed to Cape Lookout). Follow Three Capes Scenic Drive south for 8 miles then turn right into the trailhead parking area. There is adequate parking at the trailhead. The trailhead is 2.7 miles south of the entrance for the Cape Lookout State Park Campground.

THE HIKE

The Cape Lookout Trailhead, which is at approximately 800 feet elevation, is the starting point for two trails. To the right leaving the trailhead, the North Trail leads 2.3 miles north to the Cape Lookout Campground. The Cape Trail, which leads to the South Trail described here, heads west. To begin your hike of the South Trail, hike along the Cape Trail for a short distance to the junction with the South Trail. Then turn left on the South Trail, and begin your descent on the south-facing slope. The slope is forested with Sitka spruce and the ground is nearly covered with salal bushes and sword ferns. In just under 0.3 mile, the tread makes its first switchback. Some of the Sitka spruce here are fairly large but not really that big as Sitkas go.

The Coastal Sitka Spruce

Sitka spruce (*Picea sitchensis*) is a large tree, often reaching 180 feet in height and 8 feet in diameter. Being a coastal tree, it seldom grows more than 2 or 3 miles from the ocean. One exception to this is that Sitkas do grow in the Columbia River Gorge, more than 100 miles inland. It's easy to tell a Sitka by grasping one of its branches. The needles are very stiff and sharp and hurt if you grab them tightly.

Like all spruce, the 3-to-4-inch-long cones of a Sitka hang down from the branches. The wood of the Sitka spruce has the highest strength-to-weight ratio of any common timber tree. This increases the demand for Sitka spruce lumber and explains why most of the old-growth Sitka spruce forest has been logged.

In the next 0.4 mile, the route makes three more switchbacks. At the last of these three, there is a view to the right of the rugged and nearly vertical south face of Cape Lookout rising above the breakers. The track enters an area covered with large red alder trees in another 150 yards. You soon make a couple more switchbacks, then cross a small stream that flows through a culvert beneath the trail. To the left of the trail, this stream appears to flow from directly beneath a large Sitka spruce. There will be a bench next to the trail a little over 0.1 mile farther

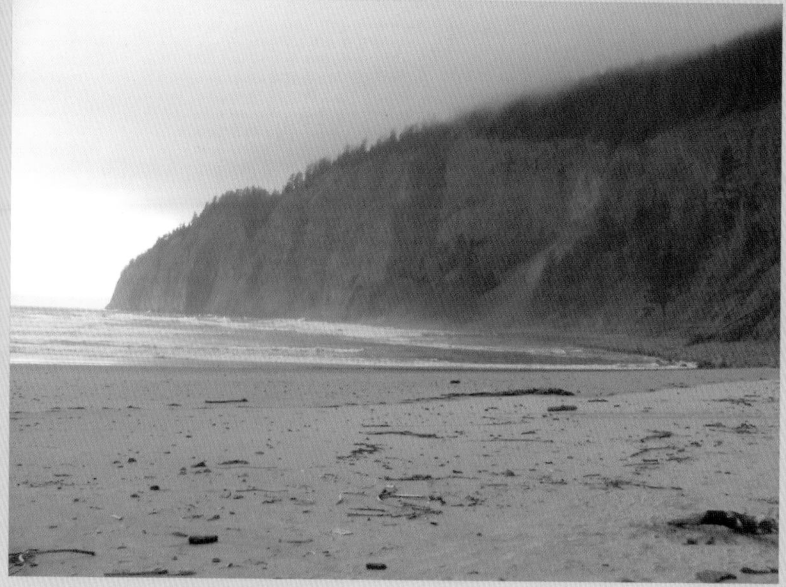

Cape Lookout from the beach

along. From the bench, there is another great view of the ocean, crashing against the dark cliffs of Cape Lookout.

The route continues downhill from the bench and viewpoint, through the now mixed forest of red alder, western hemlock, and Sitka spruce. After making five more switchbacks and descending to about 170 feet elevation, the tent frames and picnic tables of Camp Clark come into in view 100 yards to the south of the trail. The tread then makes ten more switchbacks before you reach a trail junction just above the beach. To the left at this junction it's 3.1 miles to Sand Lake. The path to the right leads a short distance to the beach. Bear right and descend the last few yards to this out-of-the-way stretch of Pacific Ocean shore. Return as you came or see the options below for an alternate return requiring a car shuttle. The return hike will probably take somewhat longer than the hike down to the beach did.

Green Tip:

Carry a reusable water container that you fill at the tap. Bottled water is expensive; lots of petroleum is used to make the plastic bottles; and they're a disposal nightmare.

Cape Lookout Cape Trail

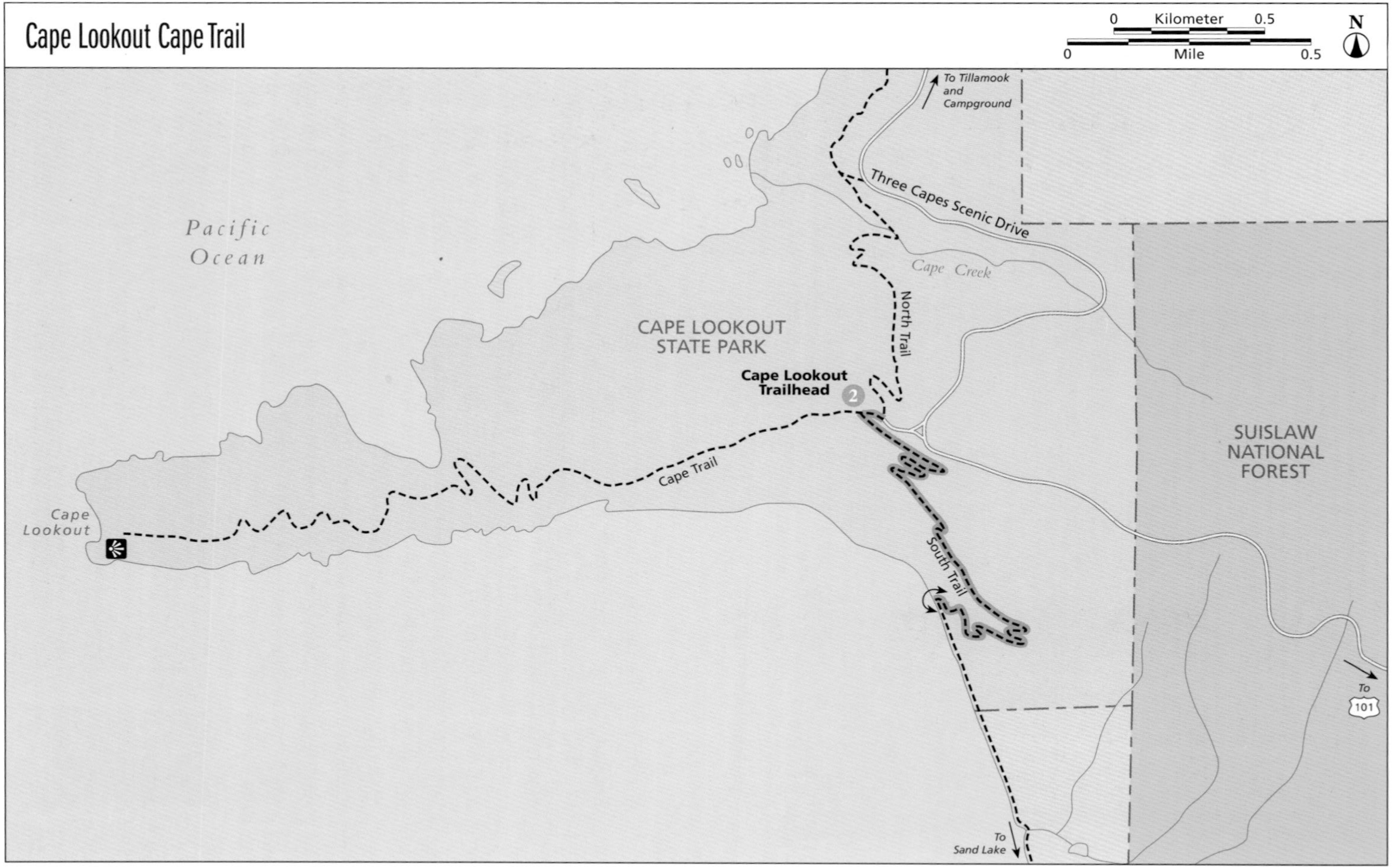

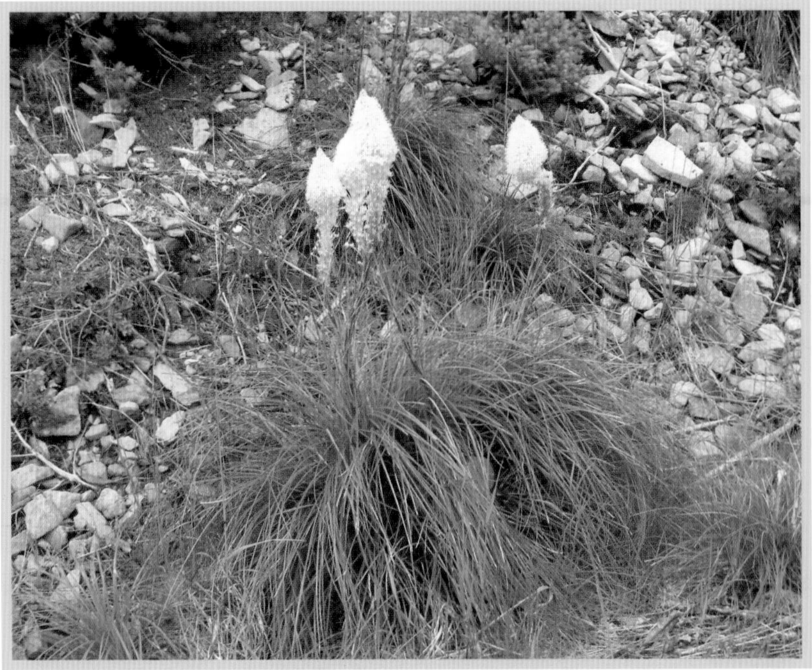

Beargrass

MILES AND DIRECTIONS

0.0 Begin at the Cape Lookout Trailhead. GPS 45 20.477N 123 58.471W. Head west then turn left on the South Trail.

1.8 Turn around at the semi-secluded beach.

3.6 Return to the Cape Lookout Trailhead. GPS 45 20.477N 123 58.471W.

Options: If you can arrange a car shuttle, the 3.1-mile hike along the beach south to Sand Lake makes a great one-way trip.

4

Neahkahnie Mountain

Neahkahnie Mountain rises abruptly from the pounding Pacific surf. In fact, a section of U.S. Highway 101 was blasted from its cliffs about 400 feet above the ocean. The steep trail to the summit starts just north of the blasted-out section, at 410 feet elevation, and winds its way through openings and dense forest to a viewpoint very close to the 1,681-foot-high summit of Neahkahnie Mountain. The Neahkahnie Mountain Trail is within Oswald West State Park and is part of the Oregon Coast Trail.

Start: North Neahkahnie Mountain Trailhead
Distance/type of hike: 5.6-mile out-and-back day hike
Approximate hiking time: 3 hours
Difficulty: Strenuous due to steep grade and sometimes rough trail surface
Best season: Year-round
Canine compatibility and other trail users: Restrained dogs are allowed, stock and mountain bikes are not.
Fees and permits: None
Maps: *Tillamook State Forest Map and Guide;* National Geographic Oregon topo on CD-ROM Disk 2; DeLorme's *Oregon Atlas and Gazetteer,* p. 64, B1
Trail contacts: Oregon State Park Information Center, (800) 551-6949; Nehalem Bay State Park, (503) 368-5154; www.oregonstateparks.org
Special considerations: Although this is a relatively short hike, it is steep in places. Good hiking boots are highly recommended, especially if the trail is wet.

Finding the trailhead:
From Portland, head west on U.S. Highway 26 to the junction with Oregon Route 53 (approximately 65 miles from downtown). Turn left (south) on OR 53 and drive 18 miles to the junction with US 101. Turn right on US 101 and go the short distance to Nehalem. Continue north on US 101 another 4.7 miles to the poorly marked North Neahkahnie Mountain Trailhead. There is parking for several cars on the left (west) side of the highway just past the trailhead, but there are no other facilities. Note that the *Tillamook State Forest Map and Guide* covers the area but shows the trail rather poorly.

THE HIKE

Walk to the south end of the parking area and carefully cross the highway to the trailhead. The route first climbs through a line of trees, then enters a slope covered with sword ferns and salal bushes.

Salal (*Gaultheria shallon*)

Salal can be either a creeping or an erect shrub. In its erect form it may reach 15 feet tall, but it is usually less than half that. Salal leaves are evergreen and leathery. The flowers are white or pink and urn-shaped. Salal, which often forms a very dense, sometimes impenetrable stand, reproduces mostly by suckering or sprouting from its roots, or by layering. Layering is when a limb lies on the ground and takes root.

Along the slope the tread follows an old abandoned phone line for a couple hundred yards, then makes a switchback to the left, away from the phone line. Arch Cape and the ocean are in view as you make the switchback. The trail makes two more switchbacks, then leaves the open slope at 690 feet elevation, 0.4 mile from the trailhead.

Leaving the open slope the route enters a forest of Sitka spruce, Douglas fir, and western hemlock. The track soon makes a couple more switchbacks then crosses a small stream in a culvert. Close to the stream grow some large old-growth trees, which have escaped logging and probably survived fires. The course makes three more switchbacks, and then the grade flattens as you traverse a section of very dense forest with lots of downed timber.

The track soon climbs again and makes a switchback to the left, at a little over 900 feet elevation, 0.9 mile from the trailhead. At this switchback there is a path that goes straight ahead but soon fades out. Be sure to make the switchback. The trail becomes a little rough just past the switchback as you climb over some tree roots. After making a couple more switchbacks, the trace traverses a slope covered with a vigorous second-growth forest of Sitka spruce and western hemlock. Beneath the straight trees, sword ferns cover the forest floor.

In places the route is quite steep and you must climb over more tree roots. You will go through a virtual tunnel cut through a grove of young hemlocks, 1.4 miles from the trailhead. Then you make another switchback and soon work your way out onto a southwest-facing slope, with the crashing Pacific Ocean some 1,400 feet below to the right. Before long the route crosses a draw, then follows a poorly defined ridgeline through a very dense and tangled stand of timber. Soon the track leaves the dense tangled timber, makes a turn to the left, and climbs the ridgeline.

4

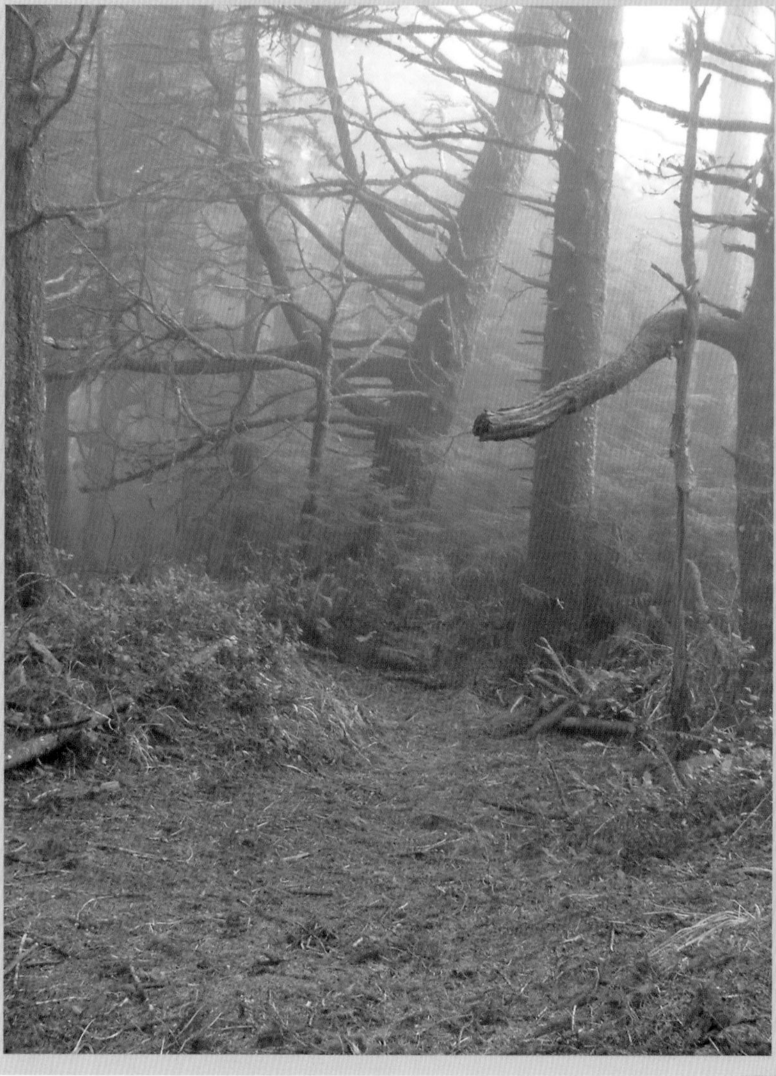

Fog-shrouded forest along Neahkahnie Mountain Trail

Soon the route bears slightly right of the ridge, then makes a couple of switchbacks. You will reach a viewpoint 0.1 mile after passing the switchbacks. The ocean view is marvelous from here. This viewpoint is at approximately 1,650 feet elevation and is 2.4 miles from the trailhead where this hike started. Although there isn't a really good place to sit here, this is the place to take a break or maybe have lunch, as this spot has the best view along the entire trail. To the right across the trail from the viewpoint, a very steep path climbs a few yards to a rocky outcrop above the

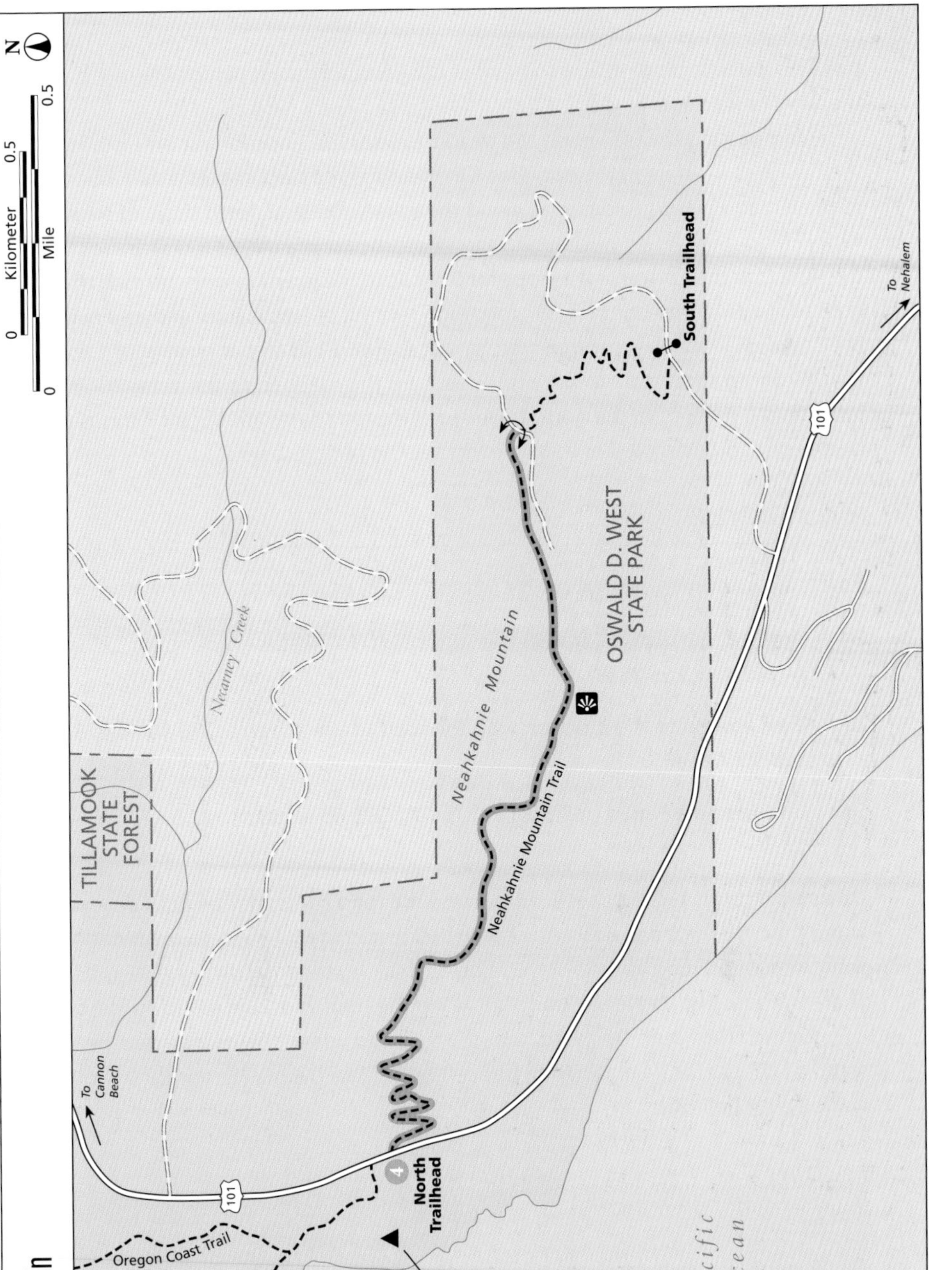
Neahkahnie Mountain
0 Kilometer 0.5
0 Mile 0.5
N
To Cannon Beach
Oregon Coast Trail
101
4
North Trailhead
Neahkahnie Mountain
Devils Cauldron
Pacific Ocean
TILLAMOOK STATE FOREST
Nearney Creek
Neahkahnie Mountain
Neahkahnie Mountain Trail
OSWALD D. WEST STATE PARK
South Trailhead
To Nehalem

trail. This is a difficult path and somewhat dangerous if its wet (which it is much of the time) or icy.

After passing the viewpoint the tread traverses the slope for a short distance, then reaches a saddle in the ridgeline. On the ridge the track makes a switchback to the left and begins to descend along the thickly forested north slope of Neahkahnie Mountain. A few yards along the slope, the course makes a switchback to the right. You then traverse the slope for 0.3 mile to the junction with the road that goes to the antennas on the 1,681-foot-high summit of Neahkahnie Mountain. By the time you reach the roadbed, you have lost about 170 feet of elevation. If you like, it's only a short walk to the right (west) up the roadbed to the summit. This junction, 2.8 miles from the north trailhead, is a good turnaround point if this is to be an out-and-back hike. For a shuttle trip, see the options below.

MILES AND DIRECTIONS

0.0 Begin at the North Trailhead on US 101. GPS 45 44.880N 123 57.734W.

2.4 Arrive at the viewpoint near the summit of Neahkahnie Mountain. GPS 45 44.603N 123 56.757W.

2.8 Turn around at the junction with the road to the summit. GPS 45 44.673N 123 56.220W.

5.6 Return to the North Trailhead on US 101. GPS 45 44.880N 123 57.734W.

Options: If this is to be a shuttle hike, cross the road and continue your descent along the trail. The tread descends about 700 feet in the 1.1 miles to the junction with the summit road at the South Trailhead, making the total distance 3.9 miles. There is a gate just above the trailhead along the road, blocking vehicle access.

To reach the South Trailhead from the trailhead where this hike started, head south on US 101 for 1.4 miles. Then turn left and follow the gravel road for 0.4 mile to the South Trailhead.

Green Tip:
Rechargeable (reusable) batteries reduce one source of toxic garbage.

5

Wilson River Trail: Footbridge Trailhead to Jones Creek Trailhead

Hike along this gentle section of the Wilson River Trail, through the lush second-growth forest, next to the always beautiful Wilson River. Bands of Roosevelt elk are often seen along this trail. An early morning hike gives you the best chance to catch a glimpse of these magnificent animals as well as other wildlife.

Start: Footbridge Trailhead
Distance/type of hike: 3.6-mile shuttle day hike
Approximate hiking time: 2 hours
Difficulty: Easy
Best season: Year-round; Footbridge Trailhead is a day-use-only area.
Canine compatibility and other trail users: Restrained dogs are allowed. This trail is open to hikers and mountain bikers; however, other uses are prohibited.

Fees and permits: None
Maps: Oregon Department of Forestry Tillamook State Forest Trail Guides, *Wilson River Trail, Jones Creek Trailhead–Keenig Creek Trailhead* and the *Tillamook State Forest Map and Guide;* National Geographic Oregon topo on CD-ROM Disk 2 (covers the area but does not show this trail); DeLorme's's *Oregon Atlas and Gazetteer,* p. 64, D4.
Trail contacts: Oregon Department of Forestry, Tillamook District Office, 5005 East Third Street, Tillamook, OR 97141-2999; (503) 824-2545; www.oregon.gov/ODF; Recorded Recreation Hotline (503) 359-7402
Special considerations: Remember that you cannot leave this trail at the Tillamook Forest Center when that facility is closed. Stop and check at the entrance for the operation times and days.

Finding the trailhead:
From the Portland metro area, drive west on U.S. Highway 26 to the junction with Oregon Route 6. Leave the freeway and head west on OR 6 for approximately 32 miles, over the summit of the Coast Range and down to the Footbridge Trailhead, at 390 feet elevation. The trailhead is on the right

(north) side of the highway some distance west of (after passing) Milepost 21. There is adequate parking and a restroom at the trailhead.

To reach the Jones Creek Trailhead, where this hike ends, backtrack to the east along OR 6 for approximately 2.5 miles, turn left (north), and cross the bridge over the Wilson River to the trailhead.

THE HIKE

The trail parallels the highway, heading west for a short distance as you leave the Footbridge Trailhead. Soon the route turns right and descends some steps before crossing a footbridge over a beautiful deep pool in the Wilson River. Once across the bridge the trail climbs out of the riverbed and soon meets the Wilson River Trail.

Turn right at the junction and head east on the Wilson River Trail. Soon the course begins to follow a long-abandoned roadbed. Beneath the mostly red-alder canopy, sword ferns cover much of the ground. You will cross a single log bridge with a handrail a little over 0.1 mile from the junction. A few Douglas firs and bigleaf maples add diversity to the alder woods. After crossing a couple more bridges over side streams, the tread begins to climb. Soon the course makes a couple of switchbacks, as it climbs to cross a ridgeline. On the ridge the track flattens for a short distance, then descends through the now mostly Douglas fir forest.

Shortly the route flattens again and traverses the slope above the Wilson River, to the creek crossing below Wilson Falls. There is no bridge here but the creek is no problem to cross. The falls are above the trail to the left at the crossing. Wilson Falls is 1.6 miles from the Footbridge Trailhead. After passing Wilson Falls, the trace descends, making a couple more switchbacks, and soon is fairly close to the Wilson River. In places you can see the Wilson River Highway across the river. Roosevelt elk are common on these flats. Their sign is often on the trail, and they can sometimes be seen. Scotch broom crowds the trail as you pass beneath some power lines.

Luebke Creek flows into the far side of the Wilson River, 0.6 mile after passing Wilson Falls. The tread passes beneath the power lines again 0.4 mile farther along, then crosses a single log bridge over Cedar Creek, a large tributary of the Wilson River. A little less than 0.4 mile farther along, the trail joins Cedar Creek Road. The GPS coordinates where the Wilson River Trail meets Cedar Creek Road are 45 34.908N 123 33. 684W. The trail follows the road for 100 yards, then bears to the right, leaving it.

Slightly less than 0.3 mile after leaving the Cedar Creek Road, the route crosses a small stream, and another 0.1 mile of gentle hiking brings you to the bridge over the Wilson River at the Tillamook Forest Center. This bridge is only open when the

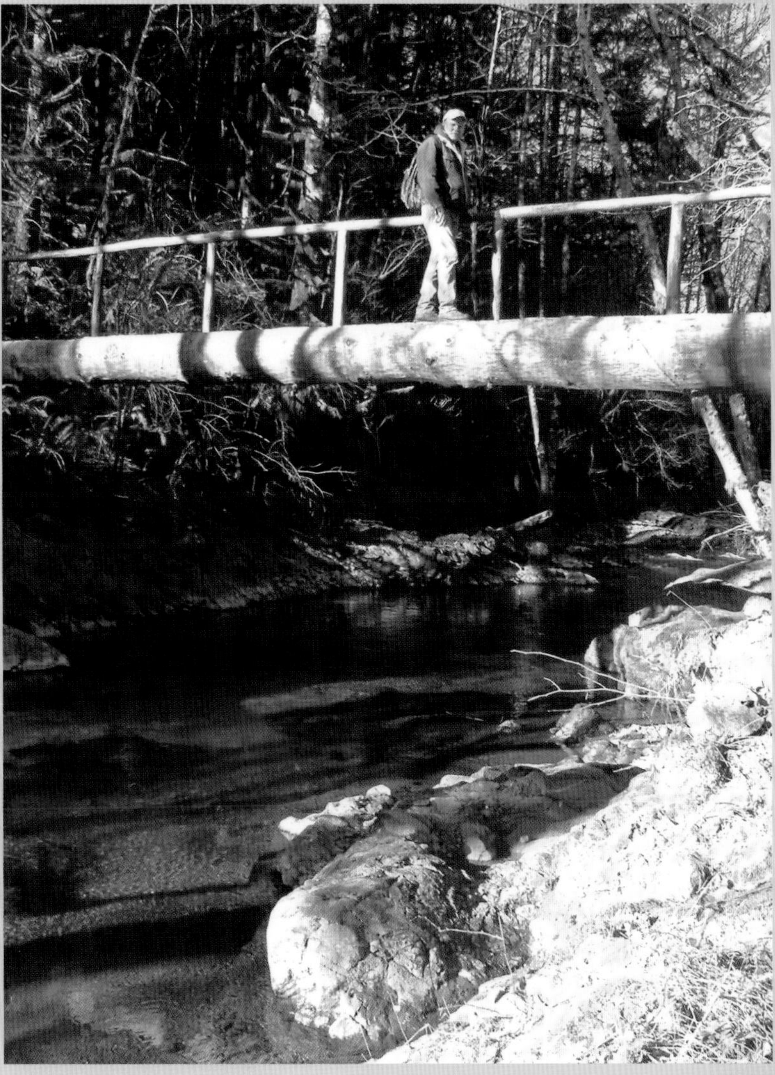

Bridge over Cedar Creek

forest center is open so if you are here early or late in the day or on the wrong day of the week, don't count on getting across the river here. At the bridge you are 3.3 miles from the Footbridge Trailhead.

If you have the time, stop at the Tillamook Forest Center and learn about the history of the Tillamook State Forest.

Wilson River Trail: Footbridge Trailhead to Jones Creek Trailhead

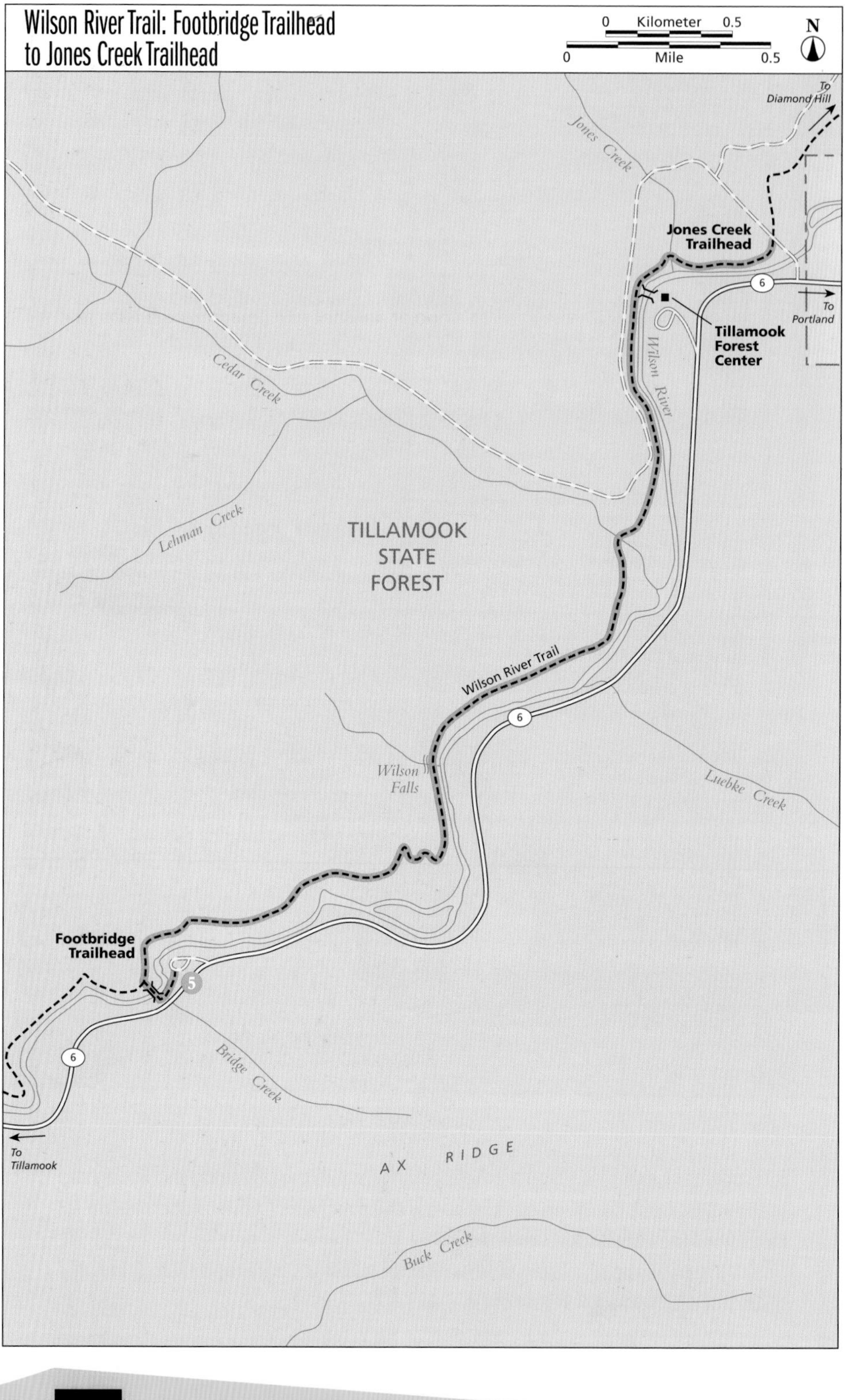

Green Tip:
Never let your dog chase wildlife.

To continue on the Wilson River Trail, head east on the gravel path. In a few yards the route crosses a small wooden bridge over a creek. In about 0.1 mile you will cross a bridge over Jones Creek. Bear right at a trail junction, just after crossing the bridge. About 150 yards farther along at another trail junction, bear left—the trail to the right goes to a day-use area. Soon the route follows a roadbed, past picnic tables and a hand water pump, where a short path to the left leads to a parking area and a restroom. Then the trail crosses a parking area at Jones Creek Trailhead. Jones Creek Trailhead is 0.3 mile from the bridge to the Tillamook Forest Center.

MILES AND DIRECTIONS

0.0 Begin at the Footbridge Trailhead. GPS 45 33.784N 123 35.118W.

0.1 Arrive at the junction with the Wilson River Trail.

1.6 Pass Wilson Falls.

2.5 Arrive at Cedar Creek.

3.3 If you have time, cross the bridge to visit the Tillamook Forest Center. GPS 45 35.217N 123 33.707W.

3.6 Arrive at the Jones Creek Campground and Trailhead. GPS 45 35.288N 123 33.328W.

Options: You can shorten this hike slightly by exiting the Wilson River Trail at the Tillamook Forest Center (if it is open).

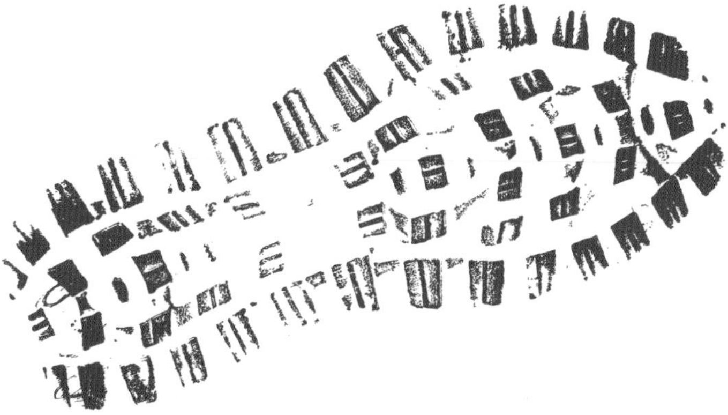

6 Wilson River Trail: Jones Creek Trailhead to Elk Creek Trailhead

This hike covers the most spectacular part of the Wilson River Trail. You climb and traverse the steep slopes above Lester Creek Canyon before descending to meet the Kings Mountain Trail. Once past the junction with the Kings Mountain Trail, the track stays closer to the Wilson River through the lush second-growth forest to the junction with the Elk Mountain Trail, then descends a short distance to the Elk Creek Campground and Trailhead.

Start: Jones Creek Trailhead
Distance/type of hike: 11-mile shuttle day hike or backpack
Approximate hiking time: 5–6 hours
Difficulty: Moderate
Best season: March through November. Some years this route may be snow-free nearly all year.
Canine compatibility and other trail users: Restrained dogs are allowed. This trail is open to hikers and mountain bikers, but other uses are prohibited.
Fees and permits: None
Maps: Oregon Department of Forestry *Tillamook State Forest Trail Guide, Wilson River Trail Elk Creek–Jones Creek Trailhead*; National Geographic Oregon topo on CD-ROM Disk 2; DeLorme's *Oregon Atlas and Gazetteer,* p. 64, D4
Trail contacts: Oregon Department of Forestry, Forest Grove District Office, 801 Gales Creek Road, Forest Grove, OR 97116; (503) 357-2191; www.oregon.gov/ODF; Recorded Recreation Hotline (503) 359-7402
Special considerations: At the Diamond Mill OHV Staging Area, there may be many off-highway vehicles driving around and making lots of noise, but don't despair: The Wilson River Trail is closed to motorized travel, and you will soon leave the commotion far behind.

Finding the trailhead:
To reach the Jones Creek Trailhead from the Portland metro area, drive west on U.S. Highway 26 for about 20 miles to the junction with Oregon Route 6. Leave the freeway and head west on OR 6 for approximately 30 miles, over the summit of the Coast Range and down to the access road for the Jones Creek Campground (Cedar Creek Road). Turn right onto Cedar Creek Road

a short distance west of (after passing) Milepost 23. Leave the highway and cross the Wilson River to the Jones Creek Campground and Trailhead. The DeLorme's *Oregon Atlas and Gazetteer* covers the area; however, the trailhead is not labeled. The National Geographic CD-ROM map also covers the area but does not show this trail. Plenty of parking and restrooms are available at the trailhead.

THE HIKE

Leaving the Jones Creek Trailhead, the Wilson River Trail angles to the left as it crosses Cedar Creek Road. Before long the trail begins to climb gently. The route crosses a single plank bridge over a creek 0.4 mile after leaving the Jones Creek Trailhead. Tiny yellow violets bloom beside this section of trail in late March. After crossing the creek, the course continues to climb gently for another 0.3 mile to the point where it crosses the North Fork Road.

After crossing the road, the trail first climbs at a moderate grade, then descends to recross the North Fork Road 1.6 miles from the Jones Creek Trailhead. After crossing the road for the second time, the route heads north between the north fork of the Wilson River and the North Fork Road. In slightly less than 0.3 mile, you will cross a creek, and the Diamond Mill OHV (off-highway vehicle) Staging Area will be to your left. At the far (north) end of the staging area, the trail will join a broad gravel path. Turn right on the path and cross the bridge over the north fork of the Wilson River.

Once across the frothing waters, the trail begins to climb and soon makes a switchback to the left. There will be a small meadow on the left side of the trail, 0.7 mile from the Diamond Mill OHV Staging Area. After passing the meadow, the route continues to climb gently through second-growth Douglas fir forest.

The course crosses a long-abandoned roadbed on a poorly defined ridgeline, at 1,160 feet elevation, 0.5 mile after leaving the small meadow. The flat area that was once a road provides a possible dry campsite if you are so inclined. The tread then continues to climb along the left side of the ridge and soon makes a switchback. A little over 0.1 mile after making the switchback, the track recrosses the ridgeline at 1,340 feet elevation. For the next 0.3 mile, the route climbs steadily, staying close to the ridgeline, and then you cross to the right side at 1,560 feet elevation. Shortly after crossing to the right side of the ridge, for the last time the timber opens up, allowing for good views into Lester Creek Canyon.

For the next 1.8 miles, the trail traverses the steep slopes around the head of Lester Creek Canyon. You cross several streams, some of them actually closer to

6

Bridge next to Diamond Mill site

being waterfalls, as you traverse the steep slopes. The route continues to climb slightly, reaching 1,860 feet elevation as you join another long-abandoned roadbed, shortly before you end the traverse.

The route crosses the ridgeline, leaving Lester Creek Canyon, 5.6 miles from the Jones Creek Trailhead, and soon bears right, leaving the roadbed. Once the Lester Creek Canyon is left behind, the route begins a steady descent through the moss-covered bigleaf maple, Douglas fir, and red alder forest. For the next 1.3 miles, the route winds its way down to a wooden bridge over a small stream. Another 0.3 mile of hiking brings you to a junction with a road. A sign next to the junction points left (north) to Kings Mountain. This is not, however, the Kings Mountain Trail. Cross the roadbed, then quickly cross a creek without the benefit of a bridge. A couple more minutes of hiking brings you to the junction with the Kings Mountain Trail, at 740 feet elevation, 7.4 miles from the Jones Creek Trailhead.

The Wilson River Trail crosses the Kings Mountain Trail. To the right (southeast) along the Kings Mountain Trail, it's only 0.1 mile to the Kings Mountain Trailhead. To the left it's 2.4 miles of steep hiking to the summit of Kings Mountain. See the options below to end your hike here. After crossing the Kings Mountain Trail, the course quickly crosses a wooden bridge over a creek. The track then climbs gently along a long-abandoned roadbed for a short distance. In 0.2 mile you pass a small pond and then a small wet meadow with a stream flowing through it. Another 0.3

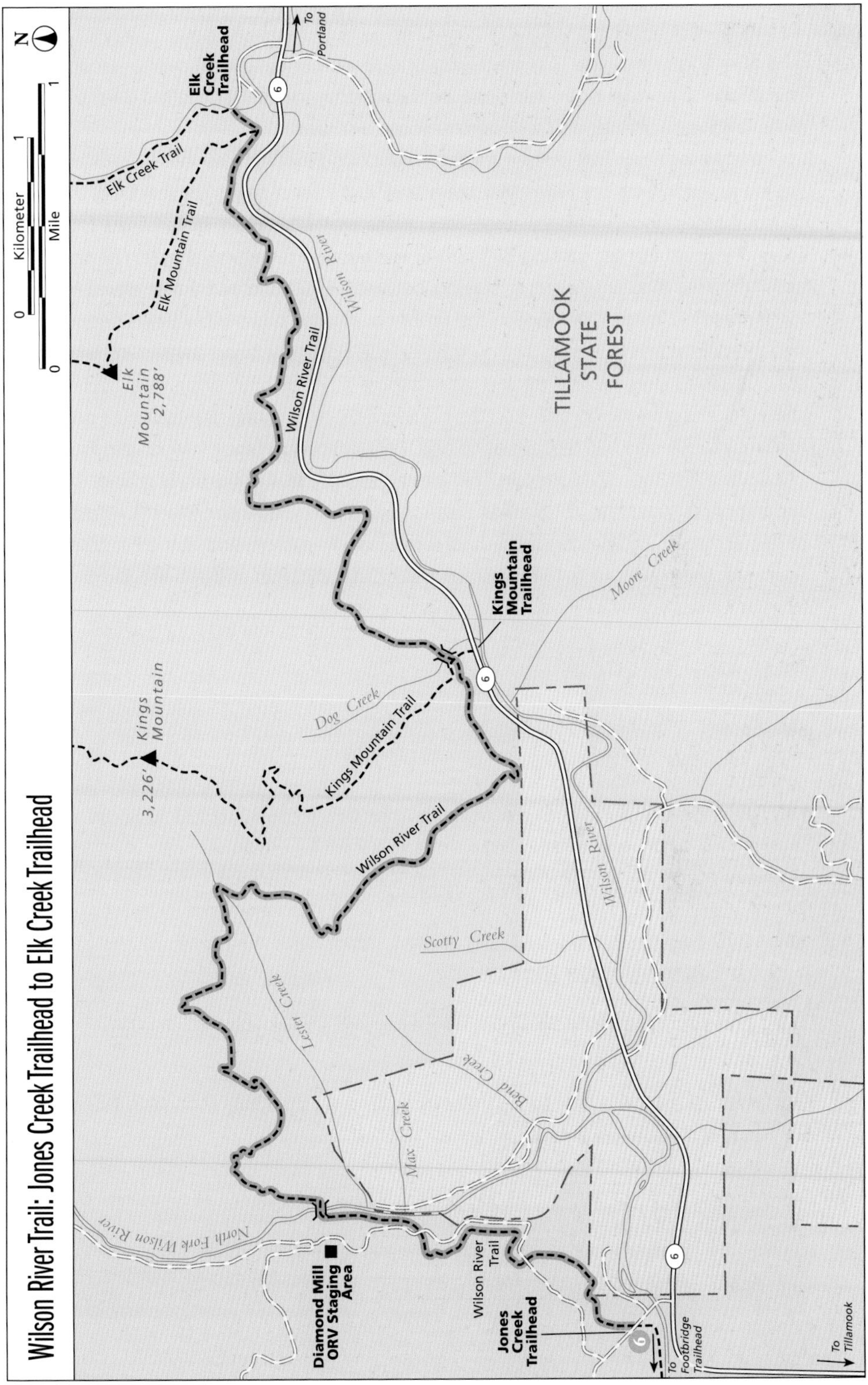

Wilson River Trail: Jones Creek Trailhead to Elk Creek Trailhead
Kilometer
Mile
0
1
0
1
N
To Portland
Elk Creek Trailhead
Elk Creek Trail
Elk Mountain Trail
Elk Mountain 2,788'
Wilson River
Wilson River Trail
TILLAMOOK STATE FOREST
Kings Mountain Trailhead
Moore Creek
Dog Creek
Kings Mountain Trail
Kings Mountain 3,226'
Wilson River Trail
Wilson River
Scotty Creek
Lester Creek
Bend Creek
Max Creek
North Fork Wilson River
Diamond Mill ORV Staging Area
Wilson River Trail
Jones Creek Trailhead
To Footbridge Trailhead
To Tillamook
6

mile of hiking brings you to a single log bridge with one handrail over a stream. This bridge is next to what was once a short earthen dam. Past the old dam the route follows an abandoned roadbed for some distance.

The Wilson River Trail crosses another abandoned roadbed, 1.3 miles after leaving the junction with the Kings Mountain Trail. Just after crossing the roadbed, the course crosses Dog Creek on a single log bridge with a handrail. Once across Dog Creek the route climbs, gaining 350 feet of elevation in the next 0.4 mile. The trail then traverses the canyon slope, staying between 1,100 and 1,200 feet elevation for the next 1.2 miles. Openings in the timber along this slope allow views deeper into the Wilson River Canyon. As you traverse the slope, the tread crosses a couple of small, steep streams. The track crosses a moss-covered talus slope, with widely spaced alders growing up between the boulders, then descends slightly for 0.3 mile to a small saddle at 1,020 feet elevation and the junction with the Elk Mountain Trail.

To the left the Elk Mountain Trail climbs steeply to the north, reaching the summit of Elk Mountain in 1.5 miles. From the junction, the Wilson River Trail turns to the northeast and descends the final 0.1 mile to its eastern end at the Elk Creek Trailhead. The elevation at the Elk Creek Trailhead is 850 feet and you are 11 miles from the Jones Creek Trailhead, where this hike started.

MILES AND DIRECTIONS

0.0 Begin at the Jones Creek Campground and Trailhead. GPS 45 35.288N 123 33.328W.

1.9 Pass the Diamond Mill OHV Staging Area. GPS 45 36.327N 123 32.858W.

7.4 Continue straight ahead (northeast) at the junction with the Kings Mountain Trail. GPS 45 35.925N 123 30.441W.

10.9 Continue straight ahead (east) at the junction with the Elk Mountain Trail. GPS 45 36.545N 123 28.117W.

11.0 End your hike at the Elk Creek Trailhead. GPS 45 36.616N 123 28.005W.

Options: Shorten your hike to 7.5 miles by exiting via the Kings Mountain Trail to the Kings Mountain Trailhead.

Green Tip:
Reuse zip-top bags.

Kings Mountain Trail

Hike via a challenging trail, with an average grade of nearly 20 percent, to the very summit of Kings Mountain. From the openings near the mountaintop, you can admire the surrounding view, which reaches from the fire peaks of the Cascade Range to the shore of the Pacific Ocean. During the spring and summer, wildflowers are an added attraction of this rewarding but difficult hike.

Start: Kings Mountain Trailhead
Distance/type of hike: 5-mile out-and-back day hike with loop and shuttle options
Approximate hiking time: 5 hours
Difficulty: Strenuous, due to the very steep grades and sometimes rough trail surface. There is minor exposure in a few places along this route, so good balance is required.
Best season: April through October. This route may be snow-free most of the year some years.
Canine compatibility and other trail users: Restrained dogs are allowed. From its junction with the Wilson River Trail north (0.1 mile from the trailhead), the Kings Mountain Trail is open to hikers only. Other means of transportation are prohibited.
Fees and permits: None
Maps: Oregon Department of Forestry *Tillamook State Forest Map and Guide* or *Tillamook State Forest Trail Guide Kings Mountain, Elk Mountain, and Elk Creek Trails;* National Geographic Oregon topo on CD-ROM Disk 2; DeLorme's *Oregon Atlas and Gazetteer,* p. 64, D4
Trail contacts: Oregon Department of Forestry, Forest Grove District Office, 801 Gales Creek Road, Forest Grove, OR 97116; (503) 357-2191; www.oregon.gov/ODF; Recorded Recreation Hotline (503) 359-7402
Special considerations: The Kings Mountain Trail is a steep and demanding hike. Be sure that all members of your party are up to it.

Finding the trailhead:
From the Portland metro area, drive west on U.S. Highway 26 to the junction with Oregon Route 6. Leave the freeway and head west on OR 6 for approximately 27 miles, over the summit of the Coast Range and down to Kings Mountain Trailhead. The trailhead is on the right (north) side of the highway just east of (before reaching) Milepost 25. The trailhead is not marked or labeled on the DeLorme's map. There is parking for several cars at the trailhead but no other facilities.

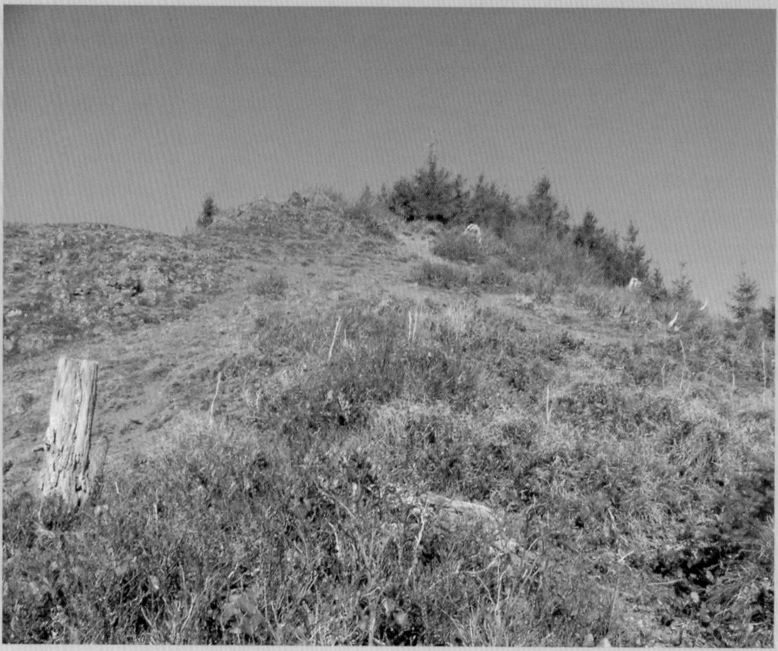

Opening near the top of Kings Mountain

THE HIKE

Leaving the trailhead, at 680 feet elevation, the Kings Mountain Trail climbs through lush second-growth forest. Red alder and Douglas fir trees make up the bulk of the timber and sword ferns cover the ground. In slightly over 0.1 mile is the junction with the Wilson River Trail. To the right it's 3.6 miles along the Wilson River Trail to the Elk Creek Campground and Trailhead. To the left it's 7.4 miles to Jones Creek Trailhead. Head northwest from the junction, staying on the Kings Mountain Trail.

The Mazamas, a Portland-based mountaineering club, has adopted the Kings Mountain Trail and takes responsibility for its maintenance.

The trail makes a switchback next to the rim of a small canyon 0.2 mile farther along. Soon the track makes another switchback and the grade becomes fairly steep. In the next 0.7 mile, the route gains nearly 600 feet, taking you up to 1,500 feet elevation. There is a sign to the right of the trail marking the 1,500-foot level. Parts of the trail here follow long-abandoned and steep roadbeds. Above 1,500 feet the course doesn't become any less steep. Much of the route continues to follow sections of very steep abandoned roadbed.

After making several more switchbacks and climbing these steep roadbeds, the trail reaches the ridgeline of Kings Mountain southwest of the peak. Where the trail reaches the ridgeline, the elevation is approximately 2,250 feet and you are 1.9 miles from the trailhead. A small sign on a tree to the right of the trail states that it is 0.63 mile to the summit from here.

On the ridgeline the route becomes even steeper. The tread winds and switchbacks up, never getting very far from the ridgeline. A couple tenths of a mile up the ridge, a small sign points left to a viewpoint. A path leads left, to the top of a rock outcrop overlooking Lester Creek and the North Fork Wilson River Canyon. Just past the path to the viewpoint, the course regains the very top of the ridge and Mount Hood comes into view ahead to the east. Three hundred yards farther along, you will find a picnic table to the left of the trail. By the time you reach the table, you have climbed to 2,950 feet elevation. This is the spot to stop for lunch or a snack—the view to the southwest is excellent. The timber is smaller up here along the ridgeline. Young Douglas firs are the predominant trees and on the ground grow salal and Oregon grape as well as beargrass.

Beargrass (*Xerophyllum tenax*)

Resembling a very large bunch-grass plant when it's not flowering, beargrass is not even a member of the grass family but rather a type of lily. This evergreen perennial lives from middle elevations up to timberline, both in shaded and open areas. Where the trees shade them, individual beargrass plants may only bloom every five to seven years. In the open, bear grass blooms more frequently, often nearly covering the slopes with a beautiful display. The small, creamy white beargrass flowers form an elongated oval, club-shaped cluster at the top of the up to 4-foot-high central stem. Blooming occurs from June to August, depending on elevation. Native Americans wove the tough leaves of beargrass plants into baskets and hats. Elk and deer often feed on beargrass flowers, usually biting off the upper part of the stem along with the entire flower cluster.

A short distance after passing the picnic table, the route leaves the timber and the view really opens up. The track climbs steeply as you approach the summit. The

Kings Mountain Trail

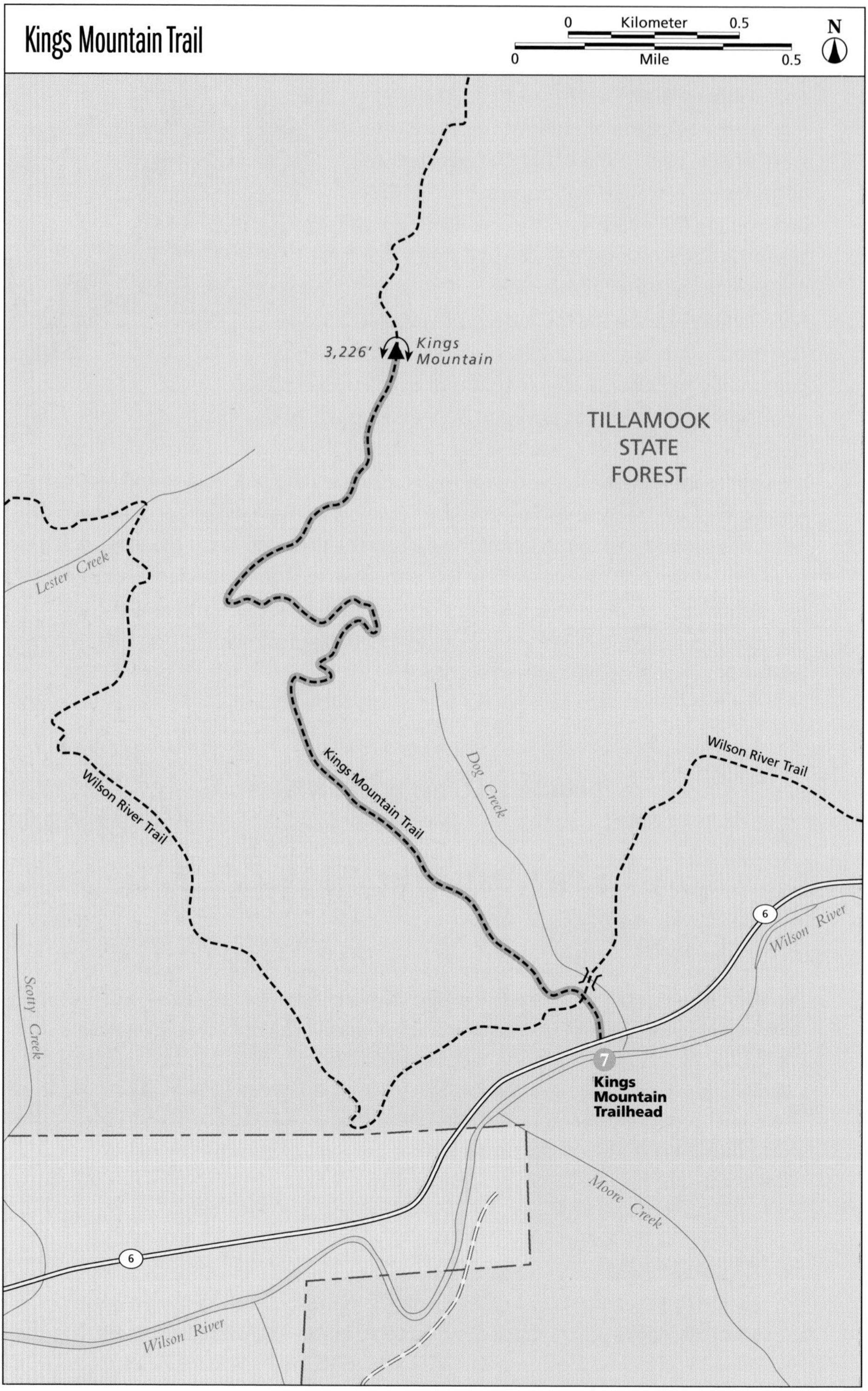

best views are just before reaching the 3,226-foot-high summit. At the very top, trees again block much of the view.

To the west the ocean is in view and to the east are Mount Hood and Mount Adams. If you look north, just the top of Saddle Mountain, in Saddle Mountain State Park north of US 26, can be seen. You may notice elk scat around the open summit area. Roosevelt elk are common here; look for them on the open slopes, which are visible in nearly all directions. The best times for seeing elk are in the early morning or evening. Return from the summit as you came, or see the options below for a loop or a shuttle return hike.

Green Tip:

Use phosphate-free detergent—it's less harmful to the environment.

MILES AND DIRECTIONS

0.0 Begin at the Kings Mountain Trailhead. GPS 45 35.830N 123 30.366W.

0.1 Pass the junction with the Wilson River Trail. GPS 45 35.925N 123 30.441W.

2.5 Arrive at the Kings Mountain summit. GPS 45 36.890N 123 30.850W.

5.0 Return to the Kings Mountain Trailhead. GPS 45 35.830N 123 30.366W.

Options: Make this a 7.4-mile one-way hike requiring a car shuttle by continuing to Elk Mountain and descending the Elk Mountain Trail to Elk Creek Trailhead. Adding another 3.5 miles of hiking along the Wilson River Trail from its junction with the Elk Mountain Trail near the Elk Creek Trailhead to the Kings Mountain Trailhead will eliminate the need for a car shuttle but makes for a long, strenuous hike.

8

Elk Mountain Loop

Climb the steep route to the summit of Elk Mountain. Then descend slightly over a very rough trail to join the abandoned road system that you will follow back, first along slopes, then close to rushing streams, to the trailhead. This loop can be hiked in either direction, but it is best to do it clockwise and get the steep parts done early in the hike.

Start: Elk Creek Campground and Trailhead
Distance/type of hike: 8.4-mile loop day hike or backpack
Approximate hiking time: 5 hours
Difficulty: Strenuous for the first 2.3 miles due to very steep grades and rough trail surface. Just past the summit of Elk Mountain, there is a short section of trail that is really a downhill scramble and somewhat exposed.
Best season: May through October. Because the route to the summit of Elk Mountain is mostly on southerly facing slopes, it may be snow-free most of the year. However, part of the route from the summit to the junction with the Elk Creek Trail is often covered by drifts into April. When the route is snow-covered, it can be rather confusing.
Canine compatibility and other trail users: Restrained dogs are allowed. The Elk Mountain Trail is open to hikers only—other means of transportation are prohibited. Along the Elk Creek Trail, the route is open to mountain bikers as well as hikers.
Fees and permits: None
Maps: *Tillamook State Forest Trail Guide Kings Mountain, Elk Mountain, and Elk Creek Trails;* National Geographic Oregon topo on CD-ROM Disk 2; DeLorme's *Oregon Atlas and Gazetteer,* p. 64, D5

Trail contacts: Oregon Department of Forestry, Forest Grove District Office, 801 Gales Creek Road, Forest Grove, OR 97116; (503) 357-2191; www.oregon.gov/ODF; Recorded Recreation Hotline (503) 359-7402

Special considerations: Some scrambling is required to reach the summit of Elk Mountain, and more must be done to continue from there on this loop hike. During wet or freezing weather, the scrambling sections of this route can be very slippery and somewhat dangerous.

Finding the trailhead:
From the Portland metro area, drive west for approximately 20 miles on U.S. Highway 26 to the junction with Oregon Route 6. Leave the freeway and head west on OR 6 for approximately 24 miles, over the summit of the Coast Range and down to the access road to Elk Creek Campground and Trailhead. The access road is on the right (north) side of the highway just west of (after passing) Milepost 28. Turn on the access road and follow it for 0.3 mile to its end at the trailhead. The elevation at the trailhead is 850 feet. There is plenty of parking at the trailhead. Restrooms and walk-in campsites are located a short distance to the southeast.

THE HIKE

Hike southwest from the trailhead along the Wilson River Trail. After climbing 170 feet in slightly over 0.1 mile, you will reach the junction with the Elk Mountain Trail, in a small saddle. Turn right at the junction and begin the steep climb to the summit of Elk Mountain. Salal, Oregon grape, and vine maple line the trail beneath the canopy of Douglas fir and bigleaf maple. The route climbs along a steep ridgeline; in several places you must scramble up and over short rock outcrops. Viewpoints overlooking the Wilson River Canyon are numerous as you make the steep ascent.

The course flattens for a short distance as you cross a false summit, 1.1 miles from the Wilson River Trail. A sign here states that you have reached the 2,500-foot level. Past the false summit the tread descends about 100 feet to a small saddle, before continuing its steep ascent toward the summit of Elk Mountain. You climb steeply for another 0.3 mile from the saddle to the top of Elk Mountain at 2,788 feet above sea level.

A small wooden sign on a dead snag marks the summit, and there is a register box where you can record your climb if you wish. If the weather is clear, the distant view is magnificent, both to the east and west. Mount Hood and the Pacific Ocean

Flood damage along Elk Creek

are both in view from the same spot. During the summer wildflowers and beargrass carpet the small meadow at the summit.

Leaving the summit is the most difficult part of this loop hike. The rocky route descends very steeply. For a short distance, you will want to use your hands for both balance and as holds in case you slip. If the conditions are wet or icy, this is a dangerous section of trail. Below the steep section the trail makes a hard turn to the right. For the next 0.7 mile, the route follows the narrow ridgeline generally heading north, then northwest. The undulating track passes beneath short cliffs, switchbacks up and down, and crosses and recrosses the ridgeline several times. The route bears right and descends slightly to the northeast, 0.7 mile from the summit. Soon it meets an abandoned roadbed at 2,610 feet elevation. Once you reach this point, the difficult part of this loop hike is over. From here on you will be following a series of abandoned roadbeds.

In 0.25 mile the route climbs slightly to a saddle on the ridgeline. In the saddle is a possible dry campsite. From the saddle the course continues on the right side of the ridgeline. In 0.2 mile you will make the first of eight switchbacks that make the gentle climb back to the ridgeline at about 3,000 feet elevation. The trail (still an abandoned roadbed) climbs a little more along the ridge, then descends slightly off the left side to the junction with the Kings Mountain Trail. This junction in a

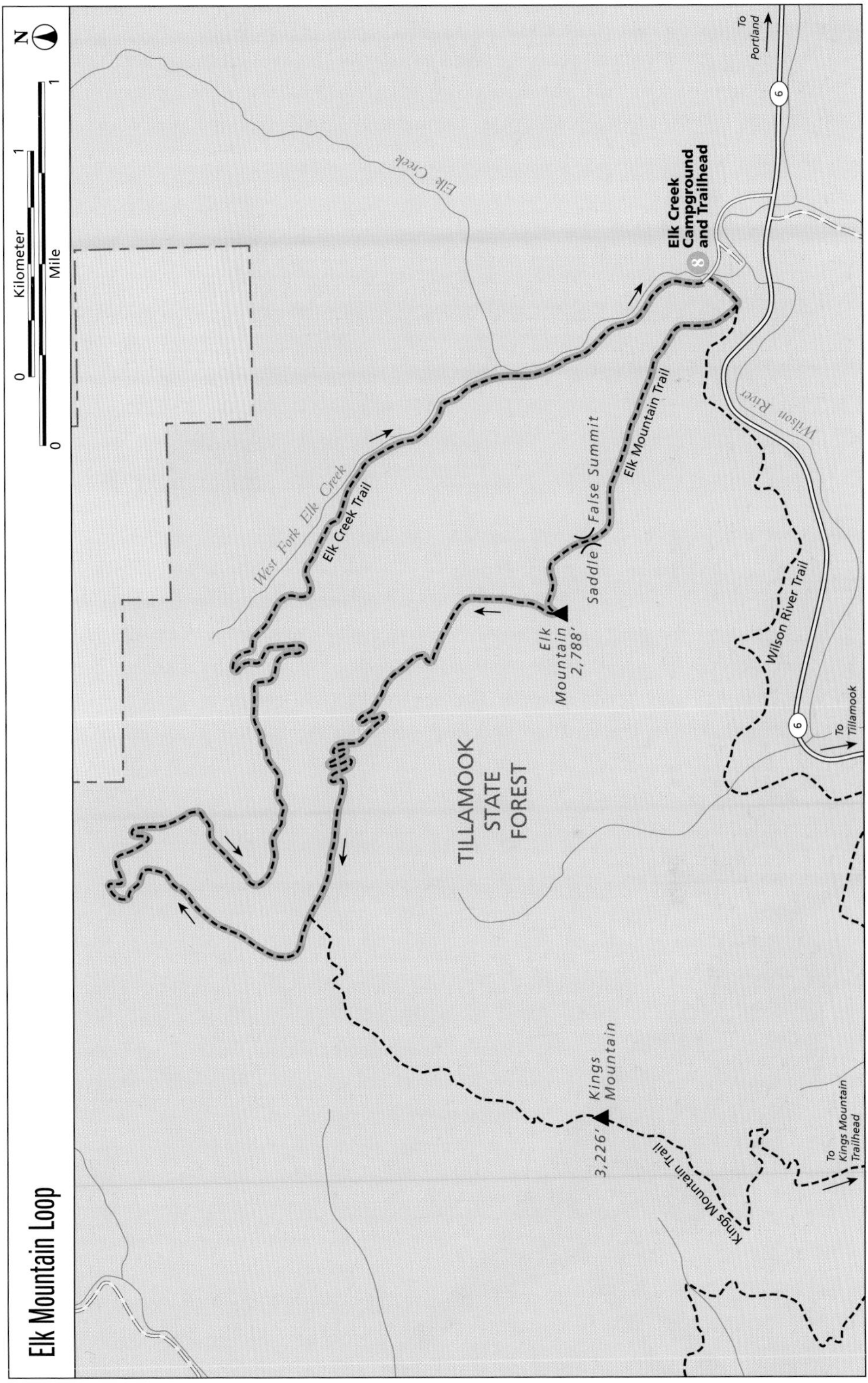
Elk Mountain Loop
Kilometer
0
1
Mile
0
1
N
To Portland
6
Elk Creek
Elk Creek Campground and Trailhead
8
West Fork Elk Creek
Elk Creek Trail
False Summit
Saddle
Elk Mountain Trail
Wilson River
Elk Mountain 2,788'
Wilson River Trail
TILLAMOOK STATE FOREST
6
To Tillamook
Kings Mountain
3,226'
Kings Mountain Trail
To Kings Mountain Trailhead

saddle, at 2,950 feet elevation, is 3.6 miles from the Elk Creek Trailhead, and it's 4.8 more miles back to the trailhead via Elk Creek Trail. To the left at the junction, it's a difficult 1.3 miles to Kings Mountain summit and 3.8 miles to the Kings Mountain Trailhead.

Green Tip:

When you just have to go, dig a hole 6–8 inches deep and at least 200 feet from water, camps, and trails. Carry a zip-lock bag to carry out toilet paper, or use a natural substitute such as leaves instead (but *not* poison oak!!!). Fill in the hole with soil and other natural materials when you're done.

Bear right (nearly straight ahead) at the signed junction and continue northwest along the right side of the ridgeline. Before long the route turns to the northeast, and 0.3 mile from the junction you will reach the highest point on this loop at 3,070 feet elevation. For the next 0.5 mile, the tread descends gently through the mostly hemlock forest to the junction with the Elk Creek Trail, at 2,840 feet elevation.

Turn right at the junction and begin the gentle but steady descent along the abandoned roadbed, which is the Elk Creek Trail. The track makes a couple of switchbacks 0.3 mile from the junction and a little farther along turns to the southwest to skirt around the head of the West Fork Elk Creek Canyon. Soon the route heads east again.

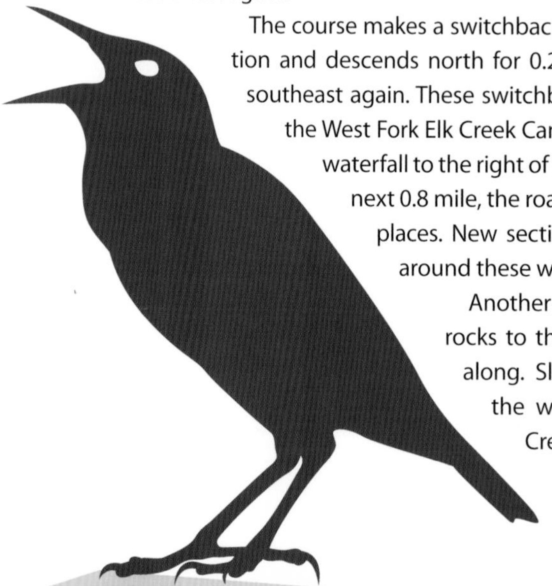

The course makes a switchback to the left 1.4 miles from the junction and descends north for 0.2 mile before switchbacking to the southeast again. These switchbacks allow for a gentler descent to the West Fork Elk Creek Canyon. A small stream plunges over a waterfall to the right of the trail 0.2 mile farther along. In the next 0.8 mile, the roadbed has been washed out in three places. New sections of trail have been constructed around these washouts.

Another small waterfall splashes down the rocks to the right of the trail 0.3 mile farther along. Slightly over 0.1 mile farther along, the west fork and the main fork of Elk Creek merge to form a larger stream. Where the forks of Elk Creek come together, you are 3.6 miles from the junction with the Elk Mountain Trail and have 0.6 mile left to hike to reach the Elk Creek Trailhead. Continuing 0.2 mile brings you to another small stream crossing, where the stream cascades over a series of small waterfalls above the trail to the right. The route continues along the gentle abandoned roadbed for another 0.4 mile to the Elk Creek Trailhead, where your loop hike began.

MILES AND DIRECTIONS

0.0 Begin at the Elk Creek Trailhead. GPS 45 36.616N 123 28.005W.

0.1 Turn right at the junction with the Elk Mountain Trail. GPS 45 36.545N 123 28.117W.

1.6 Reach the Elk Mountain summit. GPS 45 36.985N 123 29.089W.

2.3 The trail meets an abandoned roadbed and becomes much easier here.

3.6 Bear right at the junction with the Kings Mountain Trail. GPS 45 37.575N 123 30.167W.

4.4 Turn right at the junction with the Elk Creek Trail. GPS 45 38.068N 123 30.032W.

8.4 Return to the Elk Creek Trailhead. GPS 45 36.616N 123 28.005W.

Options: Combine the first 3.6 miles of this trail with the Kings Mountain Trail and the eastern section of the Wilson River Trail to make a 10.9-mile loop. This is a strenuous route much of the way, so be sure that your party is up to it and allow plenty of time—eight hours is not too much.

9

University Falls via the Gravelle Brothers Trail

The Gravelle Brothers Trail is named for the twin brothers Edmond and Elroy Gravelle, who devoted a tremendous amount of time developing the early Tillamook State Forest trail system. Hike the trail through the mixed forest of the well-regenerated Tillamook Burn to beautiful University Falls. While this is not the shortest way to reach University Falls, the ease of access and the pleasant hike through the forest make it very rewarding.

Start: Rogers Camp Trailhead
Distance/type of hike: 5.8-mile out-and-back day hike, with a shorter shuttle option
Approximate hiking time: 2.5 hours
Difficulty: Easy
Best season: All year. This is an excellent hike for a cold, clear January day, but be sure you are prepared for slippery sections of trail. It is often advisable to use four- or six-point crampons in the winter, as well as sturdy hiking boots.
Canine compatibility and other trail users: Restrained dogs allowed; also open to hikers, mountain bikers, and horseback riders
Fees and permits: None
Maps: Oregon Department of Forestry *Tillamook State Forest Map and Guide* or *Tillamook State Forest Trail Guide Historic Hiking Trail;* National Geographic Oregon topo on CD-ROM Disk 2; DeLorme's *Oregon Atlas and Gazetteer,* p. 65, C6
Trail contacts: Oregon Department of Forestry, Forest Grove District Office, 801 Gales Creek Road, Forest Grove, OR 97116; (503) 357-2191; www.oregon.gov/ODF; Recorded Recreation Hotline (503) 359-7402
Special considerations: At certain times during the winter months, there may be ice in places along the Gravelle Brothers Trail and especially on the short side trail to University Falls.

Finding the trailhead:
From the Portland metro area, drive west on U.S. Highway 26 to the junction with Oregon Route 6. Leave the freeway and head west on OR 6 for approximately 19 miles to the summit of the Coast Range. Just past the summit sign, turn left next to the Oregon Department of Transportation yard. After leaving the highway, quickly turn left again and go 0.1 mile to the large parking area at Rogers Camp Trailhead. The elevation at the trailhead is 1,600 feet. The DeLorme map does not

University Falls

show this trailhead. The National Geographic CD-ROM topo covers the area and shows the trailhead as "Rogers Forest Park" but does not show this trail. Adequate parking and restrooms are available at the Rogers Camp Trailhead.

University Falls via the Gravelle Brothers Trail

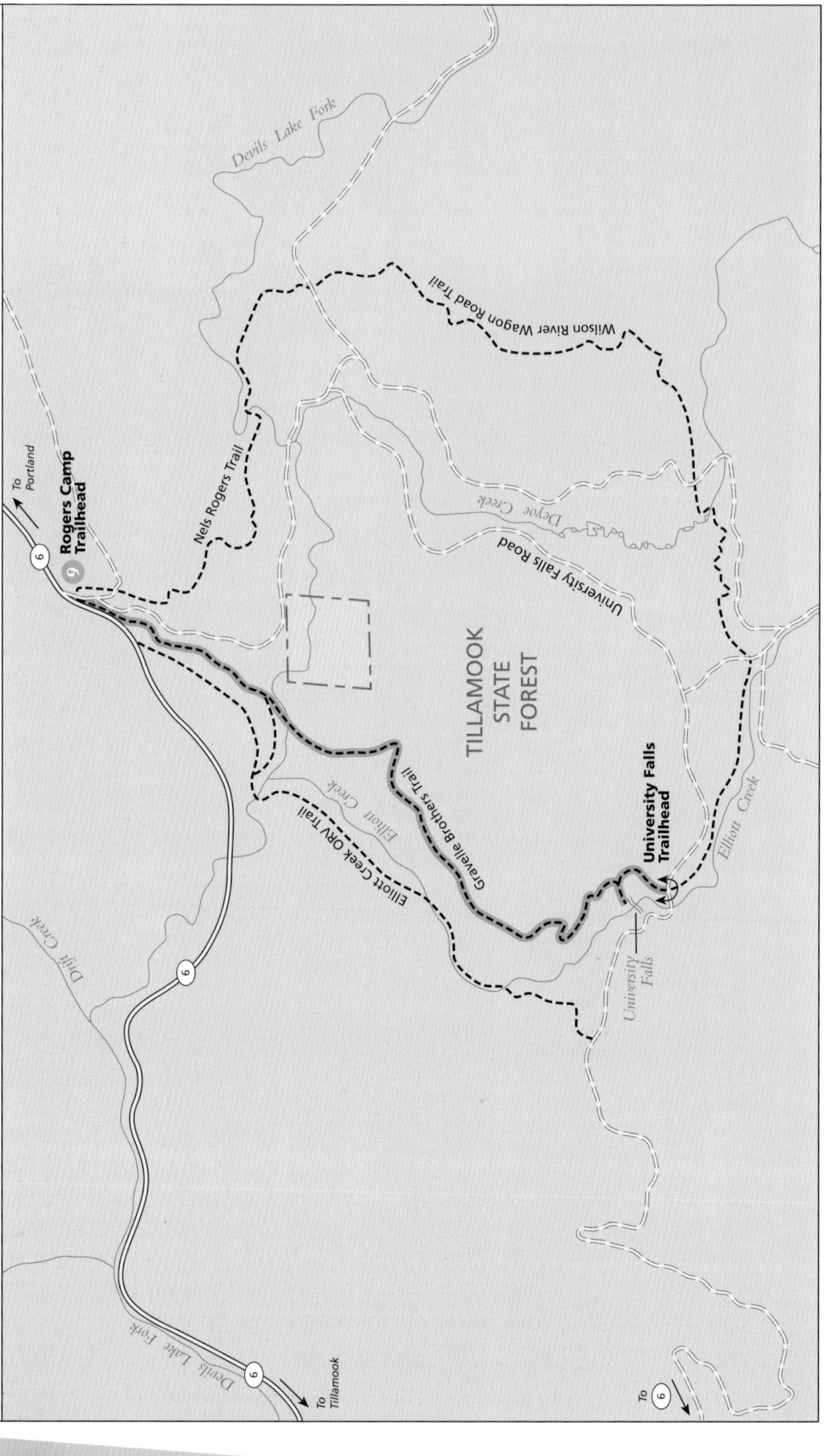

THE HIKE

To reach the trail, walk southwest from the large parking area at Rogers Camp Trailhead along the entrance road (the way you drove in), to the northeast corner of the Oregon Department of Transportation yard. This corner of the yard is next to OR 6. Turn left and follow the shared OHV and hiking trail around the east and south sides of the yard. At the southwest corner of the yard, bear left on a gravel roadbed. After following the roadbed for 0.2 mile, bear to the right on the Gravelle Brothers Trail. There is a sign marking the point where the trail leaves the roadbed.

The route descends gently through the western red cedar and Douglas fir forest for a little over 0.1 mile, where there will be a trail junction. Bear left at the junction and hike southwest to stay on the Gravelle Brothers Trail. The track descends a small ridge, then makes a couple of switchbacks before reaching the junction with the Story Burn Trail.

Bear left (nearly straight ahead) at the junction and in a short distance you will reach a single log bridge over the Devils Lake Fork of the Wilson River. The bridge has a handrail on one side making it much easier to cross. When I made this hike in late January, this bridge had ice from 0.5 to 1 inch thick all along the flattened top of the log. If it were not for the handrail, this would have been a very sporting crossing. By the time you reach this bridge, you have descended about 300 feet from the Rogers Camp Trailhead.

Green Tip:
Keep to established trails as much as possible. If there aren't any, stay on surfaces that will be least affected, like rock, gravel, dry grasses, or snow.

Once across the bridge the tread crosses the rest of the riverbed through the forest of red alder, then climbs slightly. In 0.3 mile the track crosses a creek. In the next 0.6 mile, the route climbs gently, crossing four more small streams, some of which may be dry in the summer. Just after crossing the fourth small stream, look for a very old stump that has a notch cut into its side, to the left of the trail. This notch is a springboard cut. Boards were stuck into these springboard cuts so that loggers could stand on them and thus be able to cut the tree high enough off the ground to be above the trees' butt swell. Considering the huge size of these old-growth trees and the fact that it was muscle power that was used to cut them down, this elevated stance gave the fallers a big advantage.

You will cross several more small streams in the next 1.1 miles, climbing in places as you go. The route gains about 150 feet of elevation before reaching the junction with the trail to University Falls. Turn right at the junction and hike the last 500 feet to a viewpoint near the base of the falls. The amount of water flowing over the falls varies a lot from winter to late summer; the falls are at their best from early winter through spring. Return to Rogers Camp Trailhead as you came or see the options below for a possible shuttle trip.

MILES AND DIRECTIONS

0.0 Begin at the Rogers Camp Trailhead. GPS 45 37.380N 123 22.507W.

0.2 Leave the entrance road and turn left. GPS 45 37.249N 123 22.673W.

0.5 Bear right where the trail leaves the roadbed.

0.7 Turn left at the junction with the Story Burn Trail.

2.8 Turn right at the junction with the University Falls Trail.

2.9 Turn around at University Falls.

5.8 Return to the Rogers Camp Trailhead. GPS 45 37.380N 123 22.507W.

Options: University Falls can also be reached by a short 0.4-mile hike from University Falls Trailhead, or you can make this a shuttle hike by starting or ending your hike there. To reach University Falls Trailhead from Rogers Camp Trailhead, leave the parking area and go back to Beaver Dam Road (the road you turned onto when you left OR 6). Turn left on Beaver Dam Road and follow it for 0.7 mile, then bear right onto University Falls Road. In 1.9 miles there will be another junction. Bear right here following the sign pointing to Horse Camp. In another 0.5 mile the University Falls Trailhead will be on your right. The historic Wilson River Wagon Road Trail also passes by the University Falls Trailhead. The GPS coordinates at University Falls Trailhead are 45 35.906N 123 23.538W and the elevation is 1,750 feet.

Nels Rogers Trail: Wilson River Wagon Road

Hike along gentle trails through the now regenerated Tillamook Burn. Nels Rogers, the man for whom Rogers Camp and the Nels Rogers Trail were named, was the Oregon state forester from 1940 to 1949.

Start: Rogers Camp Trailhead
Distance/type of hike: 4.6-mile shuttle day hike, with a 7.8-mile optional loop
Approximate hiking time: 2 hours
Difficulty: Easy
Best season: All year. At times during midwinter, snow may cover the area, making hiking difficult, but it usually doesn't last very long.
Canine compatibility and other trail users: Restrained dogs are allowed. This trail is open to hikers, horseback riders, and mountain bikers.
Fees and permits: None
Maps: Oregon Department of Forestry *Tillamook State Forest Map and Guide* or *Tillamook State Forest Trail Guide Historic Hiking Trail;* National Geographic Oregon topo on CD-ROM Disk 2; DeLorme's *Oregon Atlas and Gazetteer,* p. 65, C6
Trail contacts: Oregon Department of Forestry, Forest Grove District Office, 801 Gales Creek Road, Forest Grove, OR 97116; (503) 357-2191; www.oregon.gov/ODF; Recorded Recreation Hotline (503) 359-7402
Special considerations: During midwinter there can be ice on the trail and especially on the bridge over the Devils Lake Fork of the Wilson River.

Finding the trailhead:
From the Portland metro area, drive west on U.S. Highway 26 to the junction with Oregon Route 6. Leave the freeway and head west on OR 6 for approximately 19 miles to the summit of the Coast Range. Just past the summit sign, turn left next to the Oregon Department of Transportation yard. After leaving the highway, quickly turn left again and go a 0.1 mile to the large parking area at Rogers Camp Trailhead. The elevation at the trailhead is 1,600 feet. The DeLorme map does not show this trailhead. The National Geographic topo covers the area and shows the trailhead as "Rogers Forest Park" but does not show this trail. Adequate parking and restrooms are available at the Rogers Camp Trailhead.

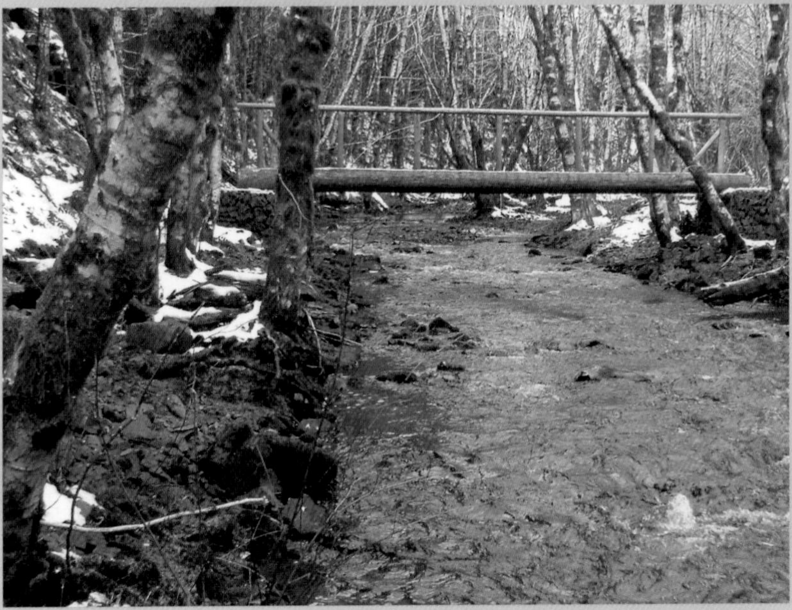

Bridge over Devils Lake Fork

To reach the University Falls Trailhead, where this hike ends, from the Rogers Camp Trailhead, first go back to Beaver Dam Road (the road you turned onto when you left OR 6). Turn left on Beaver Dam Road and follow it for 0.7 mile, then bear right onto University Falls Road. In 1.9 miles there will be another junction. Bear right here, following the sign pointing to Horse Camp. In another 0.5 mile the University Falls Trailhead will be on your right.

THE HIKE

From the southwest corner of the parking area, climb south along Firebreak 1 Road for 75 yards, then turn right on the Nels Rogers Trail. A sign where you leave the road says it is 1.45 miles to Deyoe Creek Trailhead and 2 miles to the Wilson River Wagon Road.

The trail climbs south through the second-growth forest that was planted in 1949. Douglas fir, western red cedar, and red alder are the principal trees that make up the forest canopy here. Vine maple grows as an understory shrub, and on the forest floor salal, Oregon grape, red huckleberry, and sword ferns cover the ground.

In 0.2 mile, after gaining 170 feet of elevation, the tread flattens and soon crosses an OHV trail. The route then ungulates a little, passing through some stands of bracken ferns. Roosevelt elk can often be seen along this section of the Nels Rogers Trail.

Roosevelt Elk (*Cervus elaphus roosevelti*)

The Coast Range of Oregon and Washington, as well as the damp western slope of the Cascade Mountains, is home to Roosevelt elk. Roosevelt bulls, which may weigh over 1,000 pounds, are the largest wild animals to inhabit either state. Roosevelts are common in the Tillamook State Forest.

The route crosses another OHV trail 0.4 mile farther along, then you descend for another 0.4 mile and cross Beaver Dam Road. About 300 yards after crossing the road, there will be a path to the right. This path leads to the Deyoe Creek Trailhead. Bear left and continue on the Nels Rogers Trail. The track soon makes four switchbacks as you descend to the Devils Lake Fork of the Wilson River. Along the river you are at slightly over 1,400 feet elevation. The forest in the riverbed consists of nearly all red alder. The trail crosses the Devils Lake Fork on a single log bridge.

Just after crossing the bridge, the junction with the trail to the Deyoe Trailhead is reached. To the right it's 0.2 mile to the Deyoe Trailhead. Turn left, staying on the Nels Rogers Trail. In a short distance there will be a waterfall dropping into the river from the far side. The trail soon climbs a small ridge and leaves the river. You will cross two small wooden bridges over tiny streams before reaching another junction with Beaver Dam Road and the junction with the Historic Wilson River Wagon Road Trail. This junction 2 miles from Rogers Camp Trailhead, at 1,500 feet elevation, is the end of the Nels Rogers Trail. The rest of this hike is along the historic Wilson River Wagon Road.

The route begins across Beaver Dam Road from the end of the Nels Rogers Trail. In a short distance the route passes beneath a power line and crosses several OHV trails as it climbs to about 1,900 feet elevation. Then the course descends slightly to meet the Saddle Mountain Road. Turn right on the Saddle Mountain Road and follow it for 470 feet. Then the trail bears to the left, leaving the road.

Opened in 1893, the Wilson River Wagon Road was for a time the only route that could be followed by wagons and stagecoaches between Forest Grove and Tillamook.

Leaving the Saddle Mountain Road, the route descends

Nels Rogers Trail: Wilson River Wagon Road

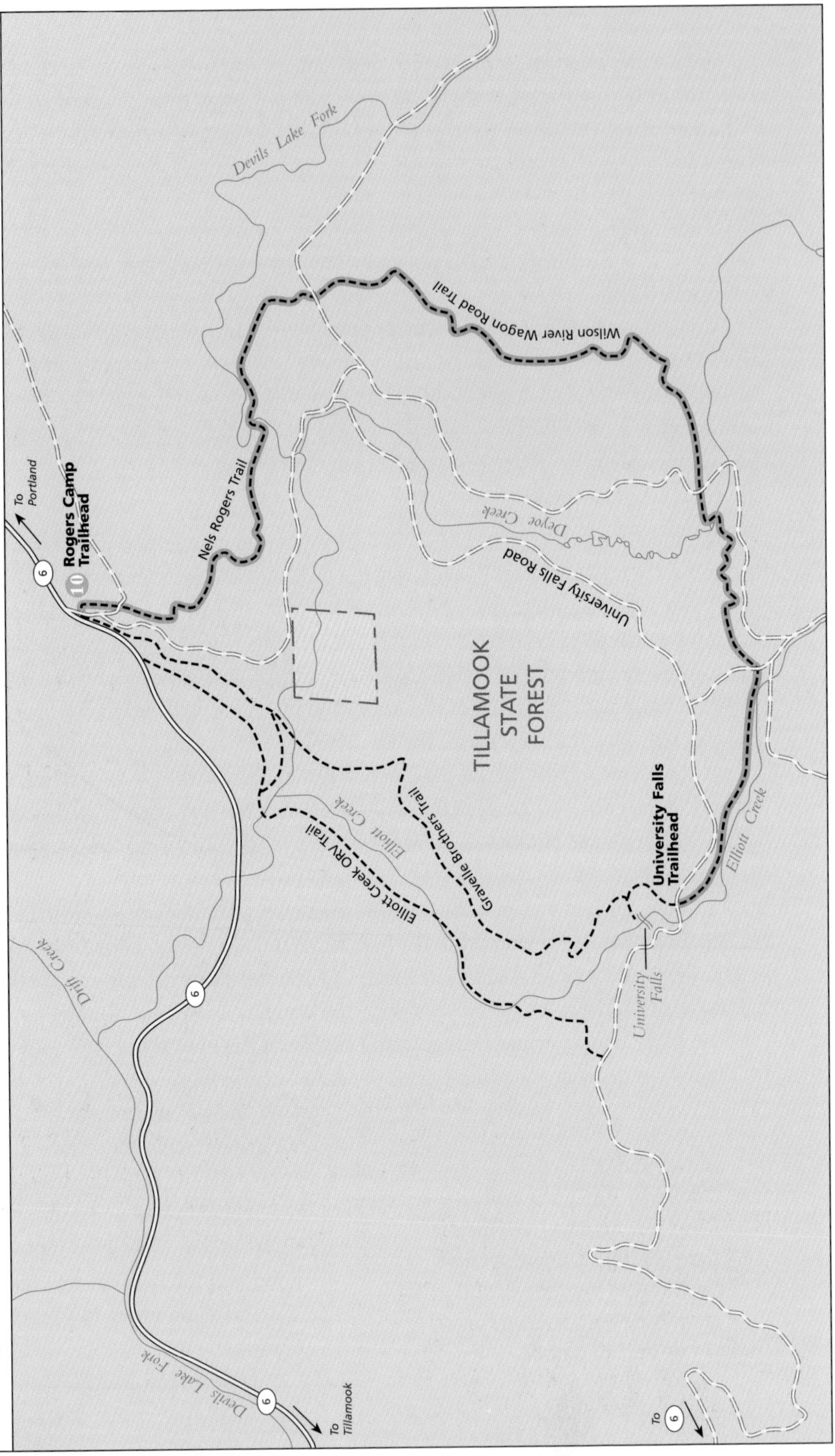

through the fir and alder forest for 0.3 mile to again meet the Beaver Dam Road. Angle to the right across the road and pick up the trail on the other side. The track then descends slightly to cross Deyoe Creek on a wooden bridge with handrails on both sides. Across the creek the trail climbs slightly and crosses the University Falls Access Road in a little over 0.5 mile. Another 0.7 mile of walking along Elliott Creek brings you to University Falls Road at the University Falls Trailhead and the junction with the Gravelle Brothers Trail. See the options below for a route from here back to Rogers Camp Trailhead.

The University Falls Trailhead, at 1,750 feet elevation, is a good place to end your hike along the historic Wilson River Wagon Road. If you wish to continue along the Wagon Road Trail, walk 0.1 mile west on the University Falls Road, then bear left on the trail. Soon the route splits. From here you may take either route. Both will reach Stagecoach Horse Camp in about 1 mile. Both of the routes follow and cross gravel roads and are well marked with signs.

MILES AND DIRECTIONS

0.0 Begin at Rogers Camp Trailhead. GPS 45 37.380N 123 22.507W.

1.3 Turn left at the junction with the trail to Deyoe Creek Trailhead. GPS 45 36.965N 123 21.931W.

2.0 Cross the road at the junction with Beaver Dam Road and the Wilson River Wagon Road Trail. GPS 45 36.804N 123 21.464W.

3.0 Turn right at the junction with Saddle Mountain Road. GPS 45 35.934N 123 21.738W.

3.9 Cross the road at the junction with the University Falls Access Road. GPS 45 35.700N 123 22.784W.

4.6 Arrive at University Falls Trailhead. GPS 45 35.906N 123 23.538W.

Options: To make this hike into a loop trip, follow the Gravelle Brothers Trail for 3.2 miles back to the Rogers Camp Trailhead, taking time to make the short side trip to University Falls along the way.

11

Soapstone Lake

Take a short hike through the second-growth timber of the Clatsop State Forest, past an abandoned homestead, and on to a small lake, enjoying a wide variety of wild-flowers as you go.

Start: Soapstone Lake Trailhead
Distance/type of hike: 3.2-mile lollipop-loop day hike
Approximate hiking time: 1.5 hours
Difficulty: Easy
Best season: All year
Canine compatibility and other trail users: Restrained dogs allowed. The trail is also open to hikers and mountain bikers.
Fees and permits: None
Maps: The map on the reader board at the trailhead and the one in this book should be all you need for this short trail. Oregon Department of Forestry *Clatsop State Forest Map;* National Geographic Oregon topo on CD-ROM Disk 2
Trail contacts: Astoria District Office, Oregon Department of Forestry, 92219 Highway 202, Astoria, OR 97103; (503) 325-5451

Finding the trailhead:
From Portland, drive 65 miles west on U.S. Highway 26 to the junction with Oregon Route 53. Turn left and head south on OR 53 for 4.8 miles to the junction with the road to Soapstone Lake Trailhead. There is a sign pointing to the trailhead here. Turn left and drive 0.3 mile east to the trailhead, at 480 feet elevation. The DeLorme map does not show this trailhead but does show Soapstone Lake. The Oregon Department of Forestry *Clatsop State Forest Map* shows the trailhead but not the trail. The National Geographic Oregon topo covers the area but shows neither the trailhead nor the trail. There is parking for a couple of cars but no other facilities at the trailhead.

THE HIKE

The route leads southeast from the trailhead, following a long-abandoned roadbed, through the second-growth western hemlock and Douglas fir forest. If you're here about the first of May, look for pink fawn lilies blooming close to the trailhead. Oxalis, aka wood sorrel or redwood sorrel (*Oxalis oregana*), covers much of the forest floor along the trail.

The course crosses a wooden bridge over a small stream 250 yards into the hike. Along the stream red alders make up the forest canopy and salmonberry bushes hug the stream banks. You will cross another wooden bridge over an often dry streambed 0.4 mile from the trailhead. Note the large but very old decomposing stumps in this area. They can attest to the size of the timber that once covered this area.

The track soon enters an opening where there are obvious signs that this spot was once inhabited. The Lindgren Cabin that once stood in this opening is now at Cullaby Lake County Park, along U.S. Highway 101 between Astoria and Seaside. As the trace leaves the open area, you must cross Soapstone Creek without the benefit of a bridge. The stream can be crossed on logs or easily forded. The logs are

Soapstone Lake

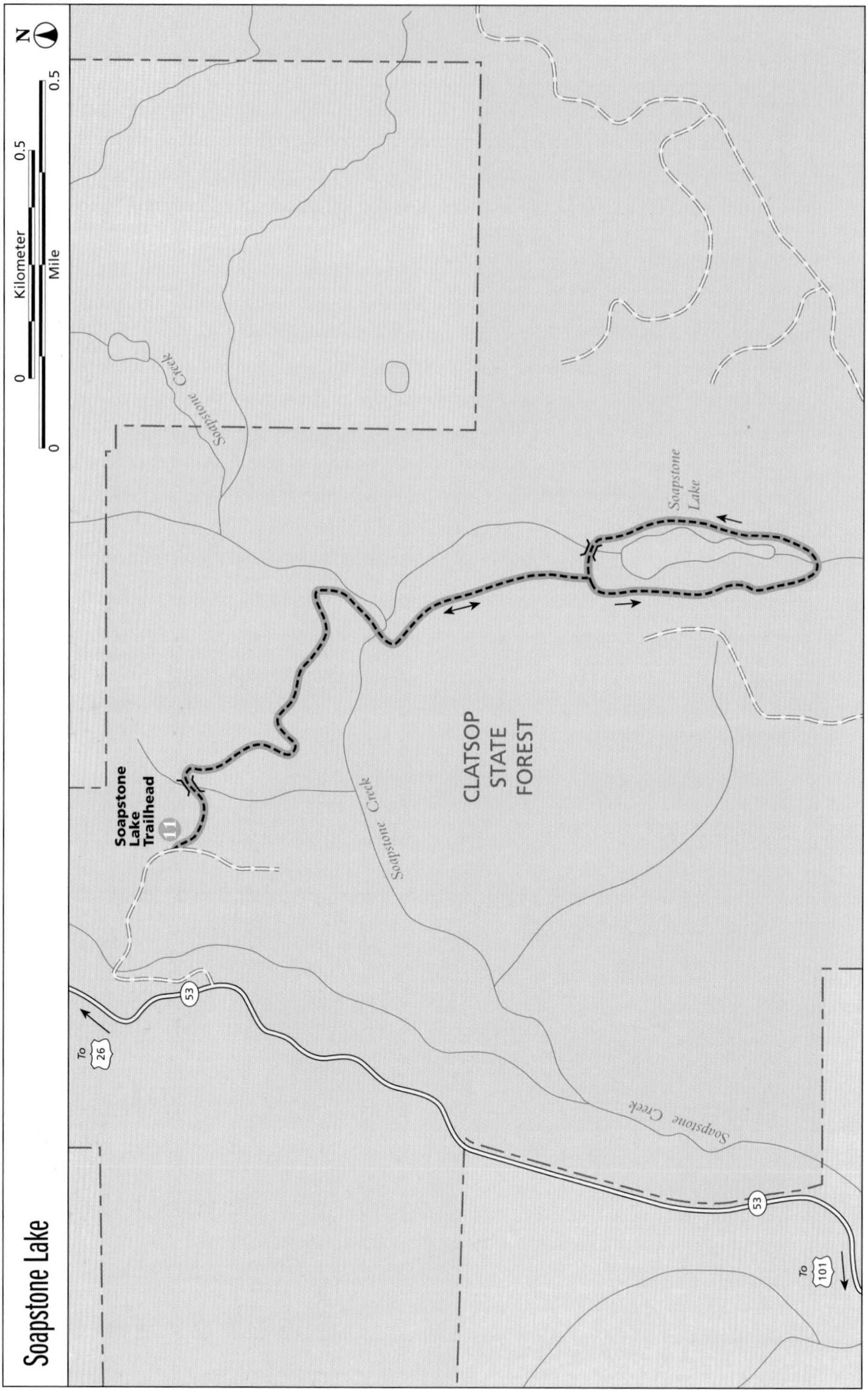
Soapstone Lake
Kilometer
Mile
0
0.5
N
Soapstone Creek
Soapstone Lake Trailhead
11
CLATSOP STATE FOREST
Soapstone Lake
53
To 26
To 101

slippery when wet, however, as are some of the "soapstone" rocks in the creek bed. At the crossing of Soapstone Creek, you are 0.7 mile from the trailhead and have descended to 390 feet elevation.

After crossing Soapstone Creek, the route soon climbs some steps. Then you follow a poorly defined ridgeline through the western red cedar, Sitka spruce, and Douglas fir forest, for another 0.3 mile to the junction where the loop around Soapstone Lake begins. At the junction you are 1.1 mile from the trailhead and have climbed to 530 feet above sea level.

Turn right at the junction on another abandoned roadbed, and climb gently to the southwest. In a short distance the trail bears to the left, leaving the roadbed. After leaving the roadbed the route climbs to the top of a small ridgeline. To your left and below is Soapstone Lake. You follow the ridgeline at 600 feet elevation, for about 0.1 mile, then the track bears slightly to the left and begins to descend closer to the lake. After passing a couple of very large Sitka spruce trees and descending to 520 feet elevation, the route crosses a wooden bridge over the inlet stream for Soapstone Lake. Beaver dams slow the flow of this stream both to the right and left of the bridge.

Once across the bridge the trail follows the inlet stream north for a short distance to the head of Soapstone Lake. You then follow the lakeshore through the red alder forest back to the junction where the loop started. Along the lakeshore look for Hooker's fairybells, bleeding hearts, and tiny yellow stream violets. All of these flowers are in bloom around the beginning of May. Turn right at the junction and retrace your steps back to the trailhead.

MILES AND DIRECTIONS

0.0 Begin at the Soapstone Lake Trailhead. GPS 45 50.817N 123 45.735W.

1.1 Turn right at the trail junction to begin the loop. GPS 45 50.313N 123 45.276W.

2.1 Turn right at the trail junction at the end of the loop. GPS 45 50.313N 123 45.276W.

3.2 Return to the Soapstone Lake Trailhead. GPS 45 50.817N 123 45.735W.

Saddle Mountain Trail

Hike from the lush second-growth forest at the Saddle Mountain Trailhead and Campground to the rocky summit of Saddle Mountain. From the summit, take in the view, which stretches from the Pacific Ocean and the mouth of the Columbia River to the ice-clad peaks of the Cascade Range. At times much of the trailside along this route is a flower garden.

Start: Saddle Mountain Trailhead
Distance/type of hike: 5.2-mile out-and-back day hike
Approximate hiking time: 3.5 hours
Difficulty: Moderate except for the last 0.3 mile to the summit, which is strenuous and somewhat rough and eroded.
Best season: March through November. There is usually snow along the upper part of this route during the winter.
Canine compatibility and other trail users: This is a hikers-only trail, but restrained dogs are allowed.
Fees and permits: None
Maps: The map on the reader board next to the trailhead and the map in this book should provide any info you might need. Also, *Oregon Department of Forestry Clatsop State Forest;* National Geographic Oregon topo on CD-ROM Disk 2; DeLorme's *Oregon Atlas and Gazetteer,* p. 64, A3.
Trail contacts: Nehalem Bay State Park, (503) 368-5154; www.oregonstateparks.org
Special considerations: The trail is very steep for the last 0.3 mile before reaching the summit. Much of this section of trail is covered with fine gravel that slides and rolls. Take your time, especially when coming down. A hiking pole, or better yet poles, can be of great help here. At times blow-downs and slides temporarily close the Saddle Mountain Trail. To check if the trail is open, call Nehalem Bay State Park.

Finding the trailhead:
From Portland, head west on U.S. Highway 26 to the junction with the Saddle Mountain Natural Area Road (approximately 64 miles from downtown). Turn right at the junction and drive 7.1 miles to the Saddle Mountain Campground and Trailhead. The elevation at the trailhead is 1,650 feet. There is adequate parking, restrooms, and a great little walk-in campground for $8 per night at the trailhead. RV camping is not allowed.

THE HIKE

Leaving the parking area, the Saddle Mountain Trail climbs moderately to the southeast through the walk-in campground and mature red alder forest. Salmonberry bushes divide the campsites, providing privacy. Shortly after leaving the campground, the route passes a water tank. If you hike here in late April or early May, the forest floor may be doted with blooming pink fawn lilies (*Erythronium revolutum*). In the same area at about the same time, the less common Hooker's fairybells (*Disporum hookeri*) are also in bloom.

Saddle Mountain

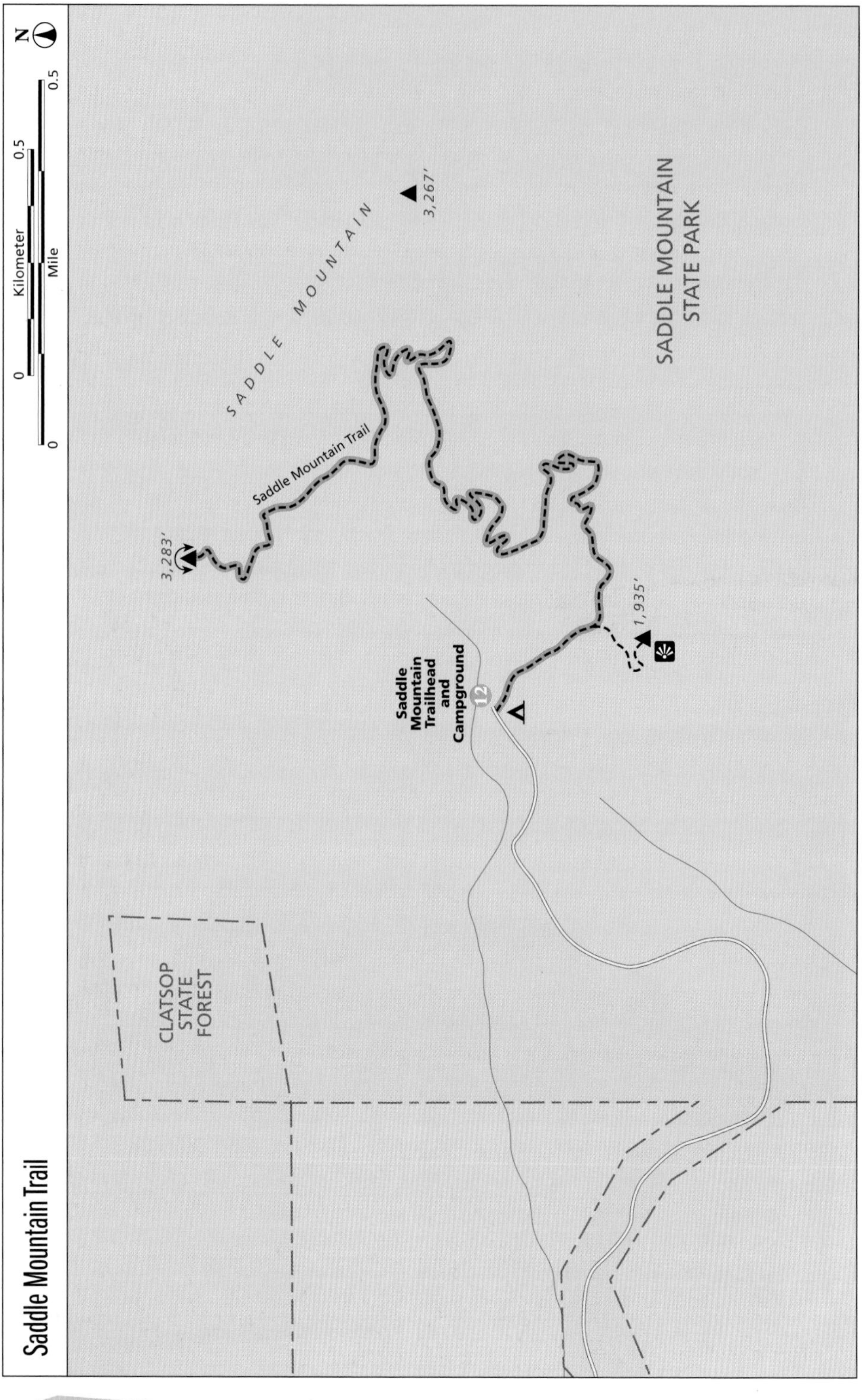
Saddle Mountain Trail
0
Kilometer
0.5
0
Mile
0.5
N
SADDLE MOUNTAIN
3,267'
SADDLE MOUNTAIN
STATE PARK
Saddle Mountain Trail
3,283'
1,935'
Saddle
Mountain
Trailhead
and
Campground
12
CLATSOP
STATE
FOREST

There is an unmarked trail junction 0.2 mile from the trailhead. The trail to the right leads to a viewpoint atop a rock outcropping. The view of the south face of Saddle Mountain is worth the short but steep (in spots) hike to the top.

To continue toward your goal, the summit of Saddle Mountain, bear left at the junction and pass through a small saddle. The track continues its climb, now heading east. In about 0.2 mile you will encounter the first of many switchbacks. As you climb, the views through the openings in the Douglas fir and western hemlock forest get better. Trilliums, Oregon grape, and sword ferns sprout beneath the forest canopy, as do red current, red huckleberry, and occasionally devil's club bushes.

At the sixth switchback, 0.9 mile from the trailhead, there will be an unusual-looking, narrow, and steep-sided rock outcropping to your left. This outcropping is a volcanic dike. This dike is visible well up the south face of Saddle Mountain.

The course passes the 1-mile marker at 2,320 feet elevation, and continues to switchback its way up the steep south side of Saddle Mountain. Before long the slope opens up allowing for almost continuous views. Woven wire covers the trail in some of the steeper spots. It seems that this would be slippery to walk on but with lug soles, the traction is fairly good even if the wire is wet. In a few spots cable handrails also assist the ascent. Sections of the trail along this slope are often wet and there may be water running down the trail in a couple of spots.

A dike is formed when magma forces its way up through a split in older rock. The older rock, being softer, erodes away faster than the cooled magma, leaving the magma in place to form a dike.

After making a total of twenty-one switchbacks, the route finally gets close to the ridgeline of Saddle Mountain at 2,900 feet elevation, slightly less than 2 miles from the trailhead. Soon the route crosses an open alp, with a view to the west of the Pacific Ocean, then descends slightly to the first saddle.

Once across the narrow saddle, the route climbs. Beside the tread, yellow glacier lilies (*Erythronium grandiflorum*), a close relative of the pink fawn lilies seen earlier, bloom about the first of May. The trail gains about 50 feet of elevation, then

Green Tip:

Wash dishes or clothes at least 200 feet from a river or lake. Bring the water to a spot with good drainage, and use only biodegradable soap in the smallest amount.

crosses a spur ridge and descends to the second saddle, at 2,820 feet elevation. From here on to the summit, the course is strenuous. The track climbs steeply and is braided in places. Wooden steps, held together with cables, aid the ascent in spots, but in many places the trail is so eroded that the steps are of little or no value. Cable handrails are of some assistance in a couple of places.

Just under 0.4 mile after passing the second saddle, the route reaches the 3,283-foot-high summit of Saddle Mountain. Around the summit area a pipe handrail keeps hikers away from the cliffs below. This rail also protects the rare plants, some of which survived the last ice age here, above the glaciers. From the summit bench, which makes a comfortable spot to rest if the wind isn't blowing, the views take in all points of the compass. To the northwest are the Columbia River Estuary and the city of Astoria. To the west is the Pacific Ocean, and to the east the Cascade Peaks rise above hazy green forested hills. A changing carpet of flowers blooms throughout the summer on the open alps near the summit. This is the end of the Saddle Mountain Trail, so you must return the way you came.

MILES AND DIRECTIONS

0.0 Begin at the Saddle Mountain Trailhead. GPS 45 57.772N 123 41.397W.

0.2 A path comes in from the right; bear left to stay on the main trail. (**Option:** This short path leads to a view of the south face of Saddle Mountain.)

2.1 Arrive at the first saddle.

2.2 Arrive at the second saddle.

2.6 Turn around at the summit. GPS 45 58.145N 123 41.122W.

5.2 Return to Saddle Mountain Trailhead. GPS 45 57.772N 123 41.397W.

Options: Make the 3.2-mile lollipop-loop hike to Soapstone Lake on the same trip. To reach Soapstone Lake Trailhead from Saddle Mountain Trailhead, first drive back to US 26. Turn right and drive west on US 26 for about 1 mile to the junction with Oregon Route 53. Turn left and head south on OR 53 for 4.8 miles to the junction with the road to Soapstone Lake Trailhead. There is a sign pointing to the trailhead here. Turn left and drive 0.3 mile east to the trailhead.

Bloom Lake Trail

From the trailhead at the side of U.S. Highway 26, hike the gentle grades of long-abandoned roadbeds, through lush second-growth forest, to a primitive picnic site on the shore of Bloom Lake. Then use your route-finding skills for a short distance cross-country to complete your circumnavigation of the lake, and return along the gentle roadbeds to the Bloom Lake Trailhead. Because most of this hike is along abandoned roadbeds and you have only a short distance where you will be bumping into trailside brush that gets very wet when it rains, this is a good trip for a rainy day.

Start: Bloom Lake Trailhead
Distance/type of hike: 3.5-mile lollipop-loop day hike or short backpack
Approximate hiking time: 2 hours
Difficulty: Easy, mostly following abandoned roadbeds, except for a 0.1-mile cross-country section where there is no trail.
Best season: March through November. Some years this route may be snow-free all year.
Canine compatibility and other trail users: This is a hikers-only trail, but restrained dogs are allowed.
Fees and permits: None
Maps: Oregon Department of Forestry *Clatsop State Forest* and *Tillamook State Forest;* National Geographic Oregon Topo on CD-ROM Disk 2; DeLorme's *Oregon Atlas and Gazetteer,* p. 64, B4. The map on the signboard at the trailhead or the one in this book is probably the only trail map necessary for this hike.
Trail contacts: Astoria District Office, Oregon Department of Forestry, 92219 Highway 202, Astoria, OR 97103; (503) 325-5451
Special considerations: Route-finding skills are required on a 0.1-mile cross-country section of the loop near the north end of Bloom Lake.

Finding the trailhead:
Drive west on the Sunset Highway, U.S. Highway 26, for approximately 50 miles from Portland. The Bloom Lake Trailhead, which is 4.5 miles west of (past) the Sunset Rest area, is on the left (south) side of the highway between Mileposts 24 and 25, just east of (before reaching) the Quartz Creek Bridge. The DeLorme's *Oregon Atlas and Gazetteer* covers the area, but this trailhead is not shown. Although this hike is in the Clatsop State Forest, the Oregon Department of Forestry's *Tillamook State Forest* map and guide (a large-scale topo map) covers this area. The National Geographic Oregon CD-ROM topo

shows most of this route as a primitive road. The parking area for this trailhead is shown but not labeled, and the lake is shown but the trail is not. There is parking for several cars but no other facilities at the trailhead. The elevation at the trailhead is approximately 1,210 feet.

THE HIKE

The Bloom Lake Trail crosses a bridge over the West Fork of Quartz Creek as you leave the trailhead. Once across the bridge the route turns right and heads west to a switchback, through the forest of red alder, with an understory of salmonberry bushes. The tread switchbacks to the left, then climbs through the woods, which in addition to the alders now includes Douglas fir and western hemlock trees.

The trail joins an abandoned roadbed 0.2 mile from the trailhead. By the time you reach the abandoned roadbed, you have gained about 120 feet of elevation. The course climbs gently to the south, following the abandoned roadbed. There is

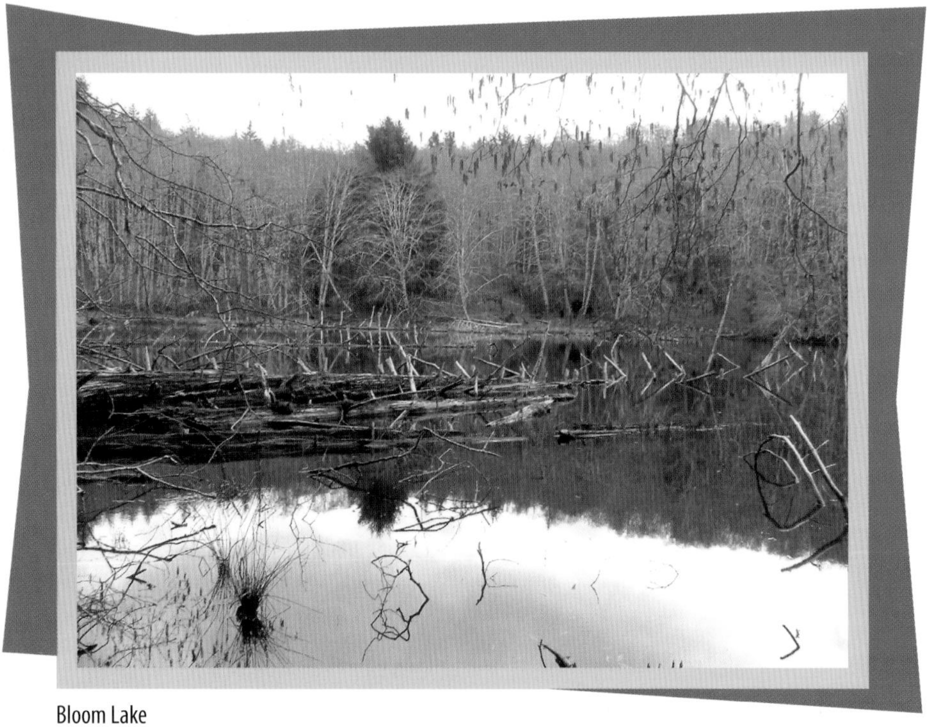

Bloom Lake

a small pond below the trail (roadbed) to the right, 0.6 mile into the hike. Here the route gradually bends around to the right (west). Another 0.5 mile of hiking brings you to the unsigned junction with the trail to the north shore of Bloom Lake, where the loop around Bloom Lake begins. At approximately 1,630 feet elevation, this junction is about as high as you get on this hike.

Red Alder (*Alnus rubra*)

Red alder, like all members of the alder family, are nitrogen-fixing plants. Nitrogen-fixing plants take nitrogen from the atmosphere and fix or deposit it in the soil. This process is tremendously important to the plants that will follow the alders, which need the soil nitrogen to live and grow. The copious amount of leaves shed by the alders each year adds large amounts of humus, also aiding in the growth of future plants.

To make the loop, don't turn onto the trail but continue on the roadbed, heading nearly straight to the west. In a little less than 0.2 mile, Bloom Lake will come into view below and to the right. The track crosses a creek 0.2 mile farther along. Salmonberry bushes hug the trail next to the water. Then you pass a marshy area covered with skunk cabbage, and in 0.1 mile more you'll reach a junction with a good gravel road. This road is open to motor vehicles.

Turn right on the gravel road and walk northwest, and soon cross another creek, as Bloom Lake comes into view to the right. After walking about 0.2 mile on the gravel road, there will be an abandoned roadbed to your right. Turn right onto the abandoned roadbed and follow it for 75 yards to the east. Then turn right on a path that leads 50 yards to a primitive picnic site along the northwest shore of Bloom Lake. The elevation of Bloom Lake is 1,552 feet.

To make the rest of the loop, go back the 50 yards to the abandoned roadbed and turn right. The next 200 yards of this route is where your route-finding skills come into play. After following the roadbed for a short distance, bear right and wind your way around the north end of Bloom Lake. Cross the lake's outlet stream and then walk a short distance northeast to pick up the trail. The trail is about 50 yards from the northern tip of the lake. There is a BLOOM LAKE sign close to the end of the trail. Once you find the trail, bear right and hike east, then southeast, along it for 0.3 mile to the junction with the abandoned roadbed, completing the loop. Turn left on the abandoned roadbed and hike back the way you came for 1.1 miles to the Bloom Lake Trailhead.

Bloom Lake Trail

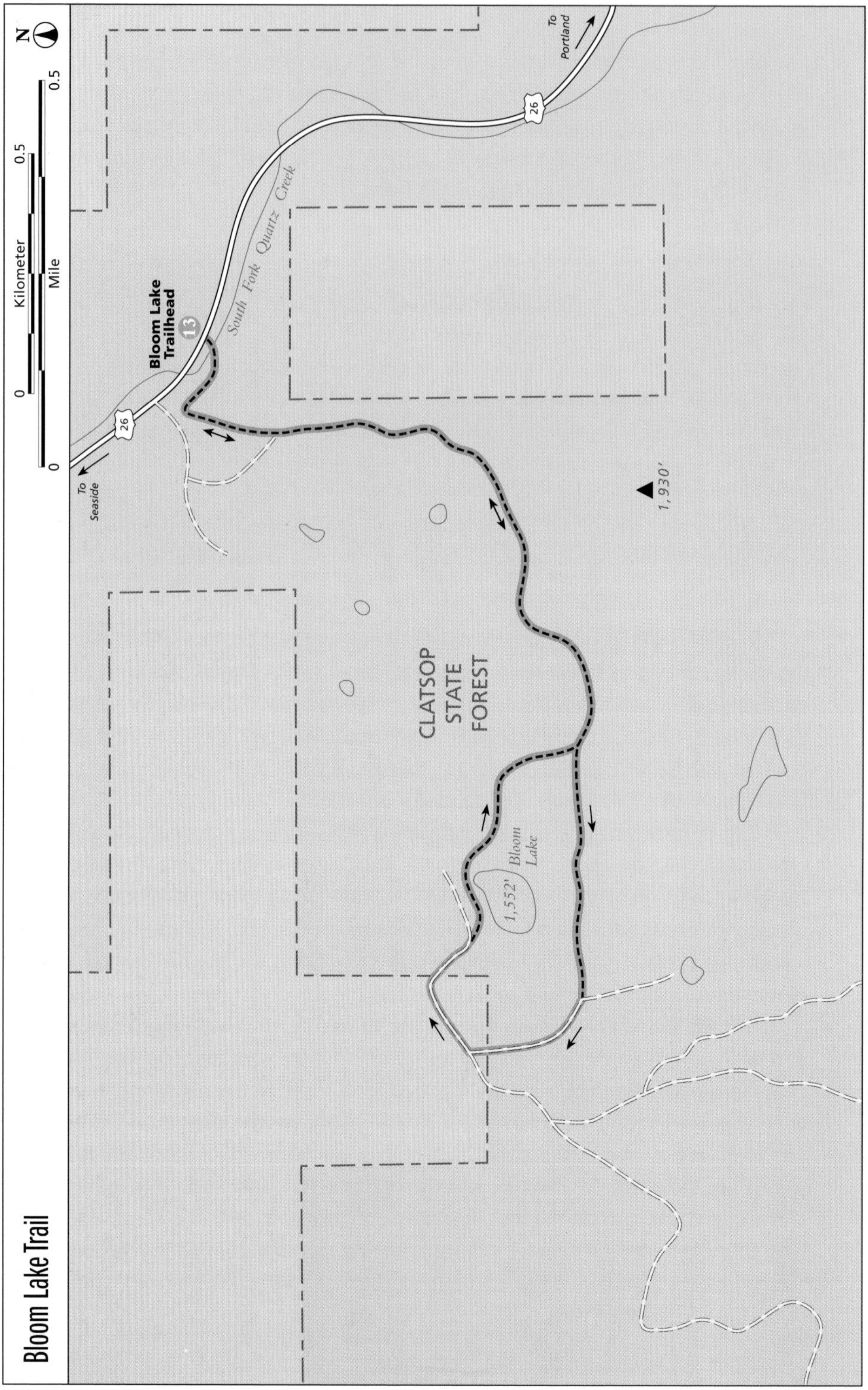

MILES AND DIRECTIONS

0.0 Begin at the Bloom Lake Trailhead. GPS 45 50.291N 123 30.819W.

1.1 Continue straight ahead on the path to the north shore of Bloom Lake. GPS 45 49.855N 123 31.486W.

1.6 Turn right at the junction, onto the gravel road.

1.9 Leave the gravel road for the abandoned roadbed near Bloom Lake and turn right. GPS 45 49.992N 123 31.803W.

2.4 Turn left on the abandoned roadbed. GPS 45 49.855N 123 31.486W.

3.5 Return to the Bloom Lake Trailhead. GPS 45 50.291N 123 30.819W.

Green Tip:
Don't take souvenirs home with you. This means natural materials such as plants, rocks, shells, and driftwood as well as historic artifacts such as fossils and arrowheads.

Willamette Valley Region

Lower South Falls in the Willamette Valley Region

These are the hikes that are closest to Portland—in fact, three of them are within the city. Hike 14 is in a great wildlife-viewing area that was once farmed and is now reverting to its natural state. Hike 15 passes several of the most beautiful waterfalls to be found anywhere.

In Forest Park within the city of Portland are Hikes 16, 17, and 18. These three are just representative glimpses of the hikes that await you in this huge urban park. Forest Park has a widely diverse and very extensive trail system, with approximately 65 miles of trails suitable for hiking, a little less than half of which are open to bikers and or equestrians. Many of the trails were once roads and their names reflect that origin, even though they are now closed to motorized travel. Leif Erikson Drive

Evening grosbeaks

was built to serve the houses that were once planned here. Soon after the road was constructed, a landslide closed it and it was not reopened. Now Leif Erikson Drive serves as an excellent bike path as well as a route for hikers and equestrians. The fire lanes, which will open to fire equipment should need arise, are also excellent routes. Several of the fire lanes are open to bikers and equestrians as well hikers and runners. The longest trail in Forest Park, the Wildwood Trail, is open only to hikers and runners. The Wildwood Trail provides a superb though gentle hiking experience without having to really leave the city.

You won't believe you're hiking so close to the urban center.

One note of caution: This is an urban environment, so don't leave anything of value in your car, whether it's locked or not.

14

Tualatin River National Wildlife Refuge

Before the establishment of the Tualatin River National Wildlife Refuge in 1992, nearly all the land that the refuge now encompasses was farmed. The portion of the refuge where this hike is located was basically a dairy farm, with crops grown mostly to feed the cows. The bottomlands here once grew some really beautiful corn, some of it 12 and 13 feet tall. Much of the refuge land, with the help of the refuge staff, is now reverting to the way it was before it was touched by the plow.

Start: Visitor Information Center parking area just north of U.S. Highway 99W
Distance/type of hike: 3.7-mile loop day hike
Approximate hiking time: 2 hours
Difficulty: Easy. The trail surface is mostly graded gravel.
Best season: May 1 to September 30 for the entire route. The 0.9-mile nature trail, which is the first part of this hike, is open year-round. Refuge hours are dawn to dusk.
Canine compatibility and other trail users: This is a hikers-only trail. Dogs and other stock, bikes, and jogging are prohibited.
Fees and permits: None at present, but in the near future there may be a charge for entering the parking area.
Maps: The map on the reader board next to the visitor center parking area and the one in this book should be all you need for this hike. Also, National Geographic Oregon topo on CD-ROM Disk 2; DeLorme's *Oregon Atlas and Gazetteer,* p. 60, A2
Trail contacts: Tualatin River National Wildlife Refuge, 16507 Roy Rogers Road, Sherwood, OR 97140; (503) 590-5811; fax (503) 590-6702; www.fws.gov/tualatinriver. Refuge information, (800) 344-WILD
Special considerations: Bring your binoculars, walk quietly, and allow lots of time for sitting and watching.

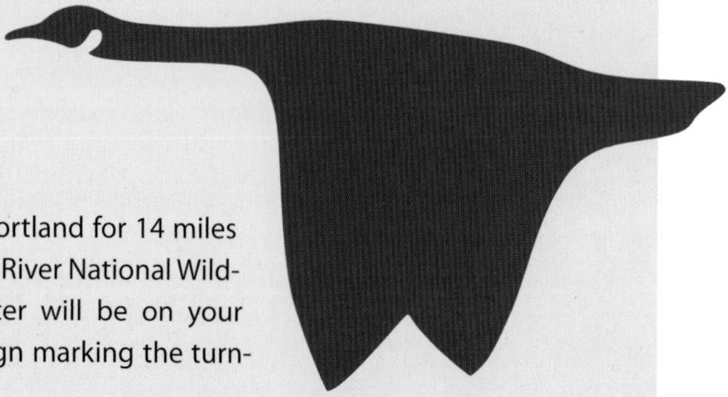

Finding the trailhead:
Drive southwest from Portland for 14 miles on US 99W. The Tualatin River National Wildlife Refuge Visitor Center will be on your right. There is a large sign marking the turn-

off. DeLorme's *Oregon Atlas and Gazetteer* map covers the area but does not show the refuge. The National Geographic Oregon CD-ROM topo covers the area but doesn't show the trails or the visitor center.

THE HIKE

The Tualatin River National Wildlife Refuge is home to almost 200 species of birds at various times of the year as well as another 75 species of mammals, reptiles, and amphibians. Take your time as you walk these trails and service roads while keeping quiet and watching the abundant life around you.

The well-graded gravel trail descends to the northeast as you leave the parking area. After descending a short distance, the route passes a bench and a switchback to the left. Unfortunately, looking to the right from the switchback, the view is of an auto-wrecking yard. Make the switchback and leave the junked cars behind as the tread passes a grove of young Douglas fir trees.

The track passes between two small ponds 0.1 mile from the parking area. Two benches are available here so you can sit quietly for a few minutes and enjoy

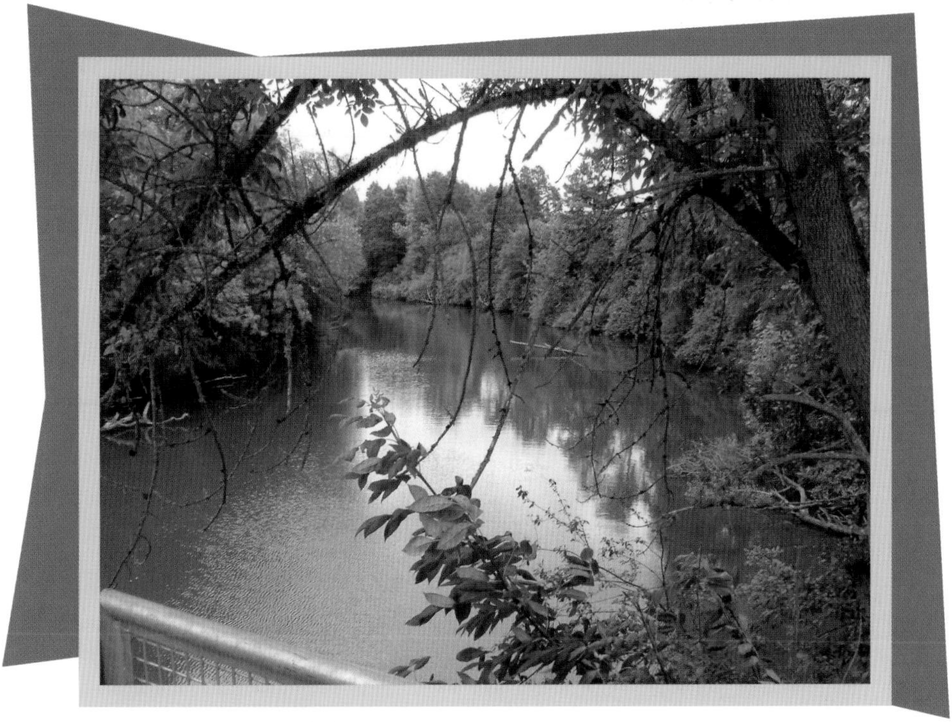

Tualatin River from viewing platform

Tualatin River National Wildlife Refuge

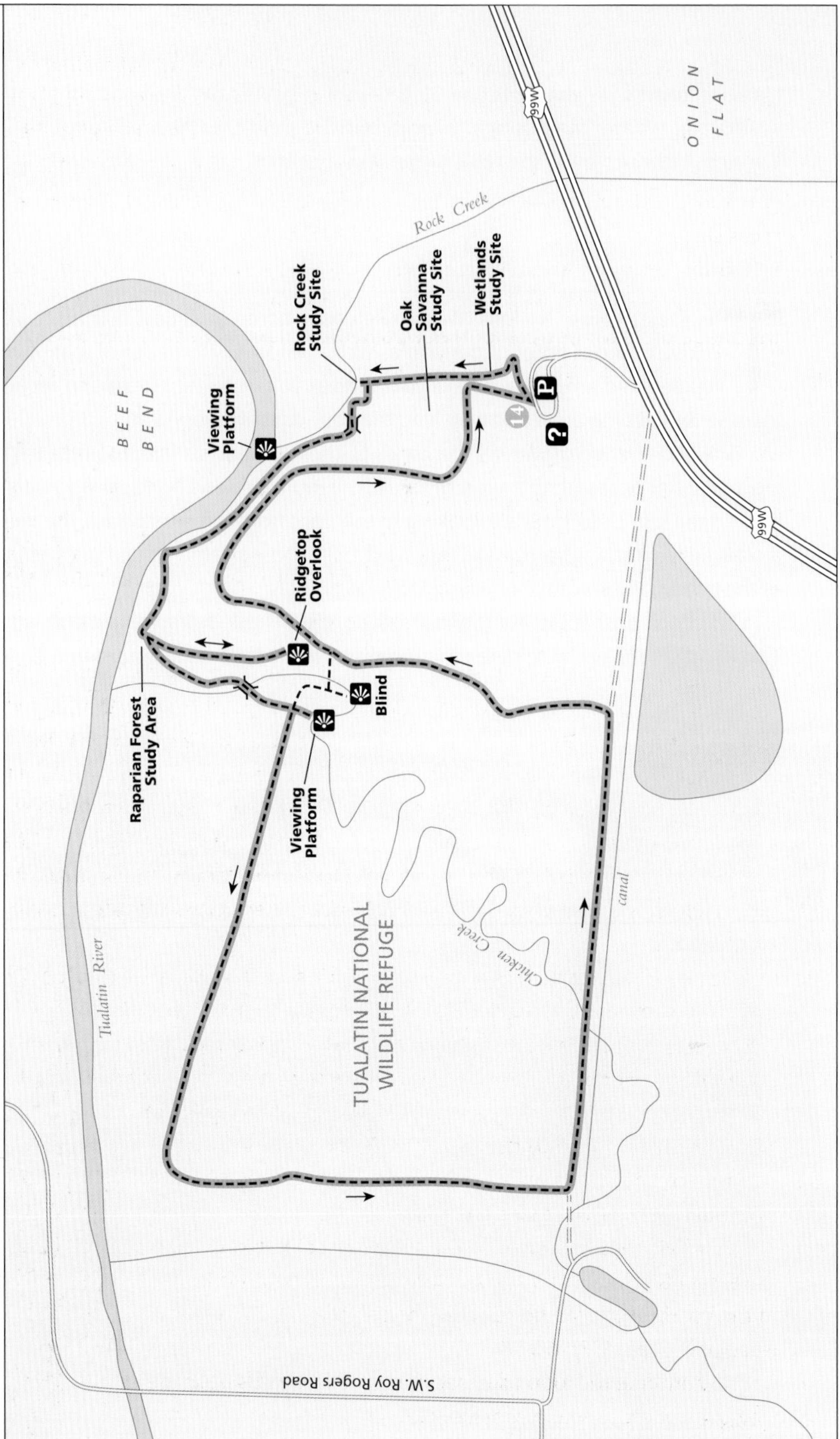

the Wetlands Study Site. Past the ponds the course passes through an area covered with scattered young Oregon white oak trees. Shortly the Oak Savanna Study Site will be a few yards to the left of the trail. Next the trail passes the Habitat Edges Study Site, which is to the right. Next is the Rock Creek Study Site, also to the right of the trail. A short side path here reaches Rock Creek. There are benches at all of these study sites.

Soon the trail crosses a bridge over a sluggish stream and gets very close to a service road, which will be part of your return hike. About 100 yards after crossing the bridge, there will be a platform viewpoint to the right of the trail, overlooking the Tualatin River. Reader boards next to the viewpoint make this an interesting stop.

Green Tip:

Even if it says it's biodegradable, don't put soap into streams or lakes. If you need to use soap, bring the water to you.

Past the platform viewpoint the trace soon enters a grove of large bigleaf maples (*Acer macrophyllum*) and quickly reaches the junction with the Ridgetop Overlook Trail. At this point you are 0.8 mile from the parking area. Turn left on the Ridgetop Overlook Trail and hike the 250 yards, through the Douglas firs, hazel brush, and Himalayan blackberries, to its end at the overlook. The route climbs a moderate grade for a short distance, gaining about 20 feet of elevation, then flattens along the ridgeline. The area around the Ridgetop Overlook is somewhat grown up with brush so the view is a little obstructed, but the short side trip is worth it anyway.

Return as you came along the Ridgetop Overlook Trail, then turn left on the main trail to continue your hike. Shortly the Riparian Forest Study Area will be to your right. Past the study area the route crosses a bridge over Chicken Creek, then quickly reaches a junction with a service road. Straight ahead (south) a few yards is the Wildlife Viewing Platform. Wild roses bloom next to the viewpoint in late June. This viewpoint is the end of the nature trail, and the turnaround point if this hike is between October 1 and April 30.

A wildlife photography blind is located a short distance to the east of this junction along the service road. A trail also leads to the blind, which can be reserved for personal use. To make a reservation, call (503) 590-5811.

To continue the loop hike, backtrack the few yards from the viewpoint to the junction with the service road and turn left (west) onto the roadbed. The route traverses areas of tall grass and passes several clumps of steeplebush (*Spiraea douglasii*). This part of the route also passes a couple of large grand firs (*Abies grandis*), which are somewhat uncommon in this area, as well as some large Douglas firs. After following the roadbed west for slightly over 0.5 mile, the route turns sharply to the left (south). You will reach a junction with another service road in a little more than 0.4 mile. Turn left here and head east along the service road, with a canal to your right. The route follows the canal for 0.5 mile, at which point you turn left again onto another service road and head north for 0.3 mile to another junction. The road to the left here will take you back to the Wildlife Viewing Platform. Turn right on this service road to continue the loop. In 0.7 mile you will reach the Visitor Information Center parking area and the end of your hike.

MILES AND DIRECTIONS

0.0 Begin at the Visitor Information Center parking area. GPS 45 22.936N 122 49.870W.

0.8 Turn left at the junction with the Ridgetop Overlook Trail, and go out and back. GPS 4523.284N 122 50.208W.

1.0 Rejoin the nature trail and turn left.

1.2 At the end of the nature trail, turn west onto the roadbed.

2.2 Turn left at the road junction.

2.7 Turn left at the road junction.

3.0 Bear right at the road junction.

3.7 Return to the Visitor Information Center parking area. GPS 45 22.936N 122 49.870W.

Options: Make this a short (1.8-mile) hike by hiking only out and back along the nature trail.

15

Silver Falls Loop

The waterfalls, most of which are accessed only by trail, are the centerpiece of Oregon's largest state park. Silver Falls State Park covers more than 5,000 acres in the foothills of the Cascade Range southeast of Silverton, Oregon. The hike described below leads the hiker to views of nine of these spectacular waterfalls, as they plunge over stacked layers of ancient lava.

Start: North Falls Trailhead
Distance/type of hike: 7-mile lollipop-loop day hike
Approximate hiking time: 3.5 hours
Difficulty: Easy, unless the trail is icy, as it sometimes is during the winter, when some spots would definitely get a strenuous rating.
Best season: The trails at Silver Falls State Park are generally open year-round. If you don't like crowds, come on a weekday in the fall, winter, or spring.
Canine compatibility and other trail users: This trail is for hikers only; dogs, horses, and bikes are prohibited. There are many miles of horse trails available in Silver Falls State Park—check the *Silver Falls Trail Guide* for their location. On many other trails in the state park, dogs are permitted on a leash 6 feet in length or shorter.
Fees and permits: Day-use parking permit $3 per car per day
Maps: *Silver Falls State Park Trail Guide,* available at the trailhead, or the map in this book are more than adequate for following these well-maintained trails. Also, National Geographic Oregon topo on CD-ROM Disk 2; DeLorme's *Oregon Atlas and Gazetteer,* p. 54, A3
Trail contacts: Oregon State Park Information Center, (800) 551-6949; Silver Falls State Park, (503) 873-8681, ext. 23; www.oregonstateparks.org
Special considerations: At times during the winter months, parts of this route can be very icy. Summer weekends are very busy at Silver Falls State Park, so don't expect to have the trail to yourself if you come at that time of the year.

Finding the trailhead:
From the Portland area, drive Interstate 5 south to Woodburn. Then follow Oregon Route 214 southeast to Silverton. From Silverton, continue 13.6 miles southeast on OR 214 to the North Falls Trailhead. The trailhead is on the right

side of the highway at 1,450 feet elevation. Adequate parking and restrooms are available at the trailhead. Trail maps are also available. This hike can also be accessed near its midpoint from the main Silver Falls Parking Area.

THE HIKE

The first 2.5 miles of this hike follows the Rim Trail. Cross the footbridge over the north fork of Silver Creek and bear left at the junction with the Upper North Falls Trail. To the right at this junction, it's only 0.2 mile to the Upper North Falls. In a few more yards, you will reach the junction with the Canyon Trail. The Canyon Trail turns to the right and follows the North Fork Silver Creek Canyon to the junction with the Winter Trail. See the options below for a possible return route along the Canyon Trail.

Bear left at the junction and hike west, climbing gently along the Rim Trail. The route parallels OR 214 through the forest of Douglas fir, western hemlock, western red cedar, and bigleaf maple. You will cross a small stream 0.2 mile after passing the junction with the Canyon Trail. Beneath the tall, sometimes moss-hung trees, Oregon grape and sword ferns cover the ground. A short distance farther along, there is a fleeting view of the North Falls, deep in the canyon to the right. The tread crosses a wooden bridge over a small stream 0.1 mile past the North Falls viewpoint. In spots salal bushes squeeze the trailside.

Green Tip:
Pack out what you pack in—even food scraps because they can attract wild animals.

The junction with the Winter Trail and the Winter Falls Trailhead are reached 0.9 mile from the North Falls Trailhead, at 1,410 feet elevation. This is the beginning of the loop portion of this hike. Bear left at the junction, staying on the Rim Trail, and cross the trailhead parking area. The route crosses the creek above Winter Falls and then heads south-southwest through the timber, climbing very gently. In slightly less than 0.3 mile, after climbing to a little over 1,500 feet elevation, the Rim Trail joins a paved bike path for a short distance. Soon the route bears to the right off the paved trail. Signs mark the route of the Rim Trail here. The Rim Trail angles across the bike path again 0.2 mile farther along. Then the route descends and crosses a road before reaching the Parking Lot A Trailhead. The Parking Lot A

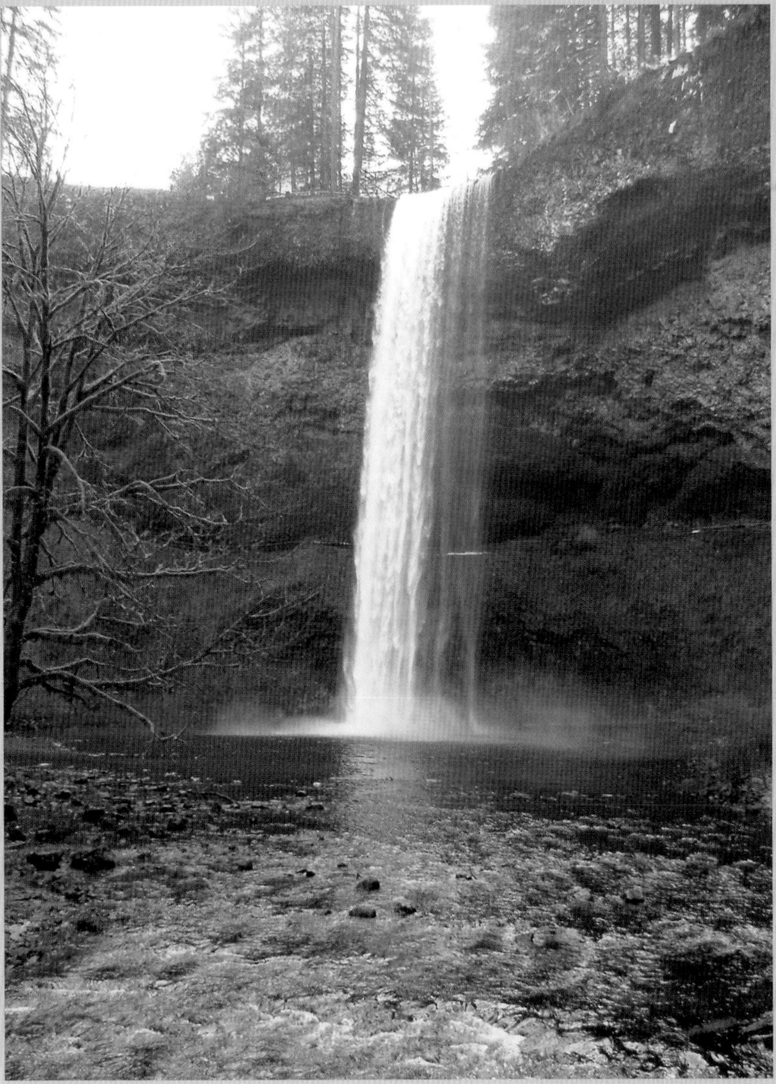

South Falls

Trailhead is 2.5 miles from the North Falls Trailhead at 1,370 feet elevation. This is the end of the Rim Trail.

For the next 3.1 miles, this hike follows the Canyon Trail. From the Parking Lot A Trailhead, the Canyon Trail heads west, crossing a picnic area, and passes a trail junction with paths to the main parking area and the South Falls Lodge, where the trail becomes paved. The historic Log Cabin will be to your right just after passing the junction. Just past the Log Cabin, another paved path to the left leads a short distance to the top of the South Falls and on to swimming and day-use areas. Bear right, staying on the Canyon Trail, and pass the junction with the Maple Ridge Trail, where you bear left. See the options below for a slightly shorter alternate hike along the Maple Ridge Trail.

Soon the route will begin the descent into the South Fork Silver Creek Canyon, passing a viewpoint, which is above to your right. After descending for a short distance, there will be another trail to the right, which leads 50 yards to a viewpoint of Frenchie Falls. Then the Canyon Trail makes a switchback to the left, continuing its descent into the canyon. Soon you will pass a bench, then make a switchback to the right. To the left a trail will take you behind the tumbling waters of the South Falls. You may take either trail here: They rejoin in a short distance next to a bridge over the south fork of Silver Creek. The bridge may be the best point from which to photograph the 177-foot-high South Falls as it plunges over the overhanging basalt cliff. Where the trails rejoin each other next to the bridge, the pavement ends and the route heads north along the shore of the south fork of Silver Creek.

In a little over 0.5 mile, you will see and hear the Lower South Falls to your right. The trail descends into the canyon bottom below the falls, via five switchbacks made up mostly of concrete steps. This spot can be very slippery during periods of subfreezing weather. During those times, if it were not for the handrail, this section of the route would become nearly impassable without the use of crampons. Even with the rail, you must be very careful here.

In the canyon bottom the tread heads upstream and passes behind the crashing waters of the 93-foot-high Lower South Falls. After coming out from behind the falls, the course soon begins to climb. At the top of the rise, after gaining about 50 feet of elevation, you will reach the second junction with the Maple Ridge Trail. This junction is 4 miles from the North Falls Trailhead at approximately 1,050 feet elevation. The Maple Ridge Trail is to the right. The track descends slightly, leaving the junction, as you head into the North Fork Silver Creek Canyon. Soon the course flattens and you pass an abandoned roadbed to your right.

A small waterfall comes into view, across the north fork of Silver Creek, 0.4 mile from the junction with the Maple Ridge Trail. In another 0.2 mile, the trail crosses the north fork of Silver Creek on a bridge above a beautiful, deep, clear, blue-green pool. A little over 0.1 mile after crossing the bridge, Lower North Falls will be to your right. Just past the falls a trail to Double Falls leads left for 0.1 mile to a viewpoint. The short side trip to the viewpoint of the two-stage falls, as it cascades 178 feet over successive layers of Columbia River Basalt, is well worth taking. Back on the main trail, you cross a bridge over the cheerfully bubbling waters of Hullt Creek, as it descends below Double Falls to join the north fork of Silver Creek.

After crossing the bridge you soon come to a viewing platform on the right

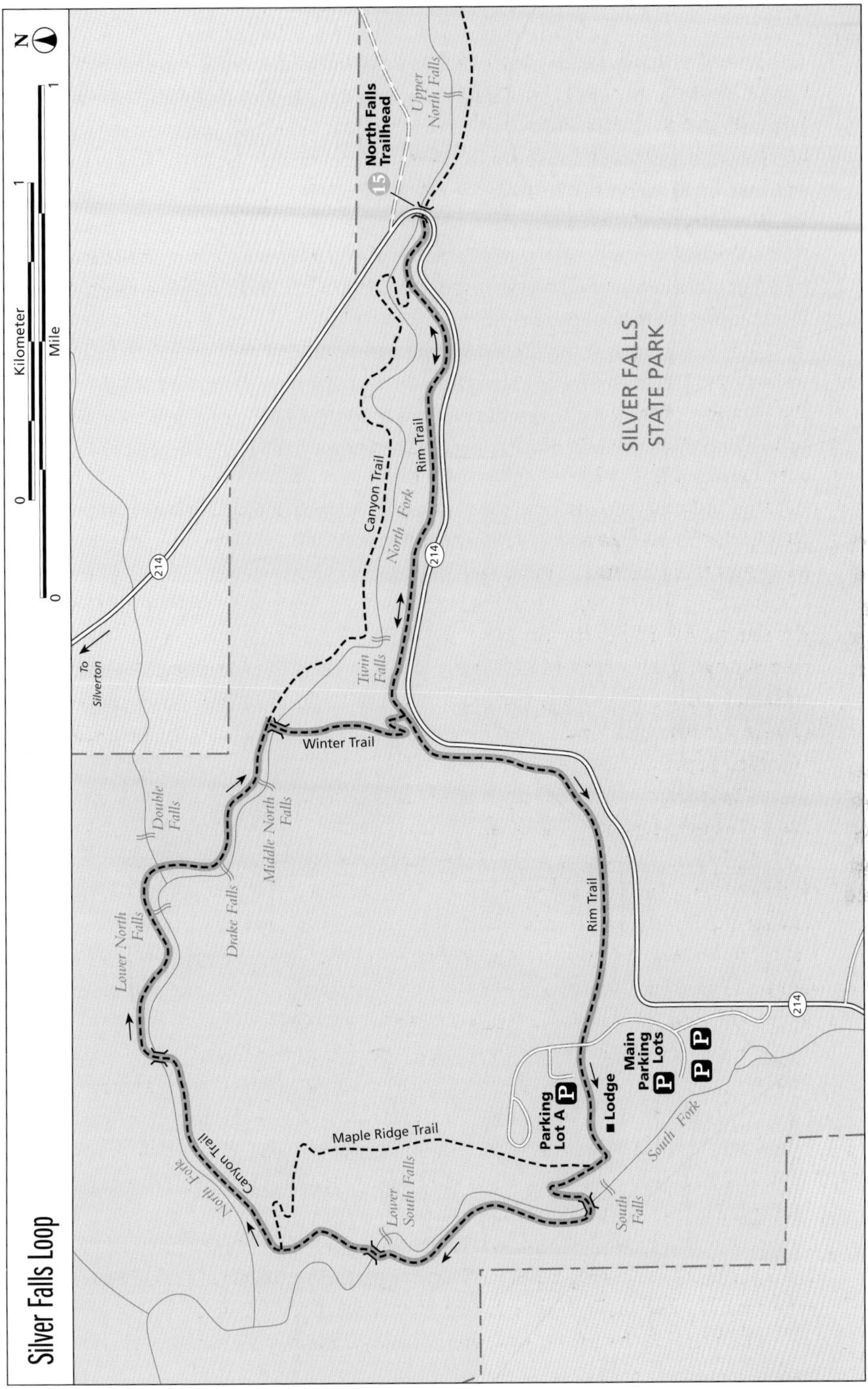
Silver Falls Loop
Kilometer
Mile
0
1
N
North Falls Trailhead
15
Upper North Falls
SILVER FALLS STATE PARK
Canyon Trail
Rim Trail
North Fork
214
To Silverton
Twin Falls
Winter Trail
Double Falls
Middle North Falls
Drake Falls
Lower North Falls
Rim Trail
Parking Lot A
Lodge
Main Parking Lots
Maple Ridge Trail
Canyon Trail
North Fork
Lower South Falls
South Falls
South Fork

side of the trail that overlooks Drake Falls. Middle North Falls comes into view to the right, 0.2 mile farther along. Just before reaching the 106-foot-high falls, there will be a path to the right that leads behind the falls. Bear left, staying on the main trail, and in a little less than 0.2 mile, there will be a reader board next to the trail with a trail map on it. In another 50 yards the route reaches the junction with the Winter Trail. This junction, at approximately 1,200 feet elevation, is 5.6 miles into the hike. At the junction the route leaves the Canyon Trail and follows the Winter Trail for 0.5 mile. For more information on the rest of the Canyon Trail and a possible alternate return route, see the options below.

Turn to the right at the junction and cross the bridge over the north fork of Silver Creek. The Winter Trail climbs gently through the moss-hung forest. Beneath the tall trees sword ferns cover much of the ground. A few Pacific yew trees also grow along this creek bed. The Pacific yew (*Taxus brevifolia*) is the source of Taxol, a cancer drug.

The route passes a bench, then makes a switchback to the left as it climbs toward the rim of the canyon. At the switchback Winter Falls is in view. The tread makes another switchback, this one to the right, and passes another bench before

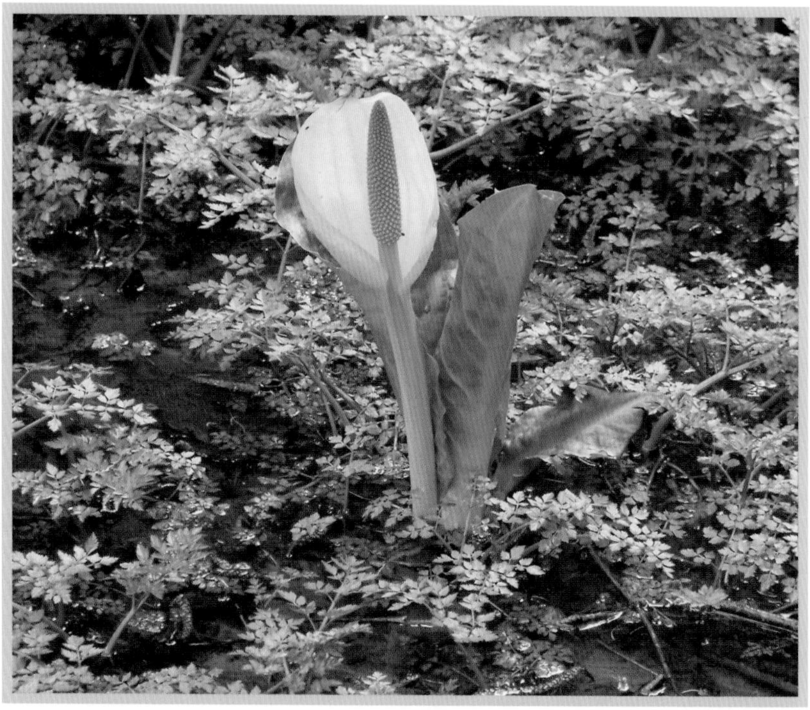

Skunk cabbage

reaching the junction with the Rim Trail near the Winter Falls Trailhead. Turn left at the junction and retrace your steps for 0.9 mile, back to the North Falls Trailhead and parking area.

MILES AND DIRECTIONS

0.0 Begin at the North Falls Trailhead. GPS 44 53.057N 122 37.225W.

0.9 Bear left at the junction with the Winter Trail at Winter Falls Trailhead, staying on the Rim Trail. GPS 44 53.074N 122 38.406W.

2.5 The Rim Trail ends at Parking Lot A, and the Canyon Trial begins. GPS 44 52.768N 122 39.266W.

2.7 Pass the junction with the Maple Ridge Trail and bear left.

2.9 Arrive at the bridge below the South Falls.

3.7 Arrive at Lower South Falls.

4.0 Pass the second junction with the Maple Ridge Trail.

5.0 Arrive at Lower North Falls.

5.6 The route follows the Winter Trail for 0.5 mile. GPS 44 53.304N 122 38.427W.

6.1 Turn left at the junction with the Rim Trail at Winter Falls Trailhead. GPS 44 53.074N 122 38.406W.

7.0 Return to the North Falls Trailhead. GPS 44 53.057N 122 37.225W.

Options: If you continue on the Canyon Trail from the junction with the Winter Trail, 5.6 miles into the hike, it is a 1.2-mile hike to the North Falls Trailhead, making it a slightly shorter alternative to the route described above. This section of the Canyon Trail passes Twin Falls and behind the 136-foot-high North Falls along the way.

The Maple Ridge Trail, 2.7 miles into the hike, can also be used as a slightly shorter alternate route for part of the hike described above. While it is about 0.3 mile shorter, it has the disadvantage of missing two of the waterfalls.

From the North Falls Trailhead, it's only a short, 0.2-mile hike, to the 65-foot-high Upper North Falls. To get there, first cross the footbridge, then turn right at the first junction and hike underneath the highway bridge to the falls.

16 Wildwood Trail: Newberry Road to Springville Road Trailhead

The Wildwood Trail makes a delightful hike through the second-growth forest of Forest Park at any time of the year. This hike covers 7.7 miles of this 30.2-mile-long route. To keep the hiker or runner advised of their location, there are mile markers at 0.25-mile intervals along the trail.

Start: Newberry Road Trailhead
Distance/type of hike: 8.1-mile shuttle day hike
Approximate hiking time: 3.5 hours
Difficulty: Smooth, easy-to-follow trails
Best season: Year-round
Canine compatibility and other trail users: This is a hikers-only trail, but restrained dogs are allowed.
Fees and permits: None
Maps: *Green Trails Forest Park,* map number 426s; National Geographic Oregon topo on CD-ROM Disk 2; DeLorme's *Oregon Atlas and Gazetteer,* p. 66, D2
Trail contacts: Portland Parks and Recreation, 1120 SW Fifth Avenue, Suite 1302, Portland, OR 97204; (503) 823-PLAY; www.parks.ci.portland.or.us
Special considerations: Don't leave valuables in your car.

Finding the trailhead:
From downtown Portland, drive west (actually northwest) on U.S. Highway 30 for approximately 10 miles, then turn left onto Newberry Road. Follow Newberry Road for 1.5 miles to the trailhead, which is on the left side of the road.

To reach the Springville Road Trailhead, where this hike ends, continue southwest and west on Newberry Road for 0.6 mile to the junction with Skyline Boulevard. Turn left on Skyline Boulevard and follow it southeast for 3.6 miles to the junction with Springville Road. Turn left on Springville Road and follow it a short distance northeast to the trailhead.

DeLorme's *Oregon Atlas and Gazetteer* does not show either of the trailheads. The National Geographic Oregon CD-ROM topo covers the area but not this specific trail. There is parking for three or four cars at the Newberry Road Trailhead and several spaces at the Springville Road Trailhead but no other facilities.

THE HIKE

The Wildwood Trail descends as you leave the Newberry Road Trailhead. At the beginning of the route, the forest is mostly made up of bigleaf maples, but soon western red cedar, Douglas fir, and western hemlock join the mix of timber. The route soon crosses a couple of small wooden bridges, then traverses a slope through the second-growth forest. You will cross six more of these small bridges before passing beneath some power lines and reaching the junction with Fire Lane 15, 1.8 miles into the hike. The track crosses a small ridgeline just before you get to the fire lane.

The Wildwood Trail crosses the fire lane and continues southeast. After crossing several more of the small wooden bridges, there is a bench with a plaque commemorating Benjamin Collins, a volunteer who was instrumental in creating this trail. A little more than 0.4 mile ahead and after crossing five more of the small bridges, the route passes the 27.5-mile mark and reaches the junction with the BPA Road. This junction is at 920 feet elevation, slightly more than 200 feet higher than the Newberry Road Trailhead.

To continue on the Wildwood Trail, turn left on the BPA Road and hike a few yards, then turn right leaving the roadbed. Upon leaving the BPA Road, the Wildwood Trail descends through the alders, maples, and firs and passes below some power lines. In about 0.25 mile the tread makes a switchback to the right. By the time you reach Mile Marker 26.75, the route has descended to about 700 feet elevation. In a few spots vine maple branches hang low over the trail.

Vine Maple (*Acer circinatum*)

A shrub or small tree, the vine maple has leaves that are easy to differentiate from those of the bigleaf maple by their size, which is much smaller, and by the number of lobes on the leaves. Vine maple leaves have seven to nine lobes, whereas bigleaf maple leaves have only five.

The route then begins to climb gently, and by the time you reach the junction with Newton Road, you are back up to 820 feet elevation. The Wildwood Trail crosses Newton Road and then descends very gently as you hike south. In 0.4 mile there will be a trail to the right, which connects with Newton Road in a short distance. Bear left, staying on the Wildwood Trail, and in a short distance there will be a wooden bridge. On the bridge is a plaque that states "Be free where you are/ In loving memory of Gaelle Anne Snell 1961–2003." Three hundred yards farther along, another trail to the right leads .08 mile (about 140 yards) to the Newton

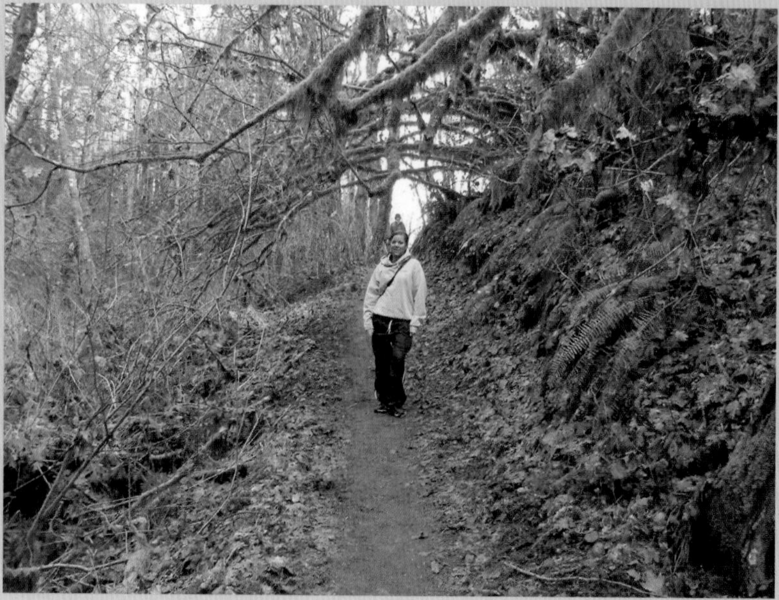

Moss-hung limbs over the Wildwood Trail

Road Trailhead. Stay on the Wildwood Trail and hike another 250 yards to the junction with Fire Lane 10. At the junction with Fire Lane 10, you are 4.8 miles from the Newberry Road Trailhead.

Cross the fire lane, staying on the Wildwood Trail, and in 0.1 mile, just after passing Mile Marker 25¼, there will be a bench on the right side of the trail. This bench is dedicated to Bruno Kolkowsky (1910–90), another dedicated volunteer who was a driving force in the trail construction. A short distance farther along, there is a view of Mount St. Helens to the left. This view is only possible in the winter, when the trees are bare of leaves. Another 0.2 mile of walking brings you to the junction with Fire Lane 8, which is an unsigned roadbed to the right. Slightly less than 0.4 mile after passing the junction with Fire Lane 8 is the Germantown Road Trailhead. The Germantown Road Trailhead is at 780 feet elevation and 5.5 miles from the Newberry Road Trailhead, where this hike started.

The Germantown Road Trailhead is a very popular starting and ending point for both hikes and runs along the Wildwood Trail. There are parking areas on both sides of Germantown Road at the trailhead. To continue your hike along the Wildwood Trail, turn right along the shoulder of Germantown Road and walk a few yards southwest. Be careful of the traffic as you cross Germantown Road, it can be

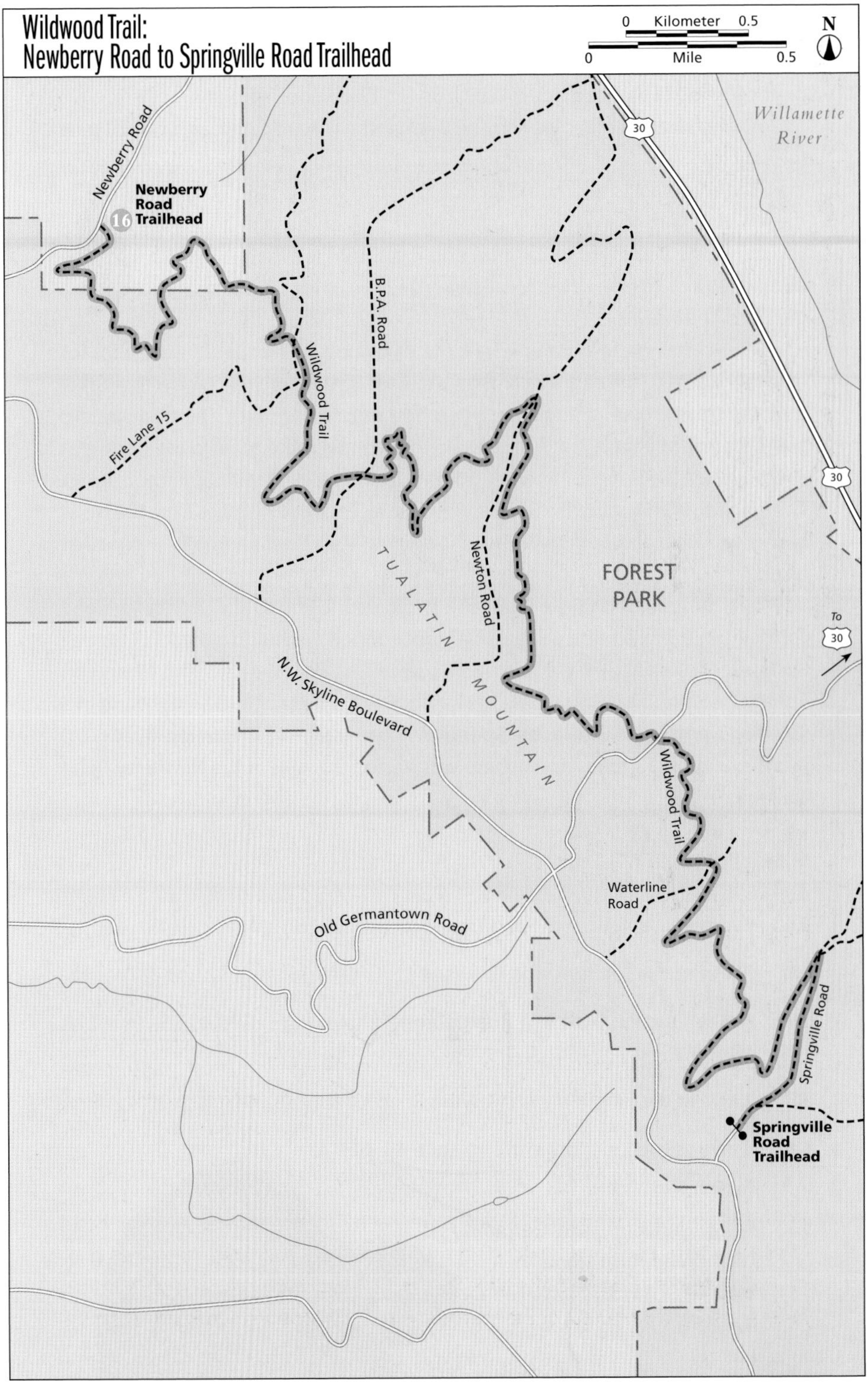
Wildwood Trail:
Newberry Road to Springville Road Trailhead
0 Kilometer 0.5
0 Mile 0.5
N
Willamette River
30
Newberry Road
Newberry Road Trailhead
16
B.P.A. Road
Wildwood Trail
Fire Lane 15
30
TUALATIN
Newton Road
FOREST PARK
To
30
MOUNTAIN
N.W. Skyline Boulevard
Wildwood Trail
Waterline Road
Old Germantown Road
Springville Road
Springville Road Trailhead

heavy and sometimes moves rather fast. At the southwest end of the parking area, on the far side of the road, you will pick up the Wildwood Trail again.

A short distance after leaving the Germantown Road Trailhead, you will pass the junction with the Canyon Trail. Bear slightly right, staying on the Wildwood Trail. The route gains about 100 feet of elevation, in the slightly over 0.6 mile to the junction with the Waterline Trail. A right turn on the Waterline Trail will take you to Skyline Boulevard in 0.4 mile, and if you turn left here, it's about the same distance to Leif Erikson Drive. Mile Marker 24 is on a tree next to the junction with the Waterline Trail.

After crossing the Waterline Trail, the Wildwood Trail leads southwest for 0.3 mile then turns to the east as it crosses a stream. Just before reaching Mile Marker 23½, the tread crosses a ridgeline, where you turn to the south. The trace crosses another small stream 0.5 mile farther along. Here the route turns to the northeast and traverses the slope for another 0.5 mile to the junction with Springville Road. The junction with Springville Road at 920 feet elevation is 7.7 miles from the Newberry Road Trailhead. Springville Road is open to equestrians and bikers as well as hikers.

Turn right on Springville Road and begin your climb to the Springville Road Trailhead. In 0.3 mile there will be a trail (abandoned roadbed) to the left. This trail leads a short distance east to join the Hardesty Trail. Bear slightly right, staying on Springville Road, and shortly pass the junction with Fire Lane 7. Bear right and in a few more yards you will be at the Springville Road Trailhead. This trailhead at 1,070 feet elevation is 8.1 miles from where you started this hike at the Newberry Road Trailhead.

MILES AND DIRECTIONS

0.0 Begin at the Newberry Road Trailhead. GPS 45 36.333N 122 49.411W.

1.8 Arrive at the junction with Fire Lane 15. GPS 45 36.089N 122 48.777W.

2.7 At the junction with BPA Road, turn left, then right. GPS 45 35.796N 122 48.606W.

3.9 Arrive at the junction with Newton Road. GPS 45 35.986N 122 48.022W.

4.8 Arrive at the junction with Fire Lane 10. GPS 45 35.421N 122 48.039W.

5.5 At the junction with Germantown Road, turn right, then left. GPS 45 35.275N 122 47.635W.

6.2 Pass the junction with the Waterline Trail.

7.7 Turn right on Springville Road at the junction. GPS 45 34.711N 122 47.295W.

8.1 End at the Springville Road Trailhead. GPS 45 34.472N 122 47.295W.

Options: If you would like to lengthen your hike along the Wildwood Trail and still exit via the Springville Road Trailhead, continue along the Wildwood Trail for another 3.8 miles past Springville Road, to the unmarked junction with the Trillium Trail. The Trillium Trail junction is just before the Wildwood Trail crosses Doane Creek. Turn right and follow the steep but short Trillium Trail for a little less than 0.3 mile to Fire Lane 7 and on to the Springville Road Trailhead. The *Green Trails* map shows this route as well as several other options clearly.

Green Tip:

Observe wildlife from a distance. Don't interfere in their lives—both of you will be better for it.

17

Loop from Springville Road Trailhead

Although this is a loop hike, nearly 3.8 of its 4.7 total miles are along the gentle Wildwood Trail and through vibrant second-growth forest. This is an excellent hike on which to begin your exploration of Forest Park.

Start: Springville Road Trailhead
Distance/type of hike: 4.7-mile loop day hike
Approximate hiking time: 2 hours
Difficulty: Moderate. Trail surfaces are good, but there are fairly steep grades in a couple of places.
Best season: All year
Canine compatibility and other trail users: Much of this hike is along the Wildwood Trail, which is a hikers-only trail with restrained dogs allowed. The other trails are also open to mountain bikes and horses.
Fees and permits: None
Maps: *Green Trails Forest Park,* map number 426s; National Geographic Oregon topo on CD-ROM Disk 2; DeLorme's *Oregon Atlas and Gazetteer,* p. 66, D2
Trail contacts: Portland Parks and Recreation, 1120 SW Fifth Avenue, Suite 1302, Portland, OR 97204; (503) 823-PLAY; www.parks.ci.portland.or.us
Special considerations: Don't leave valuables in your car. While this hike is fairly short, it does require that close attention be paid to a couple of unsigned trail junctions. All of the trails described in this hike are clearly shown on the *Green Trails* map.

Finding the trailhead:
From downtown Portland, drive west (actually northwest) on U.S. Highway 30 for approximately 7 miles. Then turn left onto Germantown Road. This junction is just past the St. Johns Bridge. Follow Germantown Road for 2.1 miles to the junction with Skyline Boulevard and turn left onto Skyline Boulevard. Drive southeast for 1 mile to the junction with Springville Road. Turn left on Springville Road and drive a short distance to the Springville Road Trailhead, at 1,070 feet elevation. The National Geographic Oregon CD-ROM topo on CD-ROM Disk 2 covers the area but this trail is not shown. The DeLorme's *Oregon Atlas and Gazetteer* does not show this trailhead. There is adequate parking at the trailhead but no other facilities.

THE HIKE

From the parking area at the Springville Trailhead, hike east along Springville Road. Shortly you will pass a gate. A few more steps brings you to the junction with Fire Lane 7. Turn right onto Fire Lane 7 and hike east for 0.1 mile to the junction with the Hardesty Trail. Bear slightly right at the junction, staying on Fire Lane 7. In slightly less than 0.1 mile, there will be a path to the right, with a gas-line marker next to it. This unmarked path is the Trillium Trail.

Turn right and begin to descend the moderately steep Trillium Trail through a forest of red alder. In a little less than 0.3 mile, you will reach a junction with the Wildwood Trail. This junction, which also has no sign, is next to the bridge where the Wildwood Trail crosses Doane Creek.

Do not cross the bridge but rather turn left on the Wildwood Trail and head downstream along Doane Creek. By the time you reach Mile Marker 18¾, the tread has moved some distance above the creek bed. The junction with Fire Lane 7 (Oil Line Road) is reached 0.7 mile from the junction with the Trillium Trail. At the junction a path to the right descends a short distance to join Leif Erikson Drive. Leif Erikson Drive is a road that is open to hikers, bikers, and equestrians but is closed to

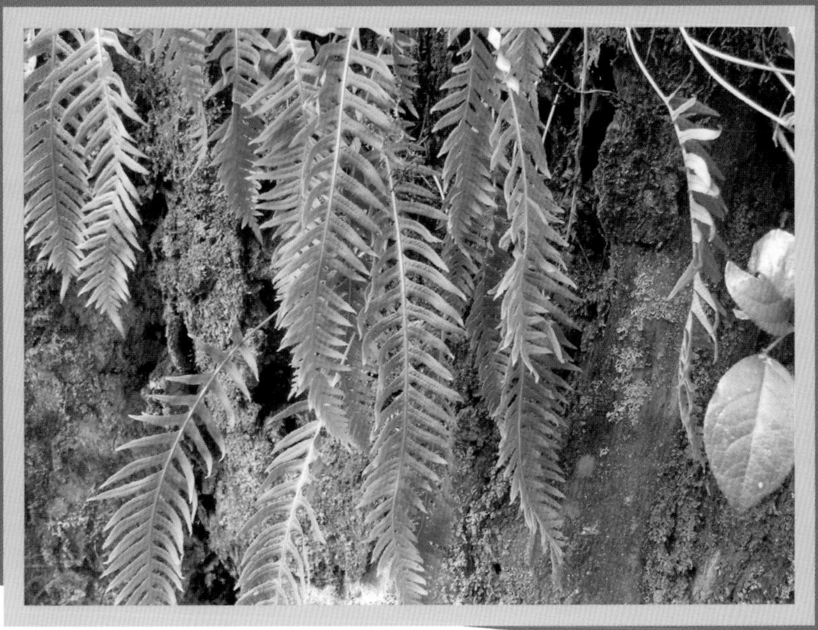

Licorice fern

motor vehicles. To the left, Fire Lane 7 leads back to the Springville Trailhead in 1.1 miles. Leaving the junction, head west, staying on the Wildwood Trail. From near the junction, Mount St. Helens can be seen through the trees to the northeast on clear days, but only in the wintertime when the limbs are bare of leaves.

The Wildwood Trail reaches the junction with Fire Lane 7a (Gas Line Road) 0.6 mile from the junction with Fire Lane 7. This junction, at 820 feet elevation, is 1.8 miles into the hike. There is a trail to the right at the junction that leads a short distance to Leif Erikson Drive. To the left, Fire Lane 7a climbs 0.3 mile southwest to join Fire Lane 7.

Continue west on the Wildwood Trail from the junction with Fire Lane 7a. The route traverses two large draws in slightly over 1 mile to the junction with the Ridge Trail. Some of the larger Douglas fir trees along the Wildwood Trail are located along the sides of these draws. While these trees are only medium-size as Dougs (as Douglas firs are commonly called) go, some of them approach 4 feet in diameter.

The junction with the Ridge Trail is reached 2.8 miles from the Springville Trailhead (via the route described here). The *Green Trails* map shows this junction somewhat incorrectly. To the left the Ridge Trail climbs to meet Fire Lane 7 in 0.4 mile. To the right it's nearly that far to Leif Erikson Drive. As you would expect, the Ridge Trail follows a ridge. The Wildwood Trail crosses this ridge and continues to the west.

Douglas fir* (Pseudotsuga menziesii) *is not a true fir but a separate and unique species.

Stay on the Wildwood Trail and climb slightly, reaching a little over 900 feet elevation, before beginning to descend. The track reaches the first junction with the Hardesty Trail 0.7 mile from the junction with the Ridge Trail. To the right from this junction, the Hardesty descends for 0.3 mile to a junction with Leif Erikson Drive. The Hardesty Trail and the Wildwood Trail follow the same route for a short distance, after which you reach the second junction with the Hardesty Trail. From this junction, the Hardesty Trail turns to the left to climb for 0.3 mile to a junction with Fire Lane 7, near the Springville Trailhead.

Stay on the Wildwood Trail and hike west for about 0.1 mile. The route then makes a turn to the northeast as you cross the bottom of a draw. In another 0.3 mile the tread turns west again, and 0.3 mile farther along you will reach the junction with Springville Road, at 920 feet elevation.

Turn left on Springville Road and begin the 150-foot climb to the Springville Road Trailhead. There will be a trail (abandoned roadbed) to the left in 0.3 mile. This trail leads a short distance east to join the Hardesty Trail. Bear slightly right staying

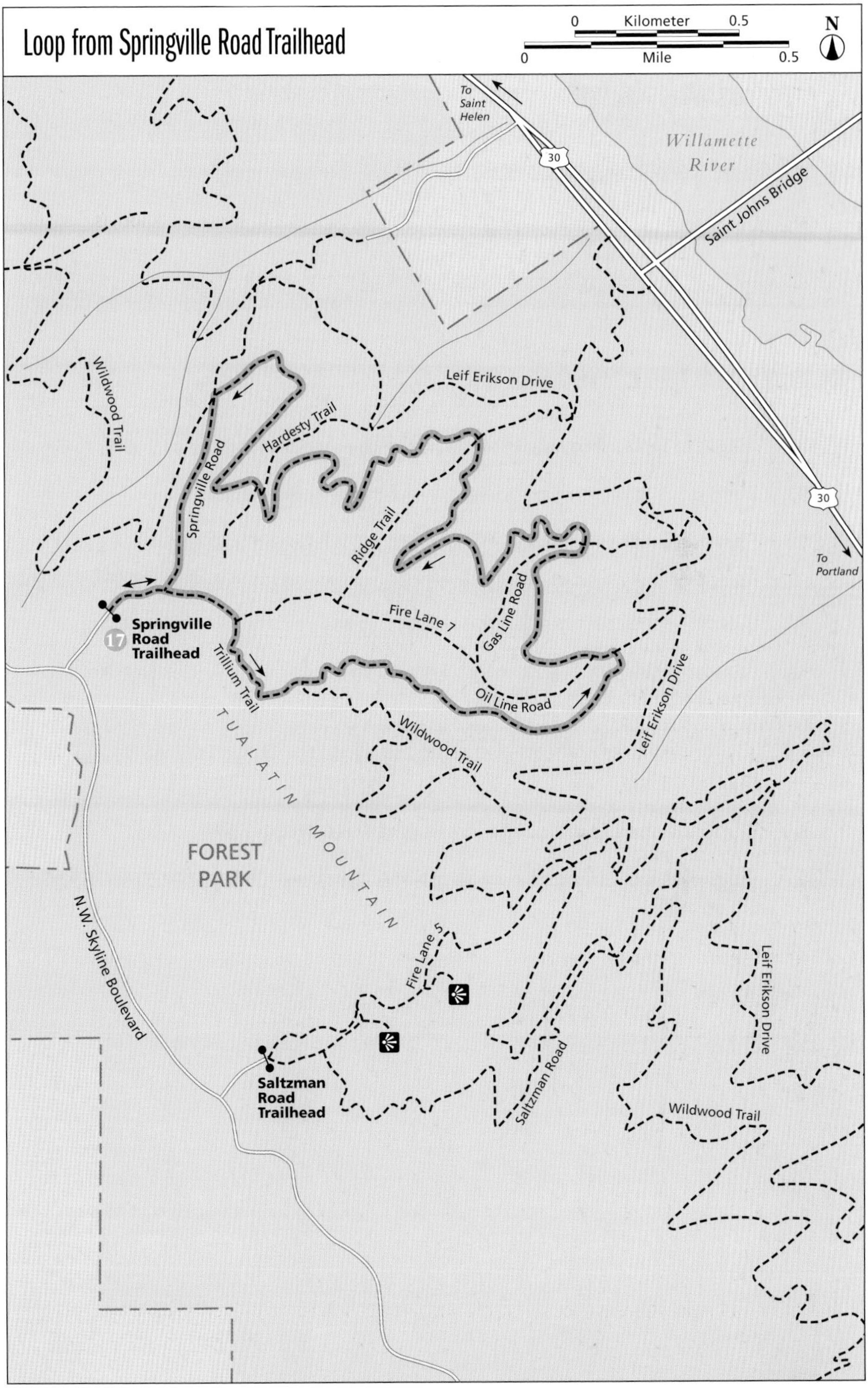
Loop from Springville Road Trailhead
0 Kilometer 0.5
0 Mile 0.5
N
To Saint Helen
Willamette River
30
Saint Johns Bridge
30
To Portland
Leif Erikson Drive
Hardesty Trail
Wildwood Trail
Springville Road
Ridge Trail
Fire Lane 7
Gas Line Road
Springville Road Trailhead
17
Trillium Trail
Oil Line Road
Leif Erikson Drive
Wildwood Trail
TUALATIN MOUNTAIN
FOREST PARK
N.W. Skyline Boulevard
Fire Lane 5
Saltzman Road Trailhead
Saltzman Road
Leif Erikson Drive
Wildwood Trail

on Springville Road and shortly pass the junction with Fire Lane 7. Bear right and in a few more yards you will be at the Springville Road Trailhead.

Green Tip:
Go out of your way to avoid birds and animals that are mating or taking care of their young.

MILES AND DIRECTIONS

0.0 Begin at the Springville Road Trailhead. GPS 45 34.472N 122 47.295W.

0.2 Turn right at the unmarked junction with the Trillium Trail.

0.5 Turn left at the unmarked junction with the Wildwood Trail. GPS 45 34.292N 122 46.003W.

1.2 Continue straight ahead at the junction with Fire Lane 7 (Oil Line Road).

1.8 Continue straight ahead at the junction with Fire Lane 7A (Gas Line Road) GPS 45 34.550N 122 46.257W.

2.8 Continue straight ahead at the junction with the Ridge Trail. 45 34.715N 122 46.495W.

3.5 Continue straight ahead at the first junction with the Hardesty Trail.

4.3 Turn left on Springville Road at the junction. GPS 45 34.711N 122 47.295W.

4.7 Return to the Springville Road Trailhead. GPS 45 34.472N 122 47.295W.

Options: Shorter hikes can be made by returning to the trailhead via the Oil Line, Gas Line, or Ridge Trails.

18

Loop from Saltzman Road Trailhead

This hike is an excellent, condensed introduction to the various types of trails that you can expect to find within Forest Park. It includes a steep fire lane and steep winding trails as well as a gentle roadbed that is also a popular bike route and a section of the very gentle Wildwood Trail, which is a hikers-only route.

Start: Saltzman Road Trailhead
Distance/type of hike: 4.1-mile lollipop-loop day hike
Approximate hiking time: 2 hours
Difficulty: Moderate. Trail surfaces are good, but there are fairly steep grades in a couple of places.
Best season: Year-round
Canine compatibility and other trail users: Some of this hike is along the Wildwood Trail, which is a hikers-only trail with restrained dogs allowed. The other trails are also open to mountain bikes and horses.
Fees and permits: None
Maps: *Green Trails Forest Park,* map number 426s; National Geographic Oregon topo on CD-ROM Disk 2; DeLorme's *Oregon Atlas and Gazetteer,* p. 66, D2
Trail contacts: Portland Parks and Recreation, 1120 SW Fifth Avenue, Suite 1302, Portland, OR 97204; (503) 823-PLAY; www.parks.ci.portland.or.us
Special considerations: Don't leave valuables in your car. While this hike is fairly short, it does require that close attention be paid to each of the trail junctions. This route makes several turns at unsigned junctions. All of the trails described in this hike are clearly shown on the *Green Trails* map.

Finding the trailhead:
From downtown Portland, drive west (actually northwest) on U.S. Highway 30 for approximately 7 miles. Then turn left onto Germantown Road. This junction is just past the St. Johns Bridge. Follow Germantown Road for 2.1 miles to the junction with Skyline Boulevard. Turn left on Skyline Boulevard and drive southeast for 1.8 miles to the junction with Saltzman Road. Turn left and go a short distance to the trailhead.

18

The National Geographic Oregon CD-ROM topo covers the area, but this trail is not shown. The trailhead is not shown on the DeLorme *Oregon Atlas and Gazetteer.* There is parking for several vehicles at the Saltzman Road Trailhead but no other facilities.

THE HIKE

From the Saltzman Road Trailhead, at 1,080 feet elevation, head east on Saltzman Road. In 0.1 mile there will be an unmarked path to the left. Turn left on the path and follow it northeast through the Douglas fir, red alder, and bigleaf maple woods for another 0.1 mile to a graveled roadbed. Turn right on the roadbed and go a short distance to its end at a viewpoint. During the winter when the leaves are off the alder trees, Mount St. Helens can be seen through the branches. Turn around at the end of the roadbed and follow it for slightly over 0.1 mile to the junction with Fire Lane 5. After you pass the path that you came in on, the roadbed descends steeply.

Turn right on Fire Lane 5 and hike downhill for 0.2 mile to the junction with another roadbed to the right. Turn right on this roadbed and climb, crossing beneath a power line to another viewpoint at the end of the roadbed. This viewpoint offers views of the city as well as Mounts Rainier and St. Helens.

Turn around at the viewpoint and return to Fire Lane 5, then turn right and continue your descent. The route heads down through the alders, maples, and Douglas fir timber; you may also notice a couple of Pacific madrone trees beside the route. Fire Lane 5 ends at a junction with the Wildwood Trail 0.4 mile from the roadbed to the second viewpoint.

> ***Pacific madrone* (Arbutus menziesii) *is a small- to medium-size broadleaf evergreen tree. The bark on mature trees is reddish brown and generally peeling.***

This is the beginning of the loop portion of this hike. Cross the Wildwood Trail and continue down the ridgeline on the twisting track, passing beneath a power line. The route passes a water tank and reaches the junction with Leif Erikson Drive 0.2 mile after crossing the Wildwood Trail. Turn right on Leif Erikson Drive and quickly cross a creek. Soon you may notice a white concrete post with "6½" written on it, on the left side of the roadbed. This mile marker is 6.5 miles from Leif Erikson Trailhead.

Mount St. Helens and Mount Rainier through the winter haze

Leif Erikson Drive will make a turn to the right 0.2 mile from the point where you started hiking along it. To the left here, in an open area, is the beginning of the Maple Trail. Turn left and hike northeast on the Maple Trail. The track crosses a small wooden bridge in the bottom of a draw, then climbs through the sword ferns to cross a small slide area.

There will be a junction with an unmarked trail to the right, 0.4 mile after you left the Leif Erikson Drive. At this junction you have descended to 620 feet elevation and are 1.8 miles into the hike. Turn right on the path and climb through the salal bushes and ivy. In slightly less than 0.2 mile, the tread reaches a confusing junction with Saltzman Road and Leif Erikson Drive. There are signs marking Saltzman Road in both directions but none marking Leif Erikson Drive. The *Green Trails* map shows a slight

Leif Erikson Drive was constructed in the early part of the last century. Not long after the road was built, a landslide closed it. This 11.5-mile-long route is open to bikers and equestrians as well as hikers, but it's closed to motorized transportation.

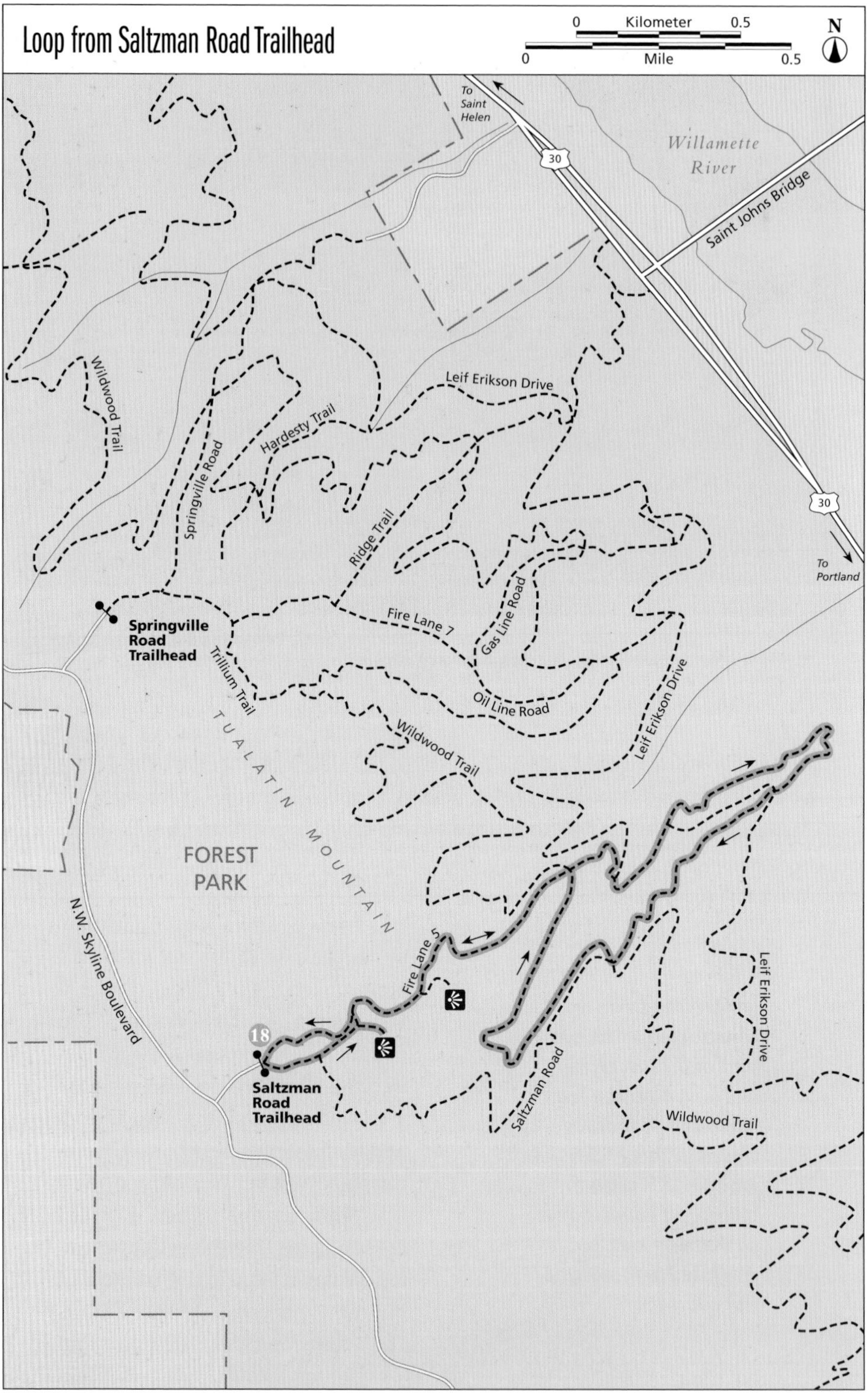
Loop from Saltzman Road Trailhead
0
Kilometer
0.5
0
Mile
0.5
N
To Saint Helen
30
Willamette River
Saint Johns Bridge
Wildwood Trail
Leif Erikson Drive
Hardesty Trail
Springville Road
Ridge Trail
30
To Portland
Gas Line Road
Fire Lane 7
Springville Road Trailhead
Trillium Trail
Oil Line Road
Leif Erikson Drive
Wildwood Trail
TUALATIN MOUNTAIN
FOREST PARK
N.W. Skyline Boulevard
Fire Lane 5
18
Saltzman Road Trailhead
Saltzman Road
Leif Erikson Drive
Wildwood Trail

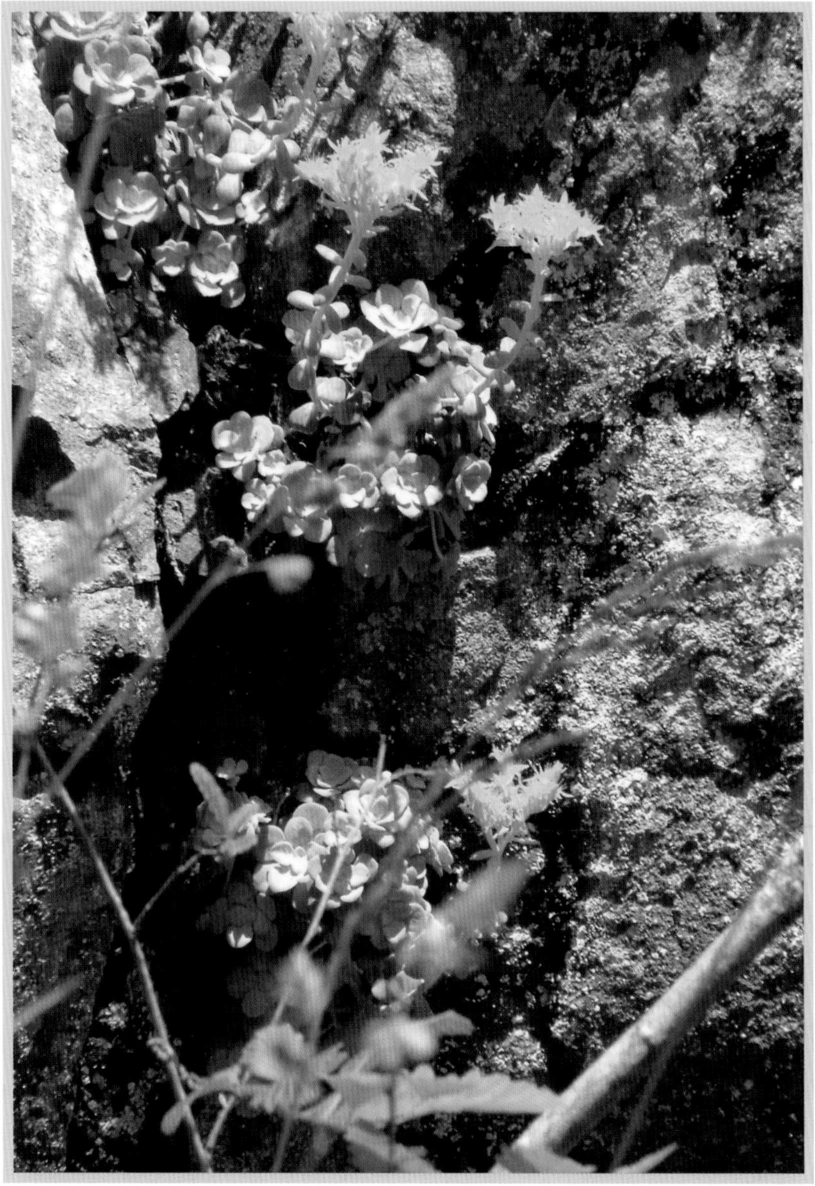

Stonecrop

error at this junction. There is a picnic table next to the junction where you can take a break.

First turn to the right, then turn left on Saltzman Road and climb. The route passes beneath a power line as you ascend the 0.5 mile to the junction with the

Wildwood Trail. By the time you reach this junction, you have climbed back up to 860 feet elevation.

Turn right at the junction and begin your walk along the well-maintained and nearly level Wildwood Trail. Just under 0.7 mile from the junction with Saltzman Road, the route reaches the junction with Fire Lane 5. This junction is the end of the loop you started 2.2 miles back. Turn left on Fire Lane 5, first retracing your steps, then continuing on the fire lane to the Saltzman Road Trailhead.

MILES AND DIRECTIONS

0.0 Begin at the Saltzman Road Trailhead. GPS 45 33.731N 122 47.006W.

0.1 Turn left on the unmarked path to the left.

0.2 At the roadbed to the right, turn right to the viewpoint and return.

0.3 Turn right at the junction with Fire Lane 5.

0.5 At the roadbed to the right, turn right to the viewpoint and return.

1.0 Cross Wildwood Trail at the junction. GPS 45 34.023N 122 46.272W.

1.2 Turn right at the junction with the Leif Erikson Drive. GPS 45 34.007N 122 46.167W.

1.4 Turn left at the junction with the Maple Trail.

1.8 Turn right at the junction with an unmarked trail to the right.

2.0 Turn right, then left, at the junction of Leif Erikson Drive and Saltzman Road. GPS 45 34.158N 122 45.772W.

2.5 Turn right at the junction with the Wildwood Trail. GPS 45 33.901N 122 46.198W.

3.2 Turn left at the junction with Fire Lane 5. GPS 45 34.023N 122 46.272W.

4.1 Return to the Saltzman Road Trailhead. GPS 45 33.731N 122 47.006W.

Options: Use this route to access the Wildwood Trail for a longer hike.

Honorable Mention

Leif Erikson Drive

This is a long and gentle trail on an abandoned roadbed that traverses the very heart of Forest Park. This one-way hiking and biking trail of 11.2 miles is accessed from Leif Erikson Drive. The trailhead is at the end of NW Aspen Avenue (near the west end of Thurman Street). The Loop from Saltzman Road Trailhead intersects Leif Erikson Drive and gives a couple of GPS coordinates at junctions.

Trail contact: Portland Parks and Recreation, 1120 SW Fifth Avenue, Suite 1302, Portland, OR 97204; (503) 823-PLAY; www.parks.ci.portland.or.us.

Green Tip:

Never feed wild animals under any circumstances. You may damage their health and expose yourself (and them) to danger.

Mount St. Helens and Washington's Southern Cascade Region

Silver Star Mountain

This region reaches from the southern flank of Mount St. Helens to the hills just north of the Columbia River. Hike 20 takes you through the longest known lava tube cave in North America. Hike 22 passes one magnificent waterfall after another as you hike up a lush canyon bottom. On Hikes 23, 24, and 25, you hike along flower-covered ridges to reach a peak with a view of the Portland metro area as well as the Columbia River, and Hike 21 leads you to the summit of an active volcano. This region is mostly accessed by Washington State Route 503.

Hikes 23, 24, and 25 can also be accessed from Washington State Route 14 at Washougal.

These hikes are just a sample of what this region has to offer, the rest of which is covered in the FalconGuides *Mount Saint Helens* and *Hiking Washington's Mount Adams Country,* by the same author.

Thread your way through a lava tube cave, admire a spectacular waterfall, or summit an active volcano . . .

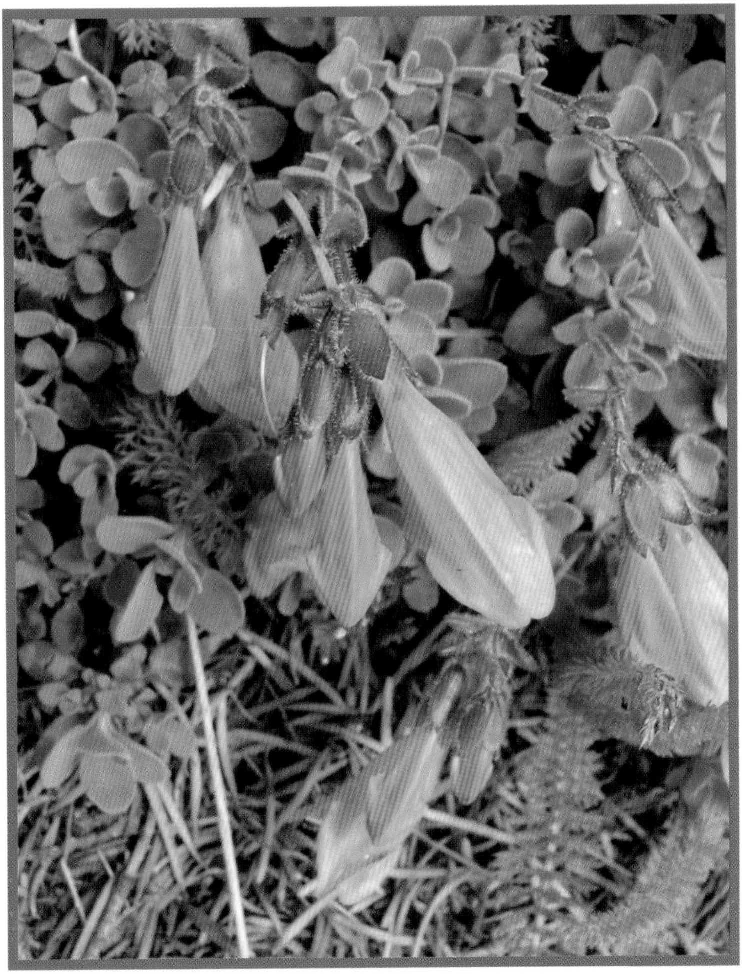

Penstemon

19

Cinnamon Loop Trails 238 and 204

The trail first follows the Kalama River, with its moss-covered banks and splashing pools, to McBride Lake. Then climb along a forested slope to the junction with the Cinnamon Trail near Redrock Pass. Continue your climb along the Cinnamon Trail to the ridgeline of Cinnamon Peak and spectacular views of the Cascades volcanoes both to the north and south. Follow the ridge west for several miles, then descend back to the Kalama Horse Camp Trailhead.

Start: Kalama Horse Camp Trailhead
Distance/type of hike: 14.1-mile loop day hike or backpack
Approximate hiking time: 6.5 hours
Difficulty: Moderate
Best season: July through October
Canine compatibility and other trail users: Restrained dogs are allowed. These trails are also open to stock users and mountain bikers as well as hikers.
Fees and permits: Northwest Forest Pass
Maps: The map on the reader board at the Kalama Horse Camp Trailhead covers the entire route. Also, *Goat Mountain* and *Mount St. Helens* USGS 7½-min. quads; National Geographic Washington topo on CD-ROM Disk 5; DeLorme's *Washington Atlas and Gazetteer,* p. 33, C6; *Green Trails* 364S
Trail contacts: USDA Forest Service, Mount St. Helens National Volcanic Monument, Monument Headquarters, 42218 NE Yale Bridge Road, Amboy, WA 98601; (360) 449-7800; www.fs.fed.us/gpnf/mshnvm
Special considerations: This route is heavily used by stock and receives some mountain-bike traffic.

Finding the trailhead:
To reach Kalama Horse Camp and Trailhead from the Portland area, drive north on Interstate 5 to exit 21 at Woodland. Then drive east on Washington Route 503 (which becomes the WA 503 spur at a junction 23 miles from I-5) for 26.5 miles to the junction with Forest Road 81. Turn left (north) on FR 81 and follow it 8.6 miles to the

Kalama Horse Camp and Trailhead. The horse camp is on the right side of FR 81, at 2,020 feet elevation.

Goat Mountain and *Mount St. Helens* USGS 7½-min. quads cover the area but don't show all of this route. The National Geographic Washington CD-ROM topo also covers the area but only shows the Toutle Trail portion of this hike. *Green Trails* 364S shows the eastern portion of this hike. DeLorme's *Washington Atlas and Gazetteer* covers the area around the trailhead, but the trailhead is not labeled on this map and only part of the trail is shown.

There is a campground for parties with stock at the Kalama Horse Camp Trailhead, so there are restrooms and horse facilities. Parties without stock are asked to camp somewhere else, but it's all right to leave your car at the trailhead.

THE HIKE

This hike begins along the Toutle Trail 238. The Toutle Trail and the Kalama Ski Trail leave Kalama Horse Camp along the same route, heading east. The ski trail is marked with blue diamond X/C ski markers, so in the places where the trails follow the same route, these markers will be visible well up in the trees along the trail.

First the path descends slightly for a few yards to a wooden bridge over a small stream. The wide trail forks a short distance past the bridge, with the Kalama Ski Trail turning to the left (northeast). Bear right (southeast) at the junction and quickly reach the first junction with the Cinnamon Trail 204, which will be your return route. Bear left at the junction, staying on the Toutle Trail, and cross another wooden bridge over a sometimes-dry streambed. The route follows the Kalama River upstream and rejoins the Kalama Ski Trail in 0.8 mile. Heading on to the east, the route stays well above the river for another 0.8 mile. At the signed junction 2 miles from the trailhead, the Kalama Ski Trail turns to the left, leaving this section of the Toutle Trail for the last time.

In another 0.3 mile you will cross Forest Road 8122. The trail climbs very gently to the east after crossing FR 8122, following the Kalama River upstream for another 1.3 miles to the junction with the Blue Horse Trail. The Blue Horse Trail, which is an abandoned road at this point, turns to the left (north).

Turn right at the junction and follow the abandoned road for a few yards, crossing the Kalama River. Just across the river the Toutle Trail turns to the left, leaving the road, and heads east. Before long the tread begins to climb above the south shore of McBride Lake. The lake, which is 4 miles from the trailhead, contains a good population of brook trout (*Salvelinus fontinalis*) and cutthroat trout (*Salmo*

19

Kalama River

clarki). The access to the lake from the trail is difficult, but there is easy access from FR 81 on the north side of the lake.

The course climbs away from the lake through old-growth forest, following a long-abandoned roadbed for a short distance, 0.3 mile after leaving the lake. The path leaves the old-growth forest 0.6 miles past McBride Lake. Then you traverse slopes covered with huckleberry bushes and vine maple (*Acer circinatum*).

One and a half miles from McBride Lake and 5.5 miles from the Kalama Horse Camp Trailhead, the route reaches the second junction with the Cinnamon Trail. Another 150 yards of walking along the Toutle Trail would take you to Redrock Pass, at 3,110 feet elevation, where the Toutle Trail crosses FR 81 and heads north. Turn right at the junction and begin your hike along the Cinnamon Trail.

From the junction with the Toutle Trail, the Cinnamon Trail climbs to the south, making seven switchbacks and gaining 560 feet of elevation in the first mile to reach the ridgeline. Along the way the route climbs through mature forest of Pacific silver fir, noble fir, and western hemlock. Devil's club grows in the damper spots beneath the large old trees, and in the openings vine maple and mountain alder make a brushy mix.

As you reach the ridgeline, there is a great view of the southern slopes of Mount St. Helens, which is close by to the north. To the east the 12,276-foot-high,

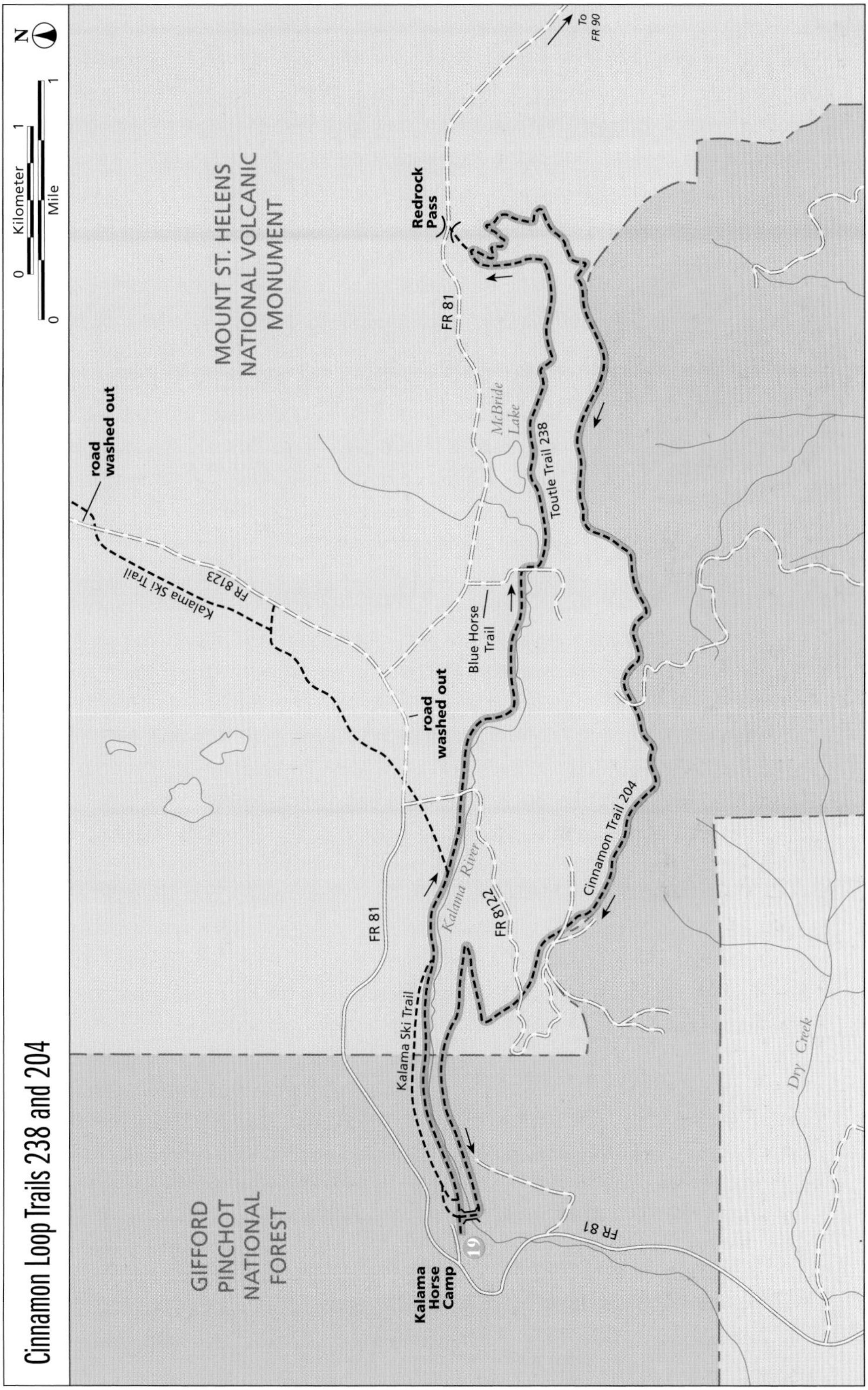
Cinnamon Loop Trails 238 and 204
0
Kilometer
1
0
Mile
1
N
MOUNT ST. HELENS
NATIONAL VOLCANIC
MONUMENT
GIFFORD
PINCHOT
NATIONAL
FOREST
Redrock
Pass
To
FR 90
FR 81
McBride
Lake
Toutle Trail 238
road
washed out
Kalama Ski Trail
FR 8123
Blue Horse
Trail
road
washed out
Cinnamon Trail 204
Kalama River
FR 8122
FR 81
Kalama Ski Trail
Kalama
Horse
Camp
19
FR 81
Dry Creek

ice-clad summit of Mount Adams rises above the hazy hills. The trail continues south along the ridge through the now smaller timber. Soon the tread swings around to the southwest, then to the west, staying close to the ridgeline. Along the ridge the trail goes through or traverses along the edge of several relatively recent clear-cuts, which are growing up with young noble and Douglas firs. In these more open areas, there is enough direct sunlight reaching ground level for foxglove (*Digitalis purpurea*) to grow and bloom.

The trail descends to a saddle on the ridgeline 2.2 miles from the junction with the Toutle Trail. At this point you are back down to 3,270 feet elevation and have lost all but about 150 feet of the elevation you gained after you left the Toutle Trail. From the saddle the tread climbs again. As you regain elevation, the sharp-pointed spire of 11,240-foot-high Mount Hood, 60 miles to the southeast across the Columbia River in Oregon, comes into view.

The grade soon moderates and the path continues to follow the ridgeline, heading generally west and crossing a gravel road, 4.7 miles from the junction with the Toutle Trail. You will soon cross this same road again, and after doing so, you quickly cross yet another road before reaching the ridgeline, and the highest point on the Cinnamon Trail at 3,930 feet elevation. As you reach the ridgeline, there will be a path that turns to the right to follow the ridge east. Don't turn on it—it is just a game trail—even though at times it may look as well used as the Cinnamon Trail. Head northwest along the ridgeline and soon begin to descend.

The route crosses another gravel road a mile into the descent. By this time you are down to about 3,300 feet elevation. In a few yards you cross one more road. In another 0.3 mile the trail reaches yet another gravel road. Cross the road and continue on a spur road, which is closed, blocked, and gradually reverting to a trail. The route follows this roadbed for a little more than 0.3 mile, then the road ends and the trail continues through the forest, descending the northwestern slope of Cinnamon Peak.

A lahar is a mixture of water, rock, sand, and soil that flows swiftly off a mountain as a result of volcanic activity or the solidified remains of such a flow.

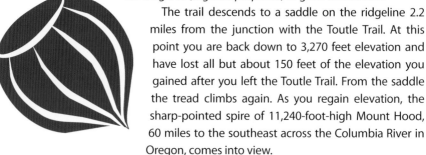

The trail finally leaves the slope 7.9 miles from the junction with the Toutle Trail. Now you hike across the old terraced lahar deposits close to the Kalama River. A quarter mile onto the relatively flat lahar deposits, there will be a trail junction. The trail to the left goes to Kalama Falls. Bear right (west-southwest) at the junction. Soon the trail makes a switchback to the right and descends a short distance to the bridge over the Kalama River at 1,980 feet elevation. A short distance past the bridge, the route rejoins the Toutle Trail, 8.5 miles from the junction where you left it. Turn left at the junction and retrace your steps for 0.3 mile to the Kalama Horse Camp and Trailhead.

MILES AND DIRECTIONS

0.0 Begin at the Kalama Horse Camp Trailhead. GPS 46 08.518 N 122 19.413 W.

0.2 Bear right where the Kalama Ski Trail and Toutle Trail separate.

0.3 Bear left at the junction with the Cinnamon Trail. GPS 46 08.532 N 122 19.389 W.

2.3 Cross FR 8122. GPS 46 08.527 N 122 17.132 W.

3.6 Turn right, then left, at the junction with the Blue Horse Trail.

4.0 Pass McBride Lake.

5.5 Turn right at the junction with the Cinnamon Trail. GPS 46 08.593 N 122 14.179 W.

10.2 Cross a gravel road. GPS 46 07.780 N 122 16.910 W.

13.8 Turn left at the junction with the Toutle Trail. GPS 46 08.532 N 122 19.389 W.

14.1 Return to the Kalama Horse Camp Trailhead. GPS 46 08.518 N 122 19.413 W.

20

Ape Cave Trails 239, 239A, and 239B

Ape Cave, the longest known lava tube cave in North America, offers a challenging scramble through the upper cave and a gentle return via a surface trail to the main entrance. Then you again descend into the cave for an easier out-and-back walk through the lower cave.

Start: Ape's Headquarters parking area

Distance/type of hike: Upper Ape Cave is a cave scramble with a surface return trail totaling 2.5 miles, Lower Ape Cave is an out-and-back 1.7-mile underground hike, for a total of 4.2 miles with 2.9 of that underground

Approximate hiking time: 2.5 hours

Difficulty: When gauged by hiking standards, the upper cave is very strenuous and the lower is moderate. Upper Ape Cave's exit is 360 feet higher than the main entrance, but you climb over several piles of boulders along the way, making the total elevation gain more like 600 feet. You descend approximately 300 feet in the lower cave.

Best season: May through October. From November through April, the gate 0.8 mile from Ape Cave is generally closed and locked, adding an extra 1.6 miles to your hike.

Canine compatibility and other trail users: This is a hikers-only route. Dogs are not allowed.

Fees and permits: Northwest Forest Pass

Maps: *Mt. Mitchell USGS* quad; National Geographic Washington topo on CD-ROM Disk 5; DeLorme's *Washington Atlas and Gazetteer*, p. 33, D7.

Trail Contacts: USDA Forest Service, Mount St. Helens National Volcanic Monument, Monument Headquarters, 42218 NE Yale Bridge Road, Amboy, WA 98601; (360) 449-7800; www.fs.fed.us/gpnf/mshnvm

Special considerations: There is no trail in Upper Ape Cave, and you must climb over and through several piles of boulders that have fallen from the sides and ceiling. The 8-foot-high vertical wall at Lava Falls must also be negotiated. There is no natural light in the cave; therefore each person should have at least two good sources of light with him or her. Headlamps are best because in many places the use of both hands is necessary. Without light, getting through this cave is virtually impossible. The temperature of the cave is about 42° F year-round.

Much of the time the cave drips almost everywhere, making the humidity nearly 100 percent, so dress for cool, damp conditions. If you wear glasses, put anti-fog on the lenses to reduce steam. Unless you have experience exploring unlit caves, don't try this one without a competent leader. Don't attempt Upper Ape Cave alone. Less ambitious cavers can explore the lower cave described below without many problems, but the upper cave is a different story.

Finding the trailhead:
Head north from Portland on Interstate 5 to exit 21 at Woodland, Washington. Then follow Washington Route 503 (which becomes the WA 503 spur) for 27.5 miles east to Cougar.

Continue east from Cougar on the WA 503 spur, which shortly becomes Forest Road 90 at the Skamania County line, to the junction with Forest Road 83, 6.8 miles from Cougar. Then turn left on FR 83 and drive 2 miles to the junction with Forest Road 8303. Turn left again on FR 8303 and follow it 1 mile north to the entrance to the Ape Cave parking area. Turn right at the sign marking the parking area.

The *Mt. Mitchell USGS* quad shows the cave entrances but nothing else. The National Geographic Washington CD-ROM topo shows the aboveground portions of this hike.

There are ample parking and restrooms at the trailhead. Ape's Headquarters, located at the trailhead, is an information station and a rental shop for the lanterns that many hikers use inside Ape Cave. Don't depend on getting your lighting equipment at Ape's Headquarters unless you are sure that they are open. To check, call Monument Headquarters at (360) 247-3900.

THE HIKE

From the parking area, at 2,120 feet elevation, walk north between the restrooms and Ape's Headquarters. In a short distance you will reach the main entrance to Ape Cave. This is the lower entrance for Upper Ape Cave and the only entrance to Lower Ape Cave. Stop at the open-air shelter and read the informational signs inside before descending into the cave.

Descend the two sets of stairs into the cave. It is a good idea to stop at the top of the second set of steps and let your eyes adjust to the lack of light before climbing on down to the cave floor. At the bottom of the second set of stairs is a sign: North leads to the upper cave and south to the lower. This is the point to stop and decide which section of the cave to do. If you are not sure of your caving skills, head into the lower cave, described below.

If you're up to the challenge of the upper cave, turn on your headlamp and head north over the rough cave floor. The next 1.2 miles of this hike is through a lava tube cave with no trail. About 400 feet up the upper cave is the Big Room, which is the largest open area in the cave. The Big Room is the turnaround point for the inexperienced. At the northwest corner of the Big Room, a short (about 160 feet long) side passage leaves the main cave; don't take it. From here on you climb over, under, and through the boulder-strewn cave for about 0.6 mile to Lava Falls. In some locations the piles of boulders reach well over halfway to the roof of the cave.

On the right side of the cave, the thin veneer of basalt has crumbled off in places, exposing the red-rock cinders that were part of the old streambed that the lava flowed

Ape Cave

Although other caves were known in the area as early as the 1890s, Ape Cave was not discovered until the mid-1900s. Probably in November or December of 1951—the exact date has been lost with the passing of time—a logger by the name of Lawrence Johnson found the main entrance to Ape Cave. Johnson descended a short distance into it by climbing down a handy tree trunk. He then tossed rocks into the darkness and realized that he had found a much larger cave than could be seen from the surface. Johnson contacted the Reese family, who owned and operated a store a few miles west of the town of Cougar and were avid cavers. A few days later Leonard Reese was the first person to be lowered to the floor of Ape Cave.

Ape Cave was formed approximately 1,950 years ago by a lava flow that originated from Mount St. Helens. This flow's unique form of lava, called "cave basalt," constructed the 12,810 feet of passages that make up the cave. Cave basalt is a form of pahoehoe (a Hawaiian word pronounced pah-*hoey-hoey*), a low-silica-content lava. In the case of Ape Cave, this very fluid pahoehoe lava flow was deepened as it flowed down a preexisting streambed, the flow rate increased, and thus it stayed hotter then the surrounding lava flow. The lava along the sides of the streambed as well as a crust over the top cooled enough to solidify, encasing the lava stream inside. Then the remaining liquid lava flowed on out of the tube, leaving the longest lava tube cave known in North America.

At some time, possibly about A.D. 1480, a sandy lahar flowed into the cave's main entrance. This lahar filled portions of the Lower Cave, blocking it about 4,000 feet below (south of) the main entrance and leaving the sand and bits of light-colored pumice we see today.

Ape's Headquarters

down. The glaze on parts of the cave ceiling and in some cases the rocks that have fallen from the ceiling is a product of the burning of superheated volcanic gasses. This happened as the flow diminished and no longer filled the cave completely. Some of this glaze flowed or dripped enough to form small stalagmites and stalactites.

In many parts of Ape Cave, you may notice that the walls and ceiling of the cave appear to sparkle in the light of your headlamp or flashlight. Tiny water droplets that are held in place by a phenomenon known as "lava tube slime" cause this sparkling. This odd slime forms in lava tube caves, but its reason for forming is not yet well understood.

Lava Falls is a vertical 8-foot semicircular wall that must be climbed to continue on up the cave. There are hand and foot holds but they can be hard to find. A quarter mile farther up the twisting cave, you will come to the Skylight. The Skylight is a place where the thin crust of lava covering the cave has collapsed, leaving an opening to the outside. You are now 1 mile from the trailhead and you have 0.2 mile to go before reaching the upper entrance. There is no exit here, so head on up the cave and plunge back into the darkness. More light is seen ahead in about another 300 yards, and soon you reach the Upper Ape Cave entrance. The upper entrance, at 2,480 feet elevation, is not the end of the cave, but it is your exit point. (The cave continues north for about another 500 feet to the point where a lava seal blocks it.) Climb the two metal ladders and reenter the outside world.

Above the ladders, climb the moss-covered lava for a few feet, then head south on the return trail. The path soon passes a small collapsed lava tube and enters a young forest. The tread descends gently and follows an abandoned roadbed for a short distance. Soon you bear right off the roadbed and enter a semi-open area that was logged long ago. In many places the trail crosses short sections of pahoehoe lava. Pahoehoe lava's surface often has the appearance of many pieces of rope laid side by side, usually in an arced position.

About a mile from the upper entrance, 2.2 miles from the starting point, the trail rounds the end of a lava flow. Soon you enter a flat sandy area. A couple hundred yards into the sandy area, a side path turns to the left (east). The side path goes a few feet to the entrance of another small lava tube, then continues along the side of a lava flow for a short distance, before ending.

The main trail continues south past the path and across the sand. The trail may be hard to see here, but there are usually human tracks on it. Shortly the trail enters an area that was burned in a 1998 arson. The tread crosses a couple of streambeds that are usually dry. The main entrance of Ape Cave and the parking area are located a few yards farther through the forest.

If you're up for a little more underground hiking, descend the steps back into the cave and turn left at the sign to enter the lower cave. The lower section of Ape Cave is a far easier hike than is the upper section. This section of the cave is very popular, so traffic may be heavy. The main hazard in this part of the cave is the darkness. As with the upper section, two good sources of light are recommended for each person entering the lower cave. The cave floor is generally fairly smooth, but there are rocks laying on it that can be real shin busters and one spot where you must step down about 1.5 feet. In one spot very tall hikers may have to duck to clear the low ceiling.

Even though Ape Cave is plugged by sand, it is believed that the tube extends on down-slope for a considerable distance. Oly's Cave, about 2 miles to the south-southwest, is thought to be part of the same lava tube.

About 150 yards into the lower cave, if you are walking close to the left wall as most hikers do here, there will be a step down of 1.5 feet. For most people this is the only place in this section of the cave where you will want to use your hand for balance.

Ape Cave Trails 239, 239A, and 239B

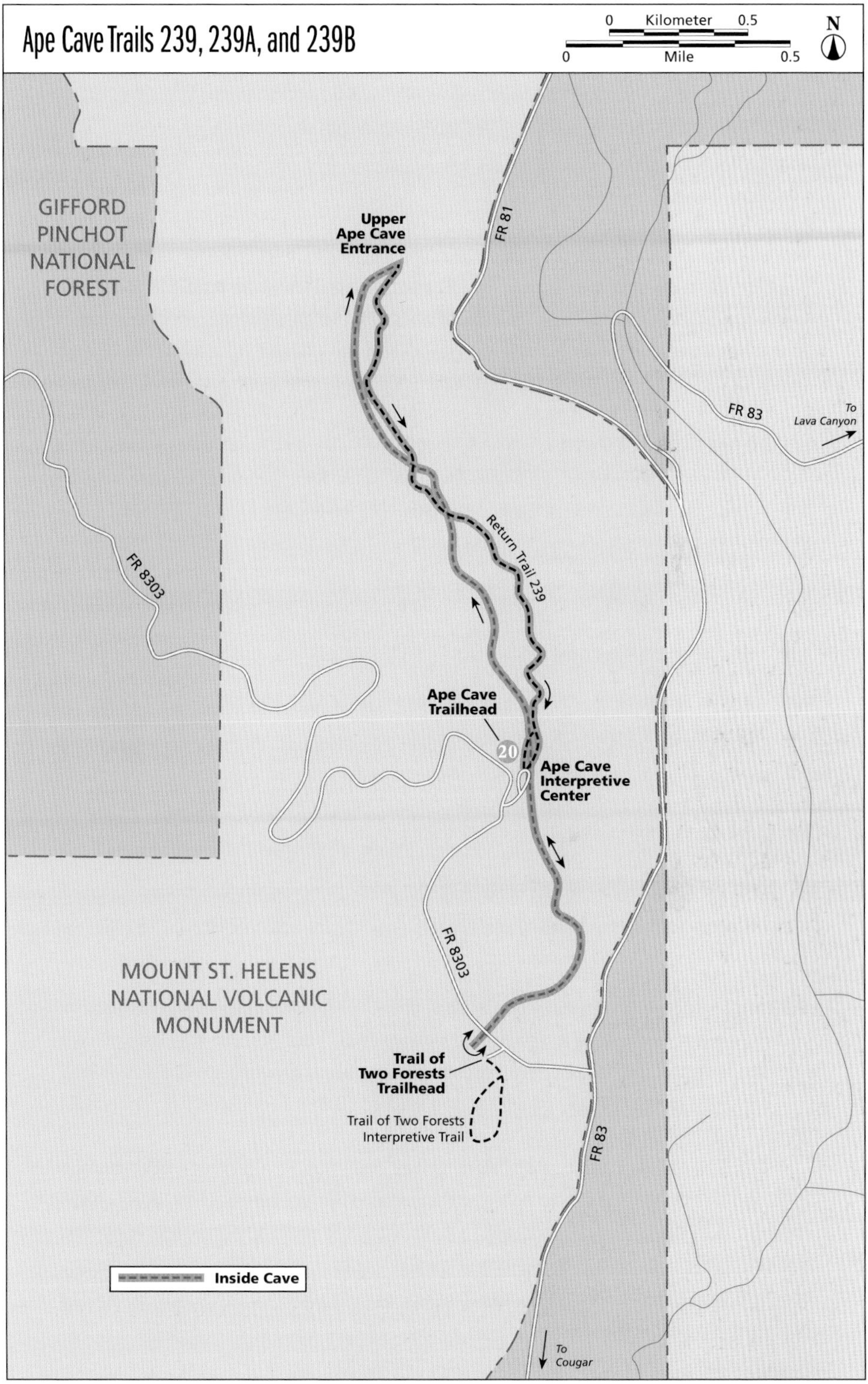

Through much of the cave, there are horizontal "flow marks" on the walls. These flow marks indicate the levels at which lava flowed through the cave as the volcano's output diminished after the cave was originally formed.

Half a mile from the cave entrance, "the Meatball" comes into view overhead. The Meatball is the last and largest of several boulders that are stuck overhead. The round Meatball is a chunk of lava that was being rafted along while the molten lava was still flowing and became stuck in a narrow spot of the cave.

The cave divides into upper and lower passages 0.2 mile past the Meatball. Continue on a short distance in the lower passage. The passage quickly gets smaller and lower, as a sand deposit that was washed into the cave by the lahar fills it from the floor up. This is the turnaround point.

MILES AND DIRECTIONS

0.0 Begin at the main Ape Cave entrance. GPS 46 06.336 N 122 12.782 W.

0.2 Arrive at the Big Room.

0.8 Pass the Lava Falls.

1.0 Arrive at the Skylight.

1.2 Arrive at the Upper Ape Cave entrance. GPS 46 07.424 N 122 12.977 W.

2.5 Reenter the cave at the main Ape Cave entrance. GPS 46 06.336 N 122 12.782 W.

3.0 Arrive at the Meatball.

3.3 Turn around here, where the cave is blocked.

4.2 Return to the main Ape Cave entrance. GPS 46 06.336 N 122 12.782 W.

Options: After exploring either or both sections of Ape Cave to your satisfaction, you may want to make the short interpretive loop hike around the Trail of Two Forests. To reach the Trail of Two Forests parking area, drive south (back the way you came in) from the Ape Cave parking area for 0.8 mile on FR 8303. Then turn west (right) and enter the parking area.

The Trail of Two Forests is an interpretive nature loop trail about a quarter mile long. Reader boards all along the route explain what you are seeing. If you have children along, don't miss "the Crawl," a horizontal tree mold about 50 feet long and about 2.5 feet in diameter that can be crawled through. If you hike this path quietly and very early in the morning, you may see one or more of the many cottontail rabbits that inhabit the area.

21

Mount St. Helens Summit via Monitor Ridge Trails 216A and 216H

Hike first through dense forest, then cross an open slope with a great view, to a junction with the Loowit Trail. Then make the nontechnical but strenuous climb up the south side of Mount St. Helens to the summit, on the rim of the 1980 eruption crater.

Start: Climbers Bivouac Trailhead
Distance/type of hike: 9.2-mile out-and-back mountain climb
Approximate hiking time: 8 hours or more depending on party's condition
Difficulty: Strenuous for hiking but easy as a mountain climb. Much of the route is without benefit of a trail over rocky footing.
Best season: June through September
Canine compatibility and other trail users: Hikers only above Loowit Trail; no dogs
Fees and permits: A Northwest Forest Pass is required to park at the trailhead, and a climbing permit is required above 4,800 feet elevation. The climbing permit, which includes parking, is sold for $22 nonrefundable, by Mount St. Helens Institute online at Active .com; (360) 449-7826. Permits are first-come, first-served; maximum of 100 climbers per day May 15 through October 15. Maximum group size 12; pick up permit at Jacks Restaurant and Store, 5 miles west of Cougar.
Maps: *USDA Forest Service Mount St. Helens National Volcanic Monument; USGS Mount St. Helens* 7½-min. quad; *Green Trails Mount St. Helens NW,* Wash No 364s; National Geographic Washington topo on CD-ROM Disk 5; DeLorme's *Washington Atlas and Gazetteer,* p. 33, C7
Trail contacts: USDA Forest Service, Mount St. Helens National Volcanic Monument, Monument Headquarters, 42218 NE Yale Bridge Road, Amboy, WA 98601; (360) 449-7800; www.fs.fed.us/gpnf/mshnvm
Special considerations: Hikers in poor condition will find this 4,615-foot climb to be grueling.
The road to the Campers Bivouac may be blocked by snow until mid-June. Check with Mount St. Helens National Volcanic Monument Headquarters if you plan an early-season trip. The road may be plowed only one lane wide so be cautious.

Climbing Monitor Ridge to the Mount St. Helens summit is not a technical climb, but a rough scramble much of the way. The weather above timberline varies greatly. There is no water along this route after the snow melts. Mount St. Helens is an active volcano. When climbing it you may be exposed to volcanic hazards, which are dangerous and possibly deadly and may happen at any time without warning. These hazards include flying rocks, ashfall, and debris flows. To improve your chances of survival in case of a volcanic event: Descend rapidly to well below the crater rim, seek cover, and protect your head, airway, and eyes; remain in a protected position until the event subsides. A hard hat, goggles, and a dust mask (N95 type) are highly recommended.

Finding the trailhead:
Head north from Portland on Interstate 5 to exit 21 at Woodland. Drive east on Washington Route 503 (which becomes the WA 503 spur, then Forest Road 90) for 34.3 miles, passing Cougar, to the junction with Forest Road 83. Turn left onto FR 83 and follow it for 3.1 miles north to the junction with FR 81. Turn left onto FR 81 and drive northwest 1.6 miles to the junction with FR 830. Turn right and head northeast on FR 830 for 2.6 miles to Climbers Bivouac Trailhead, at 3,750 feet elevation. There are restrooms and adequate parking at the trailhead. Camping is allowed at Climbers Bivouac.

DeLorme's *Washington Atlas and Gazetteer* covers the area around the trailhead, but the trailhead is not labeled on this map. The *USDA Forest Service Mount St. Helens National Volcanic Monument, USGS Mount St. Helens,* and the *Green Trails* maps all show the Ptarmigan Trail, but only the *Green Trails* map has the route marked above 4,800 feet elevation. The National Geographic Washington CD-ROM topo covers the area but doesn't show these trails.

THE HIKE

This climb to the summit of Mount St. Helens begins on the Ptarmigan Trail, which climbs gently to the north from the Climbers Bivouac Trailhead. The route is marked with blue diamond X/C ski markers.

The first mile of the trail climbs at a gentle grade, but after that it becomes somewhat steeper. The first good sighting of Mount St. Helens comes into view at 1.3 miles after you leave the parking area. The tread gets close to a lava flow 0.3 mile farther along. As you climb, Mount Hood and Mount Adams come into view to the south and east.

Two miles from the trailhead the trail makes a switchback to the left. The junction with the Loowit Trail is reached 0.1 mile after passing the switchback, at 4,600 feet elevation. This is the end of the Ptarmigan Trail. The route crosses the Loowit Trail. Just after crossing the Loowit Trail, a short path to the right goes to a restroom.

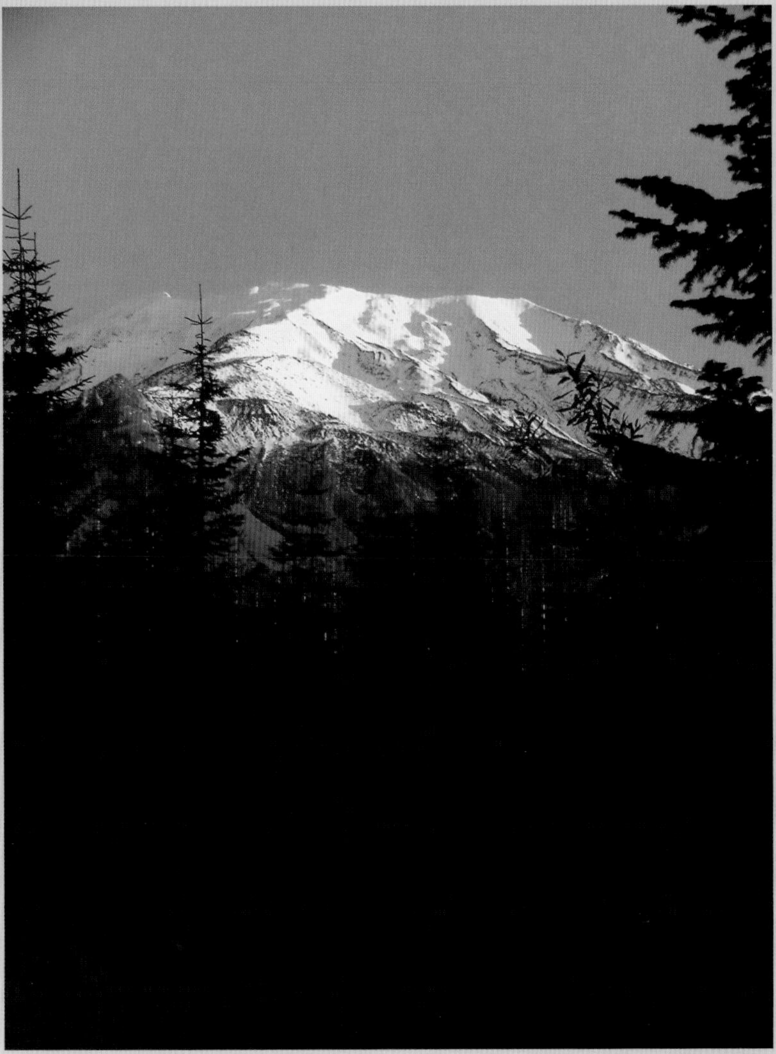

Mount St. Helens at sunrise from Climbers Bivouac

Mount St. Helens Summit via Monitor Ridge Trails 216A and 216H

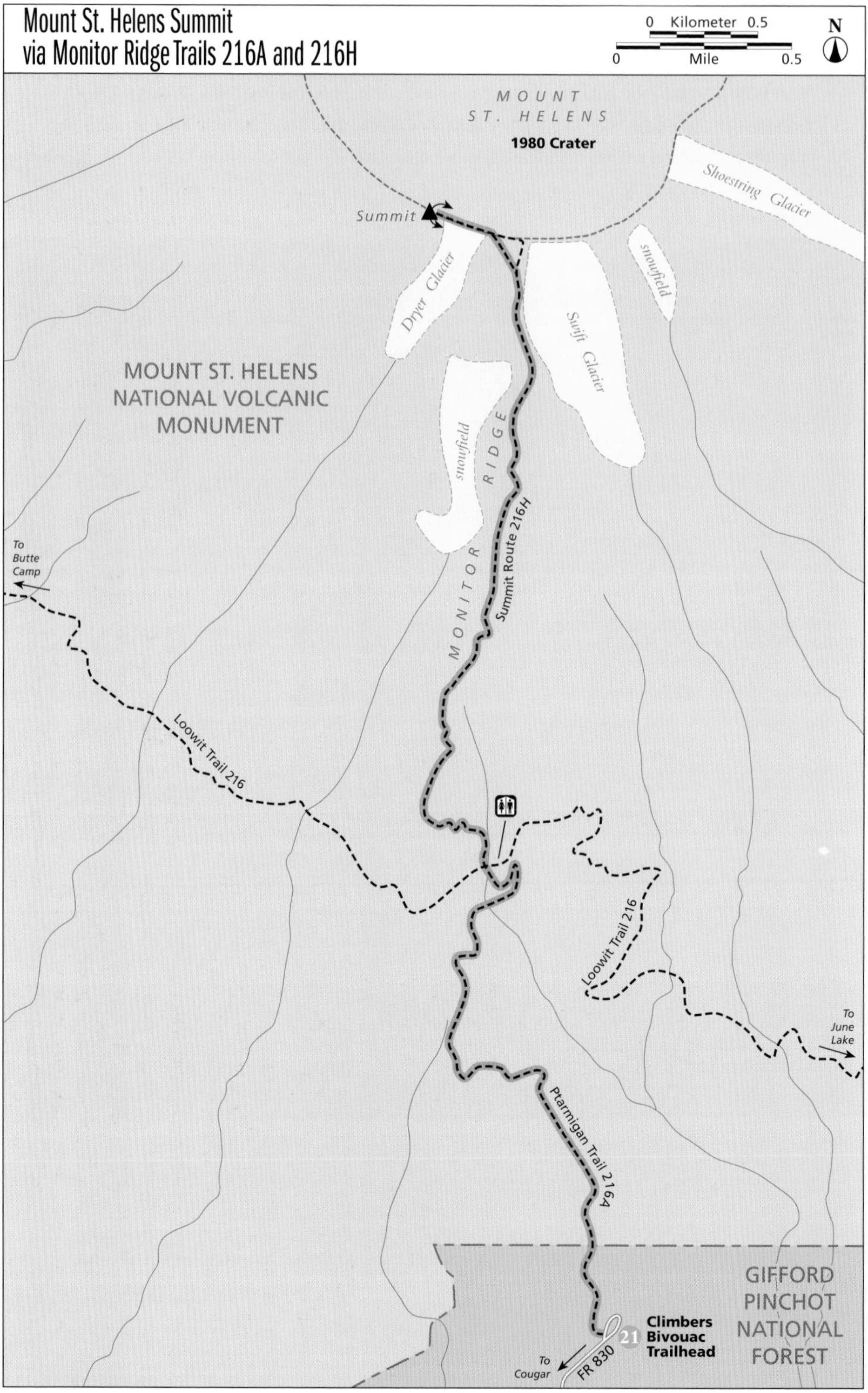

The trail soon bears to the left and leaves the larger timber 0.2 mile after crossing the Loowit Trail, at about 4,750 feet elevation. The course heads west for a short distance through the small subalpine firs. This is where the trail ends and the climbing route begins.

After heading west for a few yards, the route climbs onto a lava flow. From here up to the pumice slopes near the summit, the route is marked with wooden posts. Once you are on the lava flow, turn right and continue to climb to the north along a small ridge.

The view improves steadily as you gain elevation. Mount Adams is to the east and to the southeast is Mount Hood. If the atmosphere is really clear, you can also see Mount Jefferson slightly to the right of Mount Hood. Swift and Yale Reservoirs are far below to the south and southwest.

The line of posts and the route follow the tiny ridgeline up to 5,400 feet elevation. Then the course bears slightly left of the ridgeline. At 6,000 feet elevation the route regains the ridgeline, well above the peak marked 5,994 (elevation) on both the USGS and *Green Trails* maps. This is a good spot for a rest break.

Below peak 5,994 you may have noticed a strip of green timber reaching higher on the slope than the other timber in the area. It appears that these trees have been at least somewhat protected from volcanic action by Peak 5,994. This has

Pink mountain heather

allowed them to grow closer to what would be the natural timberline on Mount St. Helens if it weren't such an active young volcano.

The steepest part of the climb is between 6,000 and 7,000 feet elevation. You will scramble up and over several humps on the ridgeline. The route reaches the top of the dark lava rocks at 7,000 feet elevation. Above the dark rock the route becomes better defined. The path continues up a light-colored ridge to the base of the pumice slopes at about 7,800 feet elevation.

As you climb the pumice slope, you may want to bear to the left where the path forks. The left fork is a shorter way to the summit. The route reaches the crater rim at 8,280 feet elevation. On the rim, turn left and climb gently for 0.2 mile to the summit.

Try to allow yourself plenty of time to enjoy the view from the summit, 8,365 feet above sea level. Notice the crater walls, which show the layering of strata that has been put in place by the many volcanic events that have occurred over the millennia, and the fast-growing dome within the crater. Stay back from the edge of the crater, as the loose rock may give way. If there is snow, the cornices that build up along the crater rim may be unstable—don't walk out on them. To the north across the Pumice Plain is Spirit Lake and the jagged, nearly naked ridges of the Mount Margaret Backcountry. In the distance Mount Rainier rises above the lesser peaks. Return to the Climbers Bivouac Trailhead the way you came.

Green Tip:

Be courteous of others. Many people visit natural areas for quiet, peace, and solitude, so avoid making loud noises and intruding on others' privacy.

MILES AND DIRECTIONS

0.0 Begin at the Climbers Bivouac Trailhead. GPS 46 08.799N 122 10.991W.

2.1 Cross the junction with Loowit Trail. GPS 46 09.865 N 122 11.433 W.

2.3 The trail ends and the climbing route begins.

4.4 Arrive at the crater rim.

4.6 Reach the summit of Mount St. Helens. This is the turnaround point. GPS 46 11.470 N 122 11.655 W.

9.2 Return to the Climbers Bivouac Trailhead. GPS 46 08.799N 122 10.991W.

Siouxon Creek Trail 130

Hike through a lush lowland valley, passing some of the best waterfalls to be found. Then climb to the upper trailhead on Forest Road 58 near the western boundary of the Trapper Creek Wilderness. This route offers a couple of great camping spots that are not very far from the trailhead, making it an ideal backpack for families with young children.

Start: Main Siouxon Creek Trailhead
Distance/type of hike: 8.2-mile out-and-back backpack or day hike to Chinook Creek or a 9.6-mile shuttle backpack or day hike to reach the trailhead on FR 58
Approximate hiking time: 3.5 hours round-trip to Chinook Creek or 4 hours one-way to FR 58
Difficulty: Easy to Chinook Creek Trail, moderate from there on
Best season: Mid-June through October
Canine compatibility and other trail users: Trail is open to hikers, mountain bikers, and stock, closed to motor vehicles. Dogs are allowed if restrained or under close control.
Fees and permits: Northwest Forest Pass may be required in the near future.
Maps: *Siouxon Peak* and *Bare Mountain* USGS 7½-min. quads; USDA Forest Service *Gifford Pinchot National Forest* (1999); National Geographic Washington Topo on CD-ROM Disk 5; DeLorme's *Washington Atlas and Gazetteer,* p. 23, A7
Trail contacts: USDA Forest Service, Mount St. Helens National Volcanic Monument, Monument Headquarters, 42218 NE Yale Bridge Road, Amboy, WA 98601; (360) 449-7800; www.fs.fed.us/gpnf/mshnvm
Special considerations: Siouxon Creek Trail is popular with mountain bikers, so hikers should expect to meet many of them, especially on summer weekends. A couple of spots along the trail could be dangerous for children and pets, as there are drop-offs only a couple of steps to the left of the trail. One of these drop-offs is partly concealed by low brush.

Finding the trailhead:
Head north from Portland on Interstate 5 to exit 21 (21 miles north of the Columbia River Bridge) at Woodland. Drive east for 22.5 miles on Washington Route 503 to the junction with WA 503 Spur at Jack's Store. Turn right (south)

and continue on WA 503 for 6.5 miles to the Chelatchie Prairie General Store, and the junction with Healy Road. This junction is a short distance north of (before reaching) the Mount St. Helens National Volcanic Monument Headquarters.

Turn left (east) onto Healy Road, which will become Forest Road 54 in 2.4 miles, and drive 9.3 miles to the junction with Forest Road 57. The pavement on FR 54 ends at this junction. Turn left (east-northeast) onto FR 57 and follow the pavement for 1.2 miles to the junction with FR 5701. Turn left (northwest) onto FR 5701. In 0.75 mile, you will reach the first trailhead for the Siouxon Creek Trail. This trailhead, at 1,840 feet elevation, is located just after FR 5701 makes a switchback to the right to head east.

To continue to the main Siouxon Creek Trailhead (where this hike begins), drive another 3 miles east on FR 5701 to its end. The elevation at the main trailhead is 1,340 feet. The road is paved all the way to the main trailhead, but the roadbed is slipping and settling and quite rough in a few spots.

To reach the upper trailhead, where this hike ends, first backtrack along FR 5701 to the junction with FR 57. Turn left (east) on FR 57 and follow it for about 12 miles to its end at the junction with FR 58. Turn left (northwest) onto FR 58 and go 0.5 mile to the upper trailhead, on the left side of the road. This trailhead is not maintained or signed and may be hard to spot. The upper 9 miles of FR 57 is gravel and a little rough in spots.

The *Siouxon Peak* and *Bare Mountain* USGS maps show parts of this trail incorrectly. The *Gifford Pinchot National Forest* map shows the trail correctly, but the scale is too small to be very useful to the hiker. The DeLorme *Washington Atlas and Gazetteer* covers the area around the trailhead, but the trailhead itself is not labeled and only part of the trail is shown.

There is adequate parking at the main trailhead but no other facilities. The upper trailhead has very limited parking.

THE HIKE

From the main Siouxon Creek Trailhead, a path descends gently for a few yards to the north to join the Siouxon Creek Trail. Turn right on the Siouxon Creek Trail and head northeast, descending through Douglas fir and western hemlock forest. Large, tall stumps stand starkly between the medium-aged trees, attesting to this area's long ago destruction by fire. This area is prime habitat for Roosevelt elk—walk quietly and watch for them in the early morning.

After descending about 200 feet in the first 0.2 mile, the route approaches Siouxon Creek, then climbs a couple of large wooden steps to cross a single log

Falls in Siouxon Creek

bridge with a handrail, over West Creek. To the left of the trail just after crossing West Creek are the first of many campsites along this trail.

After crossing West Creek the tread continues east-northeast for 0.9 mile to the junction with Horseshoe Ridge Trail 140. The Horseshoe Ridge Trail climbs southeast for 3.7 miles to reach Forest Road 320. Hike east-northeast from the junction for 0.4 mile, then the route cuts to the right and you climb into Horseshoe Creek Canyon, with Horseshoe Creek Falls below and to your left. After the short climb the course crosses a wooden bridge above the falls, then heads north to the junction with Horseshoe Creek Falls Trail 130B. Trail 130B turns to the left off the Siouxon Creek Trail and descends 0.1 mile to a viewpoint below the falls, passing a campsite along the way.

Siouxon Creek Trail continues northeast from the junction with the Horseshoe Creek Falls Trail. In 0.3 mile you reach a viewpoint with a bench. The view is of the first of several large falls in Siouxon Creek. A deep, green pool catches the water below the falls. As you continue along the trail, another falls quickly comes into view. Slightly less than 1.0 mile past the second falls, you may notice a path descending to the left off the main trail. This path is the Wildcat Creek Trail 156, which climbs northwest to meet Trail 129 near Huffman Peak. Hike straight ahead at the junction, staying on Siouxon Creek Trail, and in 0.2 mile there will be another

Siouxon Creek Trail 130

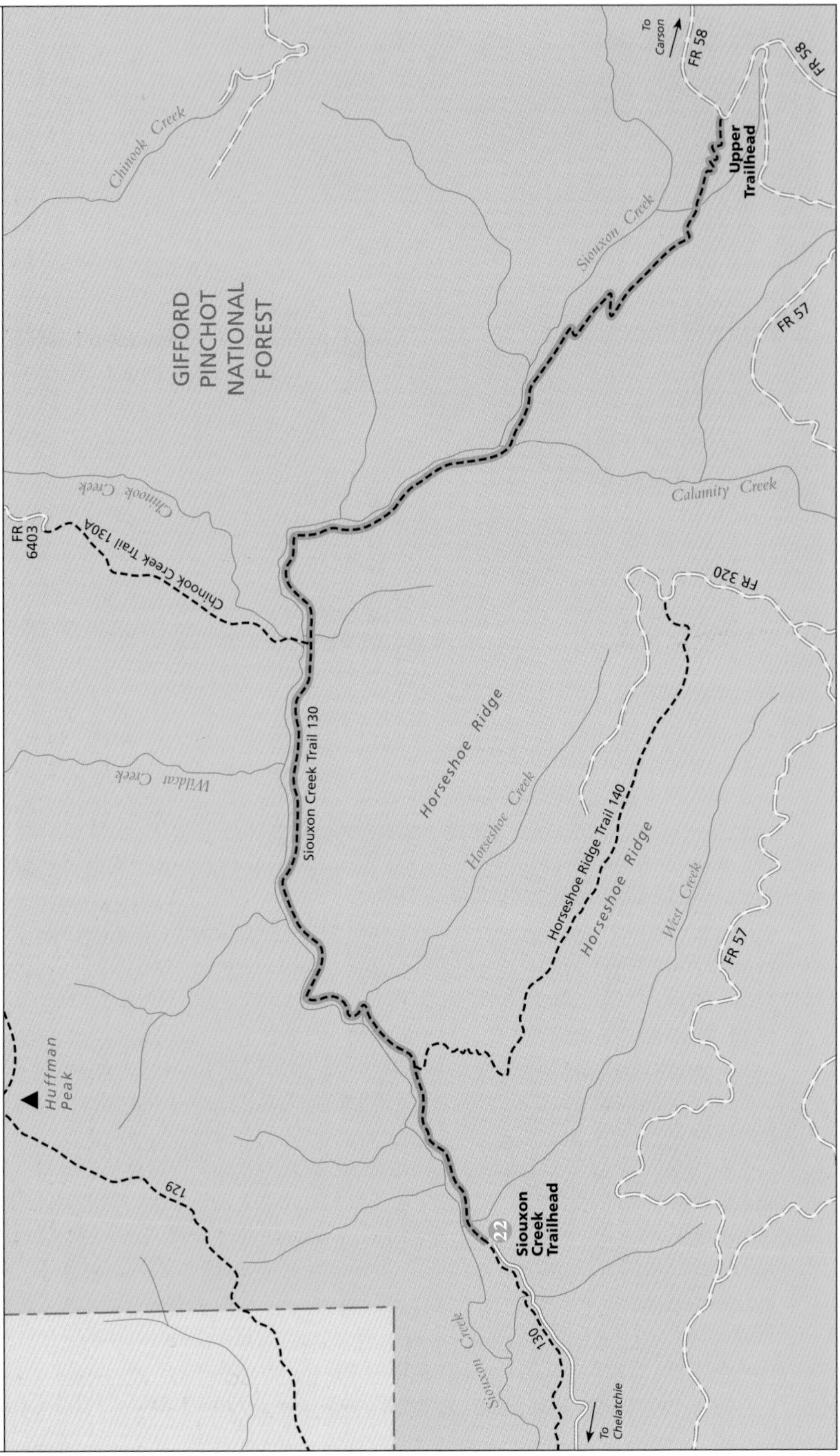

unmarked trail junction with Trail 140, just after you cross a small stream. This trail, which is a continuation of Horseshoe Ridge Trail, also climbs Horseshoe Ridge. Keep left (straight ahead) at the junction and in another 0.7 mile, just after fording an unnamed creek, you reach the junction with Chinook Creek Trail.

The unsigned Chinook Creek Trail junction is 4.1 miles from the trailhead, at 1,500 feet elevation. Chinook Creek Trail turns to the left to cross a wooden bridge over the deep, clear, and slow-moving channel of Siouxon Creek. A short hike to the north along Chinook Creek Trail will take you to a viewpoint below a spectacular falls in Chinook Creek. The Chinook Creek Trail fords Chinook Creek below the falls, then climbs north to meet FR 6403. There are a couple of nice campsites along Chinook Creek Trail just across the bridge. This is the place to turn around if this is to be an out-and-back trip.

Green Tip:
Shop for fleece clothing that is made from recycled soda bottles.

For the next 3.6 miles, the USGS quad map (*Bare Mountain* quad, 1986 vintage) shows the Siouxon Creek Trail incorrectly. The newest USDA *Gifford Pinchot National Forest* map shows this section correctly, but it's not a topo and its small scale limits its usefulness to the hiker.

To head on up Siouxon Creek, don't cross the bridge. Once past the junction with the Chinook Creek Trail, the track quickly passes another, shorter falls in Siouxon Creek. Then the course climbs, passing a few large, old-growth Douglas firs with scars from a long-ago forest fire. A quarter mile past the shorter falls, the route skirts the top of a gorge, with Siouxon Creek rushing far below. This spot could be dangerous for children and pets, as the drop-off is only a couple of steps to the left of the trail and partly concealed by low brush. After passing the gorge the tread descends for a short distance, then climbs again to the top of another large and beautiful waterfall in Siouxon Creek.

Next to the falls you are at 1,580 feet elevation and 4.7 miles from the trailhead. The route continues climbing gradually on the southwest side of Siouxon Creek for another 1.5 miles, then crosses Calamity Creek. About 0.5 miles after crossing Calamity Creek, the track begins to climb more steeply. The path makes several switchbacks as it climbs to a broad ridgeline at 2,660 feet elevation. Just before reaching the ridgeline, the course crosses a semi-open slope.

The trace makes a switchback to the left as it reaches the ridgeline. It then heads southeast, close to the edge of a clear-cut. The logged area will be on your right as you climb gently along the ridge. The route stays close to the clear-cut for about 0.4 mile. The trail crosses the south fork of Siouxon Creek 8.7 miles from the trailhead, at 2,870 feet elevation. After the creek crossing, the grade steepens. You make five switchbacks as you climb through the fir and hemlock forest to the trailhead on FR 58, at 3,520 feet elevation.

MILES AND DIRECTIONS

0.0 Begin at the main Siouxon Creek Trailhead. GPS 45 56.792 N 122 10.659 W.

1.1 Continue straight ahead at the junction with Horseshoe Ridge Trail 140. GPS 45 57.112 N 122 09.732 W.

4.1 Bear right or turn around at the junction with Chinook Creek Trail 130A. GPS 45 57.604 N 122 07.005 W.

6.2 The trail crosses Calamity Creek.

9.6 Arrive at the upper trailhead on FR 58. GPS 45 55.832 N 122 03.927 W.

Options: If your plan is to hike the entire length of Siouxon Creek Trail, you might consider starting from the upper trailhead on FR 58 where the hike description above ends. This will allow you to hike downhill most of the way.

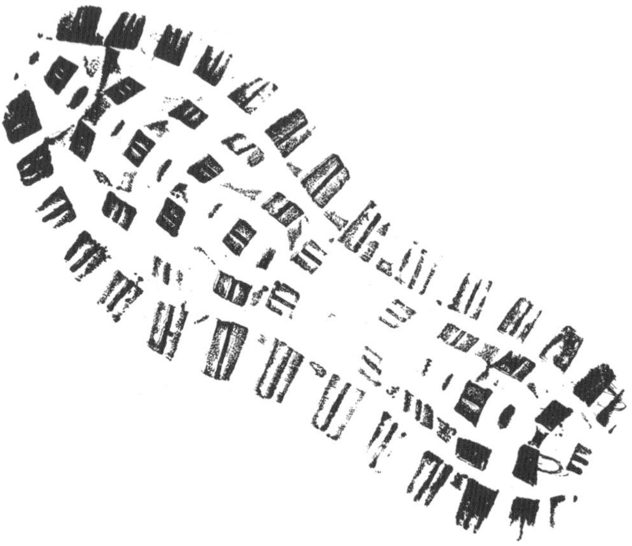

Silver Star Mountain via Silver Star Trail—Trails 180 and 180D

Hike through flower-covered ridgetop meadows nearly all the way from the trailhead to the top of Silver Star Mountain. This route is the easiest way to reach the summit. The open ridges and vistas in the Silver Star area owe their existence to the 1902 Yacolt Burn that started near Stevenson. The fire burned to the northwest, driven by strong east winds, to stop just short of Longview. The burn is named for the town of Yacolt, which was spared when the fire burned the forest surrounding it.

Start: Silver Star Trailhead
Distance/type of hike: 4.8-mile out-and-back day hike
Approximate hiking time: 2.5 hours
Difficulty: Moderate. Most of this hike is along abandoned roadbeds, some of which are a little eroded and rocky.
Best season: Mid-June through October. X/C skiers and snowshoers sometimes use this route, including part of the road leading to the trailhead, during the winter.
Canine compatibility and other trail users: Open to mountain bikes, stock, and dogs under control as well as hikers
Fees and permits: Northwest Forest Pass
Maps: *Gumboot Mountain* and *Bobs Mountain* USGS 7½-min. quads; National Geographic Washington topo on CD-ROM Disk 5; DeLorme's *Washington Atlas and Gazetteer,* p. 23, B7
Trail contacts: USDA Forest Service, Mount St. Helens National Volcanic Monument, Monument Headquarters, 42218 NE Yale Bridge Road, Amboy, WA 98601; (360) 449-7800; www.fs.fed.us/gpnf/mshnvm
Special considerations: There is usually no water along the trail. During stormy weather these open ridgetops can be a miserable place to be.

Finding the trailhead:
From Portland, drive north on Interstate 205 to exit 30. Head east on Washington Route 500 for 1.1 miles to the junction with WA 503. Don't turn at the junction, but drive straight ahead (north) on WA 503 for 13.5 miles to the junction with Rock Creek Road. Turn right on Rock Creek Road, which becomes Lucia Falls Road in 2.6 miles. Another 5.7 miles on Lucia Falls Road brings you to the junction with NE Sunset Falls Road. Turn right onto NE Sunset Falls Road and go 7.2 miles southeast and east to Sunset Campground.

23

From the campground, head south on Forest Road 41; there is no road sign at this junction. After driving southeast on FR 41 for 3.5 miles, make a hard right turn onto Forest Road 4109 (also no sign). Follow FR 4109 for 4 miles to its end at the trailhead, being careful not to bear right at Tarbell Road, which is slightly over a mile after leaving FR 41. The elevation at the trailhead is 3,090 feet.

The USDA Forest Service *Gifford Pinchot National Forest* map can be of great help in finding this trailhead. DeLorme's *Washington Atlas and Gazetteer* covers the area around the trailhead, but the trailhead is not labeled on this map and part of the trail is shown as a road. The National Geographic Washington CD-ROM topo covers the area and shows the trails very well. However, the trailheads are not labeled on this map.

There is adequate parking at the trailhead but no other facilities. There is also a great view of Mount St. Helens.

THE HIKE

The trail (not the abandoned roadbed) leaves the parking area heading south along a brush-covered slope. The course makes three switchbacks, then tops the ridgeline. As you approach the ridge, the brush becomes smaller and Mounts Adams and Rainier come into full, unobstructed view. The track crosses the ridgeline and quickly joins the abandoned roadbed that leads to the summit of Silver Star Mountain and beyond.

The Civilian Conservation Corps (CCC)

The CCC built fire-access roads and felled snags on the ridgetops to create fire breaks. The area was closed to the public until the early 1960s because of the extreme fire hazard created by the millions of dead snags. Many of the trails in the area today follow the old CCC fire roads.

Turn right on the roadbed and soon reach the junction with Ed's Trail 180A, at 3,460 feet elevation, 0.5 mile from the trailhead. See the options below for more information about Ed's Trail. Looking south from the junction, there is a view of Mount Hood, rising above the head of Star Creek Canyon. At the junction the route (roadbed) makes a hard turn to the right. The trace continues to climb, recrossing the ridgeline and passing a side trail to the left, before traversing the open slope to the junction with the Chinook

23

Trail 180B. The junction with the Chinook Trail is 1 mile from the trailhead at 3,760 feet elevation. Chinook Trail descends for 2 miles west to join Tarbell Trail.

For the next 0.7 mile, the path generally traverses just to the right (west) of the open, flower-covered ridgeline, reaching it only once in a saddle. Then the trail

Silver Star Trail

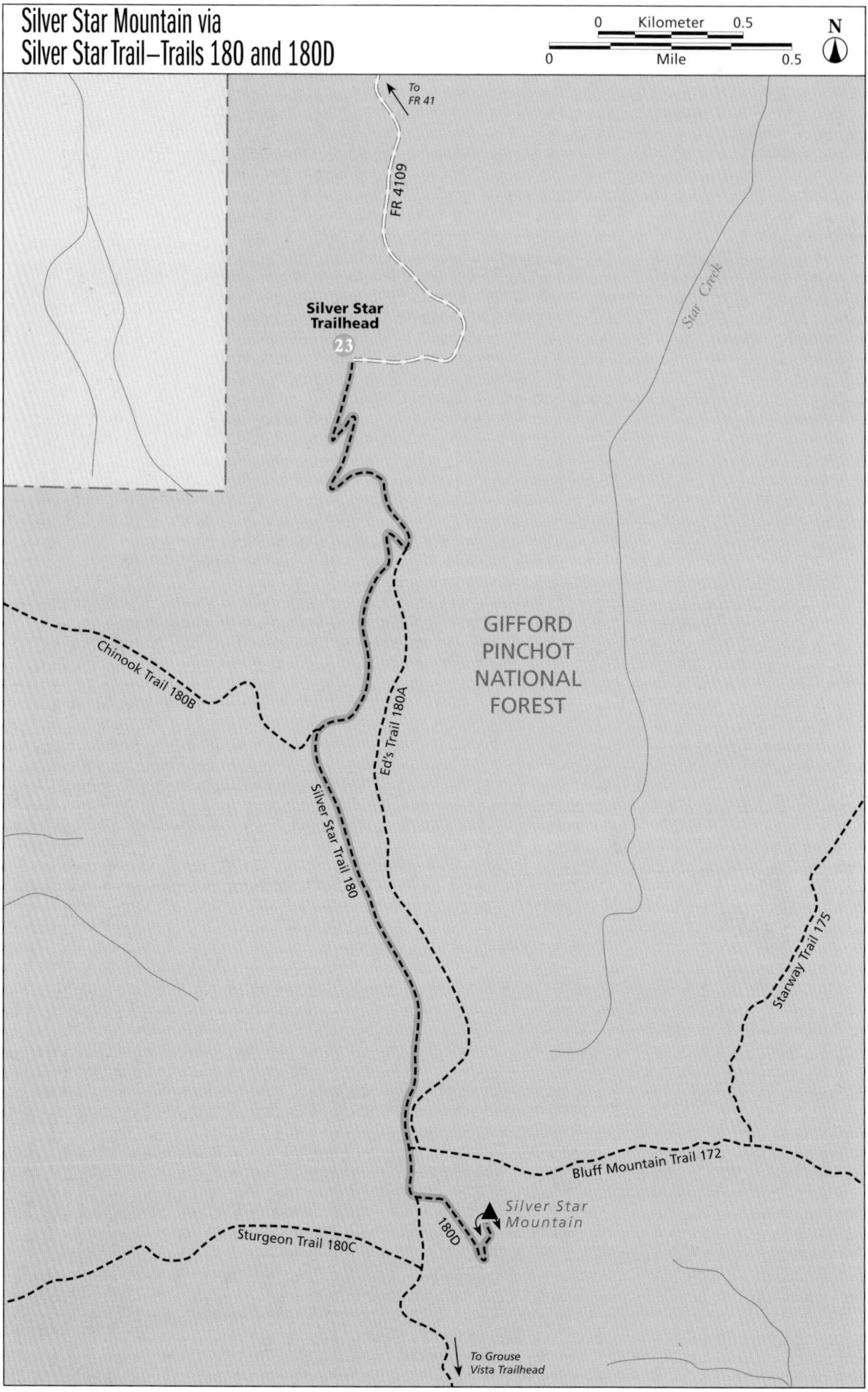
Silver Star Mountain via
Silver Star Trail—Trails 180 and 180D
0 Kilometer 0.5
0 Mile 0.5
N
To FR 41
FR 4109
Star Creek
Silver Star Trailhead
23
GIFFORD PINCHOT NATIONAL FOREST
Chinook Trail 180B
Ed's Trail 180A
Silver Star Trail 180
Starway Trail 175
Bluff Mountain Trail 172
Silver Star Mountain
180D
Sturgeon Trail 180C
To Grouse Vista Trailhead

Gray jay

flattens out and enters the timber at about 4,100 feet elevation. In the timber the track descends slightly to a saddle, then climbs gently for slightly over 0.1 mile to the junction with the Bluff Mountain Trail 172. This junction is 2 miles from the trailhead, at 4,080 feet elevation.

Past the junction with the Bluff Mountain Trail, the tread climbs moderately to the junction with Trail 180D. Turn left at the junction and climb on Trail 180D through the trees to the ridgeline just south of the summit of Silver Star Mountain. As you reach the ridge, the route leaves the woods. The trail, which is still an abandoned roadbed, makes a switchback to the left on the ridge and climbs the last few yards to the summit.

Bare, flower-covered ridges, several with trails on them, radiate from the windswept, 4,390-foot-high summit. From here the view is breathtaking in all directions. To the southwest, on a clear day, the Columbia River as well as Vancouver and Portland are visible through the haze. To the west are the forest-covered hills of the western Cascades and the Coast Range. Looking north is the squat, but still beautiful, remains of Mount St. Helens. Just to the right of Helens, far in the distance, is the ice-clad summit of Mount Rainier. To the right of Rainier to the northeast, the jagged peaks that make up Goat Rocks are on the horizon. To the right of Goat Rocks but still to the northeast is the glacier-covered bulk of Mount Adams. Looking southeast, the sharp peak of Mount Hood rises high above the green ridges of the Oregon Cascades.

MILES AND DIRECTIONS

0.0 Begin at the Silver Star Trailhead. GPS 45 46.360 N 122 14.672 W.

0.5 At the junction with Ed's Trail 180A, turn right, staying on the roadbed. GPS 45 46.046 N 122 14.537 W.

1.0 Bear left (straight ahead) at the junction with the Chinook Trail 180B. GPS 45 45.735 N 122 14.746 W.

2.0 Bear right (straight ahead) at the junction with Bluff Mountain Trail 172. GPS 45 44.989 N 122 14.528 W.

2.1 Turn left at the junction with Trail 180D.

2.4 Turn around at the summit of Silver Star Mountain. GPS 45 44.864 N 122 14.339 W.

4.8 Return to the Silver Star Trailhead. GPS 45 46.360 N 122 14.672 W.

Options: A one-way hike can be made by combining this hike with the Grouse Vista Trail 180F to Grouse Creek Vista Trailhead on the south side of Silver Star Mountain.

To reach the Grouse Creek Vista Trailhead by road, first backtrack to Sunset Campground. Then drive west on Sunset Falls Road for 5.3 miles to the junction with Dole Valley Road. Turn left (south) on Dole Valley Road (which becomes Road 1000) and drive for 5.2 miles to the junction with Road W 1200. Turn left on W 1200 and drive 5 miles over the fairly rough gravel road to the Grouse Creek Vista Trailhead.

Another option is to return via Ed's Trail 180A. To hike back along Ed's Trail, first backtrack from the summit for 0.4 mile to the junction with Bluff Mountain Trail. Turn right (east) on Bluff Mountain Trail and hike a short distance to the junction with Ed's Trail. Turn left on Ed's Trail, and follow it 2 miles north along the canyon wall of Star Creek Canyon to the junction with Trail 180. Then retrace the route you came in on for 0.5 mile north back to the trailhead. Ed's Trail is not suitable for mountain bikes or stock.

24

Bluff Mountain to Silver Star Mountain Summit Trails 172, 180, and 180D

Hike along a mostly open ridgeline with fantastic views and tons of flowers, from a poorly marked trailhead on Forest Road 41 to the summit of Silver Star Mountain. This entire area was burned in the 1902 Yacolt Burn. Much of the burned area has not naturally reforested itself and has not been replanted with trees, leaving many ridges and slopes mostly open. This openness gives the area a more alpine character than the altitude would suggest.

Start: The poorly marked Bluff Mountain Trailhead on FR 41
Distance/type of hike: 13-mile out-and-back day hike or backpack
Approximate hiking time: 6 hours
Difficulty: Moderate. Much of this route is along closed roadbeds that are reverting to trails.
Best season: Late June through mid-October. Flowers are best in early July.
Canine compatibility and other trail users: Restrained dogs, mountain bikes, stock
Permits and fees: Northwest Forest Pass
Maps: *Gumboot Mountain* and *Bobs Mountain* USGS 7½-min. quads; USDA Forest Service *Gifford Pinchot National Forest;* National Geographic Washington topo on CD-ROM Disk 5; DeLorme's *Washington Atlas and Gazetteer,* p. 23, B7.
Trail contacts: USDA Forest Service, Mount St. Helens National Volcanic Monument, Monument Headquarters, 42218 NE Yale Bridge Road, Amboy, WA 98601; (360) 449-7800; www.fs.fed.us/gpnf/mshnvm
Special considerations: Early in the season steep lingering patches of snow may make this trail difficult and dangerous in spots. The only water along this route is the streams you cross at the head of Copper Creek about 2.5 miles from the trailhead. Late in the season these streams may not be dependable so it's best to take along all the water you will need. If you get water from the stream, be sure to filter or treat it before drinking.

Finding the trailhead:
From Portland, drive north on Interstate 205 to exit 30, Washington Route 500. Travel east on WA 500 for 1.1 miles to the junction with Washington Route 503. Don't turn at the junction, but drive straight ahead (north) on WA 503 for 13.5 miles to the junction with Rock Creek Road. Turn right on Rock Creek Road, which becomes Lucia Falls Road in 2.6 miles. Another 5.7 miles on Lucia Falls Road brings you to the junction with NE Sunset Falls Road. Turn right onto NE Sunset Falls Road and go 7.2 miles southeast and east to Sunset Campground. From the campground, head south on Forest Road 41; there is no road sign at this junction. FR 41 is a gravel road that is usually in fairly good condition, but you may have to ease your vehicle through a few rough spots and around a few rocks. After driving southeast on FR 41 for 9 miles, you will reach the trailhead at 3,550 feet elevation. The trailhead is on the right side of FR 41 as it crosses through a saddle. There is plenty of parking but no other facilities at the trailhead. The DeLorme *Washington Atlas and Gazetteer* covers the area around the trailhead, but the trailhead is not labeled on this map and part of the trail is shown as a road.

THE HIKE

The first 2.2 miles of this hike follow an old abandoned roadbed. Leaving the trailhead, the route heads south-southwest, climbing gently along a brushy slope. Scattered fir trees rise above the vine maple bushes, while penstemon and paintbrush add cheer to the trailside. In 0.1 mile Mount Hood comes into view to the left as the course reaches a saddle in the ridgeline. The route then traverses along the right side of the ridgeline for 0.4 mile, through a dense stand of small firs. Back on the ridge, at 3,650 feet elevation, the tread crosses to the more open east slope. Shortly you reach the ridgeline again, and just after crossing it you reach a junction. The trail to the right is an abandoned four-wheel-drive road that descends about 3 miles to Copper Creek and a group of mines.

At the junction you are at 3,610 feet elevation, 0.7 mile from the trailhead, and back into patches of stunted fir trees. As the trace recrosses the ridgeline 0.6 mile farther along, Mount Jefferson can be seen far to the south, as well as the much closer Mount Hood. Soon the trail turns to the west-southwest and starts to descend from 3,680 feet elevation. The route descends for slightly over 0.7 mile, losing 350 feet of elevation. A few yards before the road-

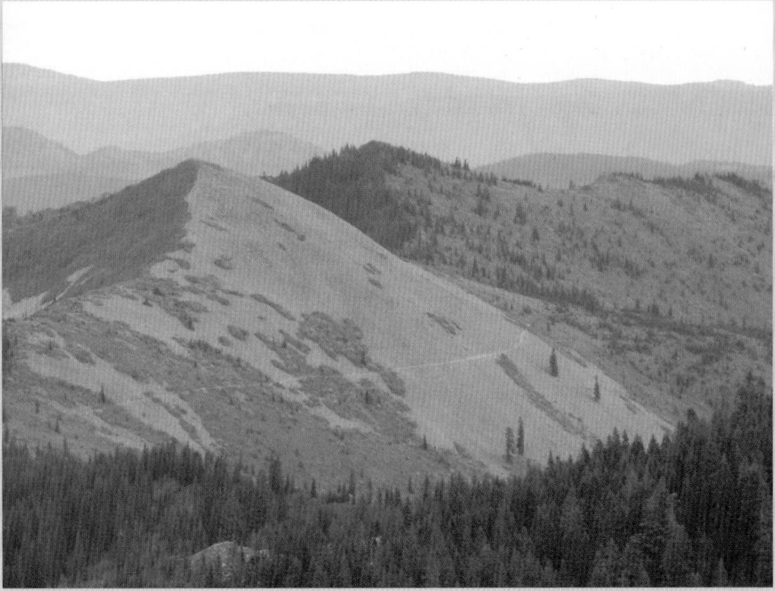

Little Baldy and Bluff Mountain

bed ends, the trail bears to the right and continues its descent another 0.4 mile to a large saddle, making a switchback along the way. This saddle, at 3,120 feet elevation, is the low point of this trail.

Leaving the saddle, the trail climbs across talus slopes and below the dark cliffs that are the northwest face of Bluff Mountain. After traversing and climbing, around the head of Copper Creek Canyon for 0.7 mile, the track enters a stand of old, fairly large timber. In the timber on the steep north-facing slope, the tread crosses a couple of small streams. If you are here early in the season (June), there may be snow on this slope and in the saddle ahead. On this steep slope, crossing snow can be difficult and in some cases dangerous. Be prepared.

After crossing a mostly brush-covered talus slope, the route reaches the timbered saddle west of Bluff Mountain. If there is snow in the saddle, head west, climbing just slightly to the left of the ridgeline, and pick up the route as it begins its traverse around the south side of Little Baldy. The south slope of Little Baldy is mostly talus. Looking southwest from the open talus slope, the Columbia River and Portland can be seen in the distance through the haze. The course reaches the ridgeline, at 3,460 feet elevation, on the west side of Little Baldy, 0.6 mile after leaving the timbered saddle.

The route now follows the ridge, heading west and climbing for 0.2 mile. Then you traverse, still climbing along the south side of the ridge crest and passing an outcropping before regaining the crest at 3,820 feet elevation, where you reach

Bluff Mountain to Silver Star Mountain Summit Trails 172, 180, and 180D

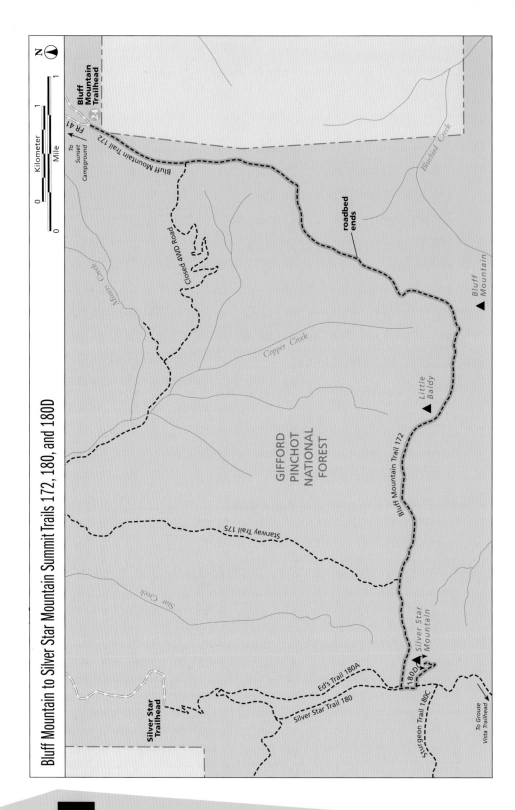

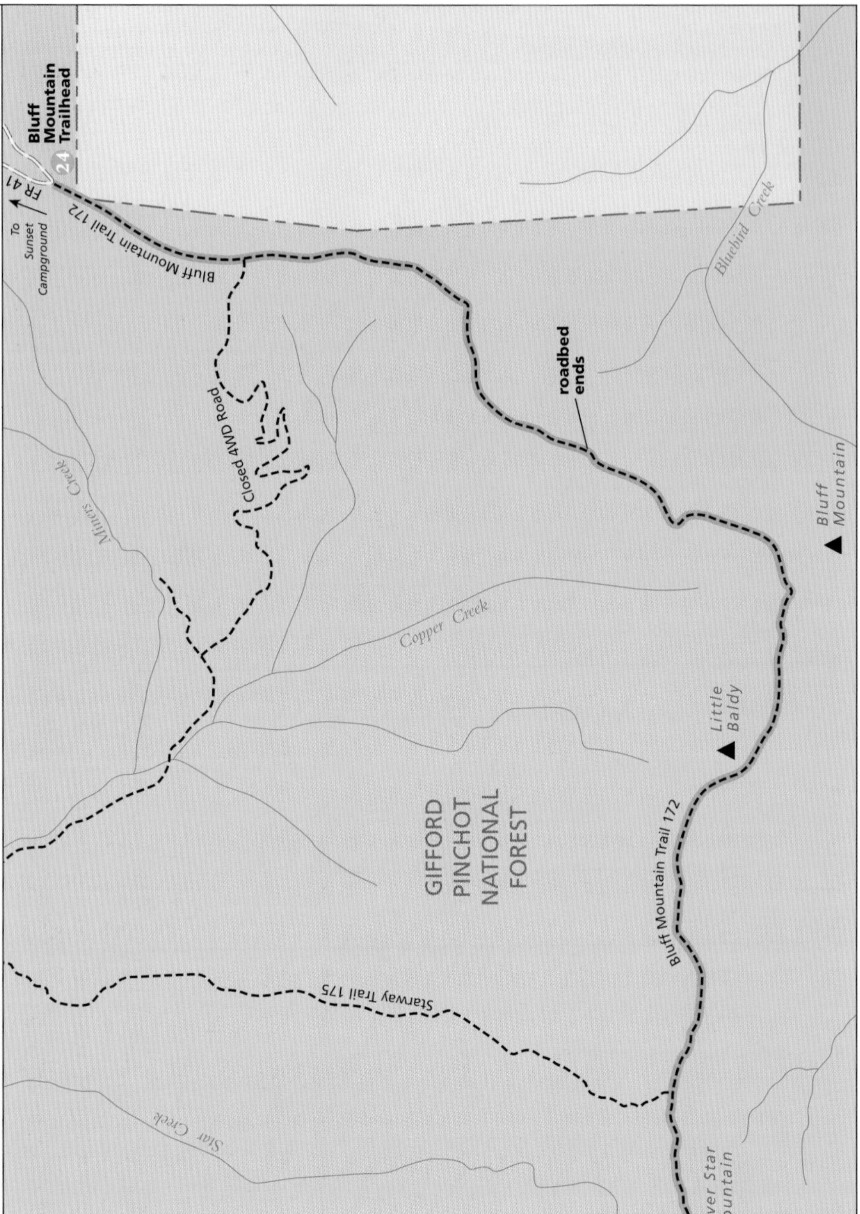

the junction with the Starway Trail 175. This junction is 5.3 miles from the trailhead. The Starway Trail turns to the right (north) and follows the ridgeline for a little over 2 miles, before descending the last 2 miles to Copper Creek.

Past the junction the trail continues to climb the open slope just left (south) of the ridgeline, then traverses the steep timbered slope north of Silver Star Mountain, passing the junction with Ed's Trail 180A and the junction with the Silver Star Trail 180, at 4,080 feet elevation. Ed's Trail 180A and the Silver Star Trail 180 are parallel routes leading 2 miles north to the trailhead at the end of Forest Road 4109.

To continue to the summit of Silver Star Mountain, turn left (south) at the junction and climb moderately along Trail 180 (which is an abandoned CCC fire road) for 0.1 mile to the junction with Silver Star Summit Trail 180D.

Turn left at the junction and climb on Trail 180D, through the trees to the ridgeline just south of the summit of Silver Star Mountain. As you reach the ridge, the route leaves the woods. The trail, which is still an abandoned roadbed, makes a switchback to the left on the ridge and climbs the last few yards to the summit, at 4,390 feet elevation. Return as you came or see the options below for a one-way hike, requiring a car shuttle.

MILES AND DIRECTIONS

0.0 Begin at the Bluff Mountain Trailhead. GPS 45 46.800 N 122 10.015 W.

0.7 Bear left at the trail junction.

2.2 The trail leaves the roadbed. GPS 45 45.287 N 122 11.056 W.

5.3 Bear left at the junction with Starway Trail 175.

6.1 Turn left at the junction with Silver Star Trail 180. GPS 45 44.989 N 122 14.528 W.

6.5 Turn around at the summit of Silver Star Mountain. GPS 45 44.864 N 122 14.339 W.

13.0 Return to the Bluff Mountain Trailhead. GPS 45 46.800 N 122 10.015 W.

Options: A one-way hike can easily be made by combining this hike with the Silver Star Trail 180. To make this hike, backtrack along Trail 180D for 0.3 mile and turn right (north) on Silver Star Trail 180. Then follow the Silver Star Trail for 2.1 miles north to the Silver Star Trailhead.

Doing this will shorten the trip by 4.1 miles but will require a car shuttle. To reach the Silver Star Trailhead, where you will end your hike, first drive back the way you came on FR 41 for 5.5 miles, then turn left on FR 4109 (there is no sign at the junction). Follow FR 4109 for 4 miles to its end at the Silver Star Trailhead.

25 Silver Star Mountain via the Grouse Vista Trail—Trails 180F, 180, and 180D

Hike through the second-growth forest, leaving the Grouse Creek Vista Trailhead to the open flower-covered ridges high above. Then traverse the open slopes to the summit of Silver Star Mountain. The area was burned in the 1902 Yacolt fire, leaving the open slopes, which are reforesting very slowly.

Start: Grouse Creek Vista Trailhead
Distance/type of hike: 7.6-mile out-and-back day hike
Approximate hiking time: 4 hours
Difficulty: Moderate grade, but the surface of nearly the entire route is eroded and rocky.
Best season: June through October. The best flower bloom is in late June and July.
Canine compatibility and other trail users: Mountain bikes, stock, under-control dogs
Fees and permits: None
Maps: *Bobs Mountain* 7½-min. USGS quad; National Geographic Washington topo on CD-ROM Disk 5; DeLorme's *Washington Atlas and Gazetteer,* p. 23, C6
Trail contacts: USDA Forest Service, Mount St. Helens National Volcanic Monument, Monument Headquarters, 42218 NE Yale Bridge Road, Amboy, WA 98601; (360) 449-7800; www.fs.fed.us/gpnf/mshnvm
Special considerations: There may be no water along this trail, so take all you will need.

Finding the trailhead:
Drive north from Portland on Interstate 205. Just after crossing the Columbia River, turn east on Washington Route 14 and drive about 10 miles to the town of Washougal. Get on the Washougal River Road (WA 140) and follow it 10.4 miles northeast to the junction with Skye Road. Turn left (north) onto Skye Road and drive 3.7 miles to the junction with Skamania Mines Road. Turn right (north) and follow Skamania Mines Road 2.7 miles to the junction with Road W 1200. You will leave the pavement 1.3 miles before reaching the junction. Bear left (really almost straight ahead) at the junction and follow Road W 1200. In 0.1 mile the road forks. Bear left and stay on Road W 1200, heading north. In another 5.6 miles you will reach Grouse Creek Vista Trailhead.

The National Geographic Washington CD-ROM topo covers the area and shows the trails very well, however, trailheads are not labeled on this map. DeLorme's *Washington Atlas and Gazetteer* covers the area around the trailhead, but the trailhead is not labeled on this map and part of the trail is shown as a road.

There is adequate parking at the trailhead but no other facilities. The elevation at the trailhead is 2,380 feet.

THE HIKE

Cross the road from the parking area, then climb for 150 yards to a fork in the trail. There is no sign at the fork. The left fork is the Tarbell Trail, which can be used as part of a return route from the summit. Bear right at the fork and climb over the end of a nearly rotted log, which was put here to keep out vehicles. This entire trail, as well as many other now-abandoned roads in the area, were built by the CCC as fire break roads.

Past the fork the tread becomes very rocky and stays that way all the rest of the way to the top. The route climbs fairly steeply through the second-growth forest. In places the forest canopy completely covers the course, giving the trail a tunnel effect. In another 0.6 mile the grade moderates for a short distance at 2,860 feet elevation. Soon you climb steeply again for another 0.2 mile. Here, at slightly over 3,000 feet elevation, the trace leaves the forest and traverses brushy slopes. Soon the brush becomes shorter; much of the slope is now covered with short huckleberry bushes, beargrass, and paintbrush as well as many other varieties of flowers.

In about another 0.4 mile, the tread passes through two small groves of fir trees at 3,270 feet elevation. Flowers bloom all along these open slopes once the snow has gone; avalanche lilies are among the first to show. Shortly after passing through the second grove, you reach another trail junction. The trail to the right climbs a few yards to a saddle on the ridgeline, where there is a good view of Mount Hood.

Green Tip:

Stay on the trail. Cutting through from one part of a switchback to another can destroy fragile plant life.

From the junction, the main trail descends slightly, then crosses a short talus slope, before resuming its climb to the north-northeast. After crossing the flower-covered slope for 0.8 mile, the track reenters the timber at 3,600 feet elevation. If you are here early in the season, this is where you will hit snow. In another 0.4 mile is the junction with Silver Star Trail 180, at 3,800 feet elevation, where you'll bear

25

Lower Grouse Vista Trail

left (straight ahead) on Trail 180. The trail will be quite close to the ridgeline 0.3 mile farther along. If the ground is snow-covered, climb right here to the ridge and work your way up the ridgeline to the summit.

Silver Star Mountain via The Grouse Vista Trail—Trails 180F, 180, and 180D

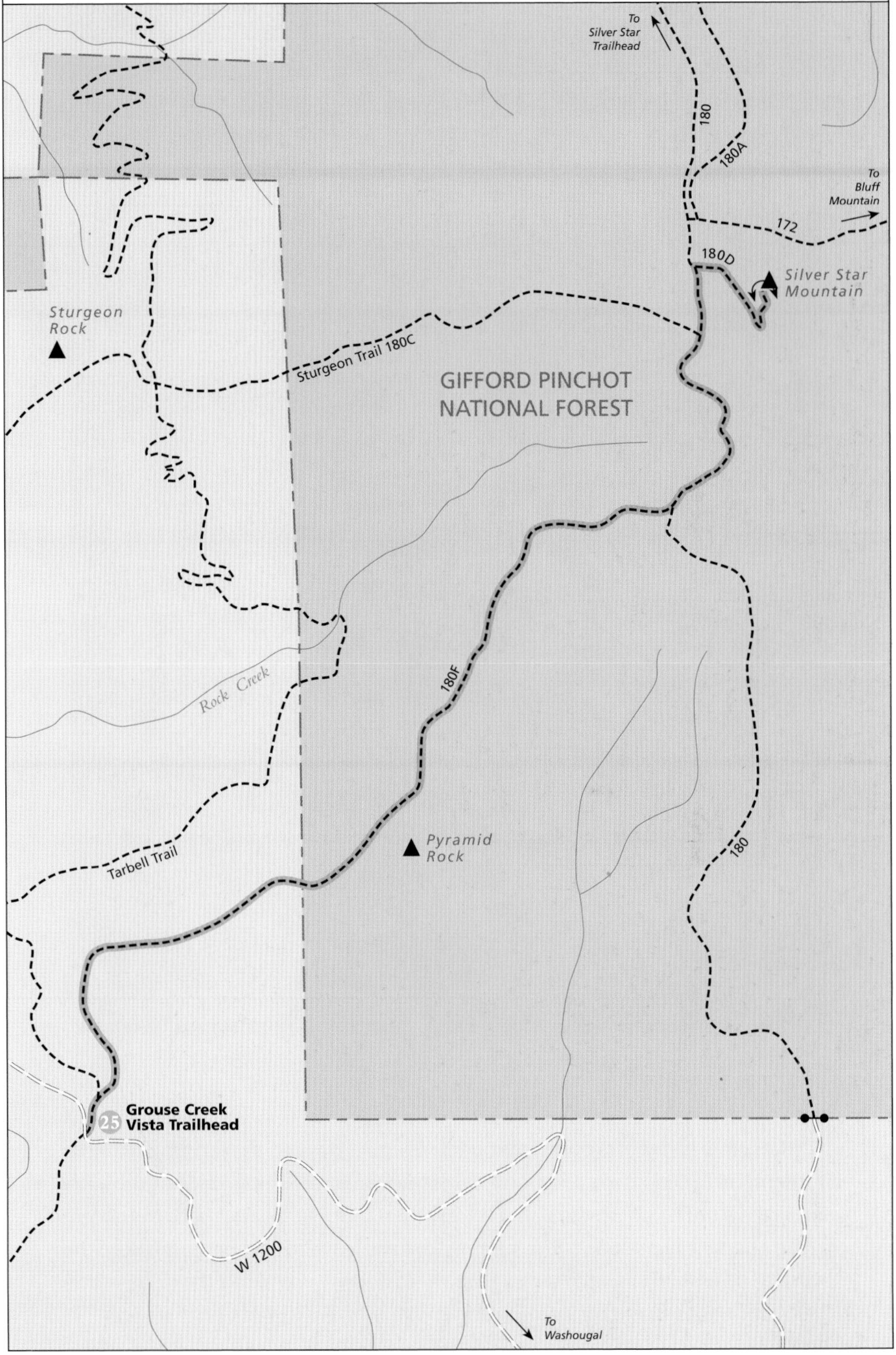

Foxglove

If the trail is clear, follow it for another 0.5 mile, passing the junction with the Sturgeon Trail 180C, to the junction with Silver Star Summit Trail 180D. At the junction make a right turn on the summit trail. Then climb to a switchback to the left, on the ridgeline just south of the summit. You will leave the timber just before the switchback. From the switchback, climb the last few yards along the ridge to the 4,390-foot-high summit of Silver Star Mountain, where a lookout once stood.

Bare ridges radiate from the summit, most with trails on them. The view sweeps around the compass: Mount Hood is to the southeast, Three Corner Rock, with a tower next to it, is to the east. To the northeast is Mount Adams and Goat Rocks. Far to the north-northeast is Mount Rainier, and to the north is Mount St. Helens. To the southwest are Vancouver, Portland, and the Columbia River. Cell phone service is generally good from the summit.

MILES AND DIRECTIONS

0.0 Begin at the Grouse Creek Vista Trailhead. GPS 45 43.313N 122 16.168W.

0.1 Bear right at the junction with Tarbell Trail.

1.4 Bear left (nearly straight ahead) at the trail junction. GPS 45 43.988N 122 15.257W.

2.7 Bear left (nearly straight ahead) at the junction with Trail 180-2, the southern section of 180. GPS 45 44.486N 122 14.556W.

3.0 Use the side path to the ridge when the route is snow-covered.

3.5 Turn right at the junction with Silver Star Summit Trail 180D.

3.8 Turn around at the summit. GPS 45 44.864N 122 14.339W.

7.6 Return to the Grouse Creek Vista Trailhead. GPS 45 43.313N 122 16.168W.

Options: An alternate return may be made by first backtracking to the junction with the Sturgeon Trail. Then follow the Sturgeon Trail west to the junction with the Tarbell Trail. Turn left on the Tarbell Trail and hike southeast back to the junction 150 yards from the trailhead.

Columbia River Gorge Region

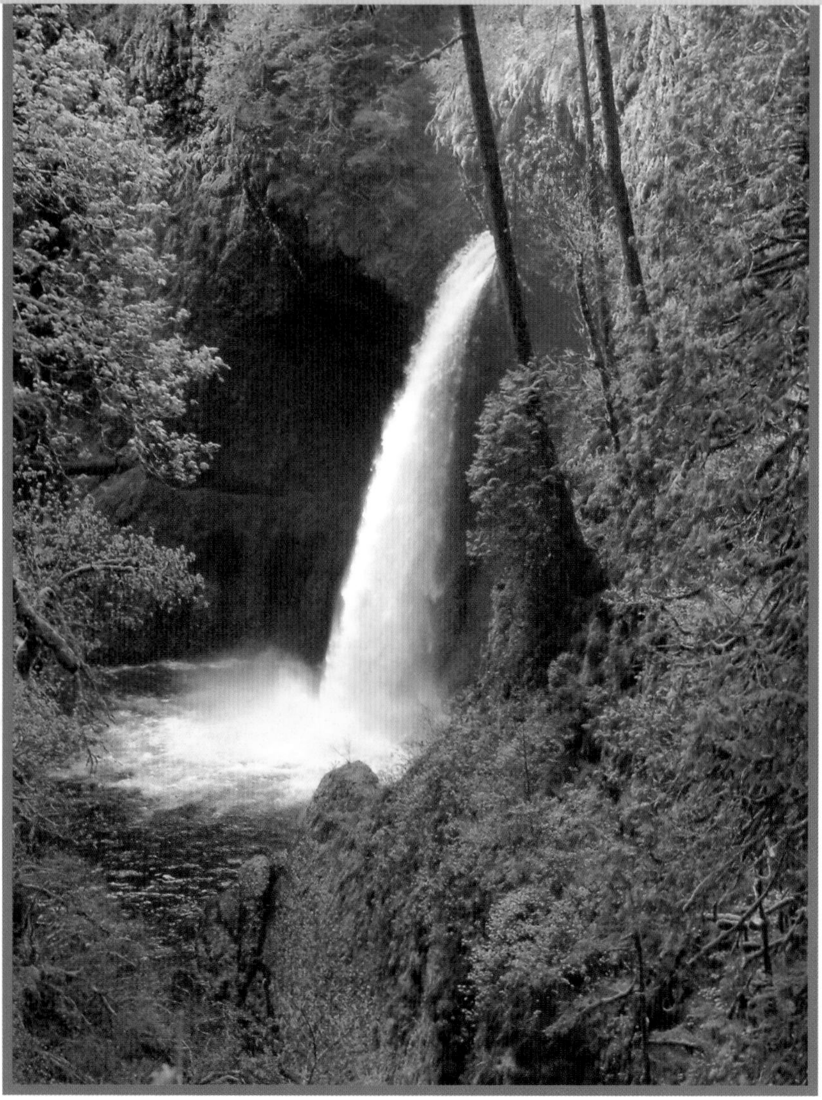

Metlako Falls in the Columbia Gorge Region

The huge gash through the Cascade Mountains that was cut by the mighty Columbia River has created some of the best and also most challenging hiking country to be found. All three of the hikes featured here begin at river level,

Columbine

and two of them reach rocky summits with wonderful views. Hike 28 follows a crystal-clear creek into the heart of a deep canyon, passing several outstanding waterfalls along the way. This region is accessed by Interstate 84.

Enjoy the magnificent scenery of the mighty Columbia River.

Because of the limited space available here, this book barely touches on the hikes and trips that can be made in this tremendous gorge. The FalconGuide *Hiking the Columbia River Gorge,* by Russ Schneider, will lead you into nearly every nook and cranny of this fabulous hiking area.

26

Angels Rest—Wahkeena Falls Trails 415 and 420

Hike to the flat-topped summit plateau of Angels Rest and return or continue through the old-growth forest, passing the large Wahkeena Springs to the Wahkeena Falls Trailhead. Much of the forest that this route passes through before reaching Angels Rest summit was burned in 1991. In places there are silvered snags, but a large percentage of the mature trees survived the fire. This fire opened up the woods enough to make this trail more scenic than it previously was.

Start: Angels Rest Trailhead
Distance/type of hike: 4.6-mile out-and-back day hike to Angels Rest summit or 6.4-mile shuttle day hike one-way to Wahkeena Falls Trailhead
Approximate hiking time: 2.5 hours round-trip to Angels Rest summit; 3.5 hours to Wahkeena Falls Trailhead
Difficulty: Moderate. Trail surfaces are generally fairly smooth, but there is considerable climbing involved on this hike.
Best season: March through November. Some years this route is snow-free nearly all winter; however, at times ice can be a problem.
Canine compatibility and other trail users: Hikers only; dogs if restrained
Fees and permits: None
Maps: *Bridal Veil* and *Multnomah Falls* USGS 7½-min. quads; Geo-Graphics *Trails of the Columbia River Gorge;* National Geographic Oregon topo on CD-ROM Disks 2 and 4; DeLorme's *Oregon Atlas and Gazetteer,* p. 67, D7 and D8
Trail contacts: Columbia River Gorge National Scenic Area, Waucoma Center, 902 Wasco Avenue, Hood River, OR 97031; www.fs.fed.us/r6/columbia/forest
Special considerations: Lock your car at either trailhead; don't leave any valuables inside. Unfortunately, break-ins have become fairly common at Columbia Gorge trailheads.

Finding the trailhead:
Drive east from Portland on Interstate 84; get off at exit 28. Drive southeast a short distance to the junction with the Columbia Gorge Scenic Highway. The Angels Rest Trailhead parking area is to your right next to the junction. The trailhead is just across the Scenic Highway from the parking area. The DeLorme's *Oregon Atlas and Gazetteer* covers the area but does not show the Angels Rest Trailhead; however, it does show the Wahkeena Falls and Multno-

mah Falls Trailheads. Parking is limited at this popular trailhead. There is an overflow parking area a short distance to the southwest along the Columbia Gorge Scenic Highway.

To reach the Wahkeena Falls Trailhead where this hike ends, head east for 2.5 miles from the Angels Rest Trailhead on the Columbia Gorge Scenic Highway.

THE HIKE

From the west end of the parking area, angle across the Columbia River Scenic Highway to the trailhead, and begin your climb through the bigleaf maple and Douglas fir forest. In a short distance there will be a trail junction. The trail to the right leads to the Angels Rest overflow parking area. If you are here on a busy summer weekend, this may be where you meet the Angels Rest Trail, as you may be parked in the overflow lot. The route crosses a talus slope 0.3 mile from the trailhead. Pikas inhabit this slope and can often be seen, or their shrill call can at least be heard.

The first viewpoint overlooking Canopy Falls is to the left of the trail 0.6 mile from the trailhead. Over the next 0.1 mile, several more short side paths to the

Angels Rest plateau in the fog

left offer views of the main falls and smaller ones in the creek above it. The course crosses a wooden bridge over the creek, well above Canopy Falls, 0.7 mile from the trailhead.

You will make a switchback 0.1 mile after crossing the bridge. This is the first of sixteen switchbacks that the ascending track will make in the next 1.3 miles. As you climb, the route passes several viewpoints overlooking the Columbia River. The trail rounds a ridgeline and nearly disappears as it enters a talus slope, 2 miles into the hike. Be cautious as you cross the talus: Some of the rocks are not solid and if they are wet, they can be very slippery. Once across the talus the trail continues its traverse through an area of low brush for a short distance, then makes a switchback to the left. In a little less than 0.1 mile, you will reach the junction with the path to Angels Rest summit plateau. This junction at 1,600 feet elevation is 2.2 miles from the Angels Rest Trailhead.

Take the time to visit the summit plateau. Bear left (really straight ahead) at the junction and follow the ridgeline, heading northwest. This is a rough trail and you will have to climb over some boulders before reaching the nearly flat plateau. In 0.1 mile you will reach the plateau. The view from the plateau nearly 1,600 feet above the broad Columbia River is great in all directions. After you have finished admiring the view and perhaps had lunch, return the 0.1 mile to the junction. If this is to be an out-and-back hike, bear to the right and descend the way you came back to the Angels Rest Trailhead.

To continue toward the Wahkeena Falls Trailhead, bear left and continue along the rocky ridgeline, heading east. The route climbs, makes a couple of switchbacks, and gains about 130 feet of elevation in the 0.2 mile to the first junction with the Foxglove Trail. This junction may or may not have a sign marking it. To stay on the Angels Rest Trail 415, heading toward Wahkeena Springs and Trailhead, bear left at the junction. The track crosses a wooden bridge over a small stream 0.5 mile from the first junction with the Foxglove Trail. Just past the bridge there is a campsite with an old picnic table on the left side of the trail.

Once past the campsite the track climbs for a short distance then flattens out again. There will be another junction with the Foxglove Trail 0.5 mile from the bridge and campsite. This junction at approximately 1,800 feet elevation is close to the highest point reached on this hike. When I hiked this trail, there was a small sign marking this junction.

Bear left (straight ahead) at the junction, staying on the Angels Rest Trail. A short distance after passing the second junction with the Foxglove Trail, there is a

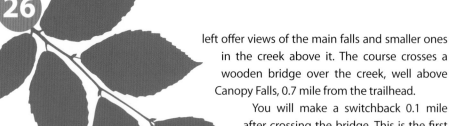

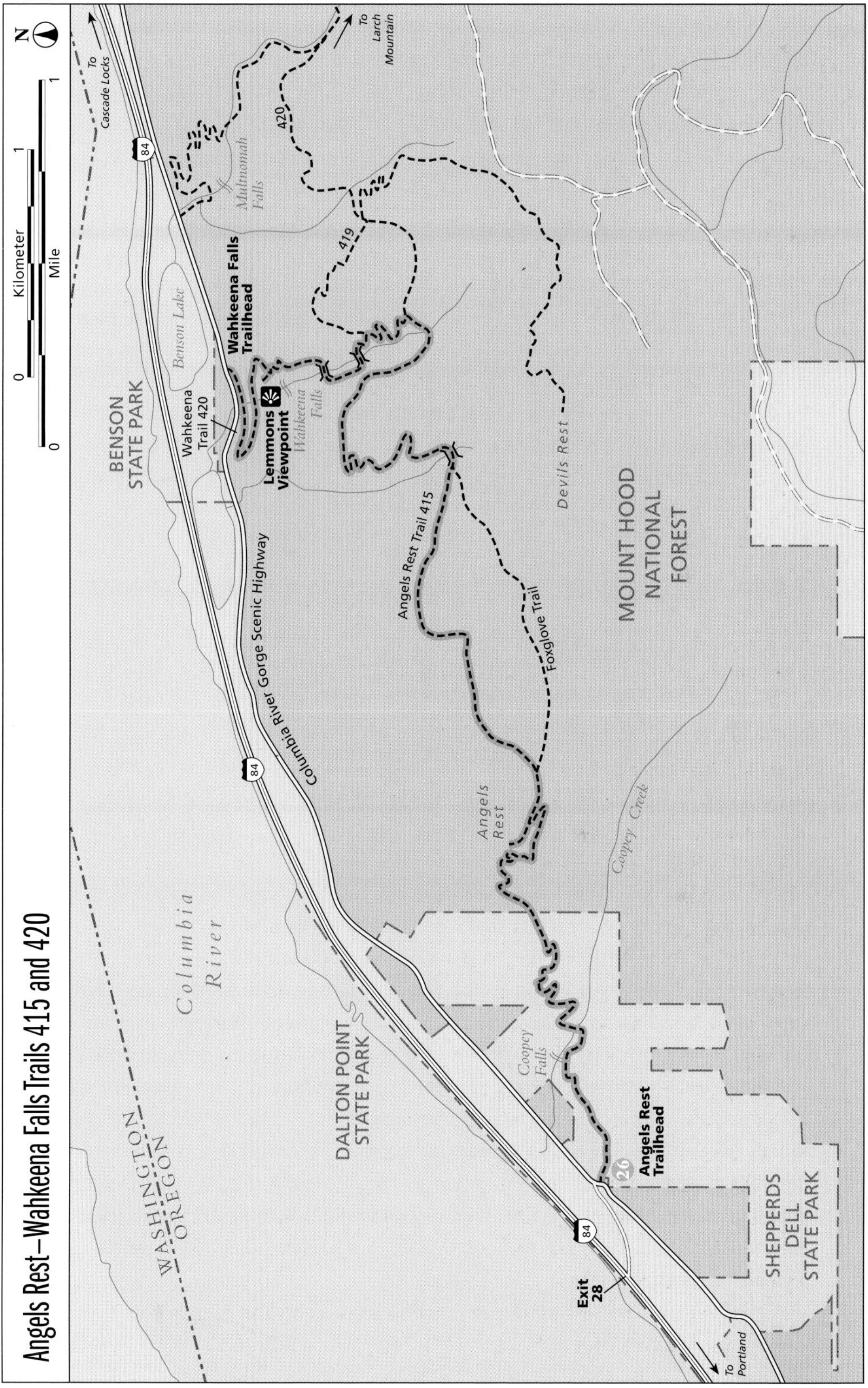

Angels Rest—Wahkeena Falls Trails 415 and 420
Kilometer
Mile
0
1
WASHINGTON
OREGON
Columbia River
To Cascade Locks
To Larch Mountain
84
Multnomah Falls
420
419
BENSON STATE PARK
Benson Lake
Wahkeena Falls Trailhead
Wahkeena Trail 420
Lemmons Viewpoint
Wahkeena Falls
Devils Rest
Columbia River Gorge Scenic Highway
Angels Rest Trail 415
Foxglove Trail
MOUNT HOOD NATIONAL FOREST
Angels Rest
Coopey Creek
Coopey Falls
DALTON POINT STATE PARK
Angels Rest Trailhead
26
Exit 28
SHEPPERDS DELL STATE PARK
To Portland

single log bridge over a small stream. The route crosses another small stream without the benefit of a bridge 0.2 mile farther along, as you begin the descent toward Wahkeena Springs. The route gently winds its way down for 0.8 mile, then climbs slightly to Wahkeena Springs. Another 100 yards of nearly flat hiking and the junction with the Wahkeena Trail 420 is reached at 1,240 feet elevation. This junction is 4.8 miles from the Angels Rest Trailhead and the end of the Angels Rest Trail 415. To the right the Wahkeena Trail leads east for 1.2 miles to meet the Larch Mountain Trail 441. See the options below for descending via the Larch Mountain Trail.

Turn left at the junction and descend 250 feet, in three switchbacks, to the junction with the Vista Point Trail 419. Bear left at this junction and continue the downhill hike. The route makes six more switchbacks, then crosses a fork of Wahkeena Creek. After crossing the creek and making six more switchbacks, the trail crosses Wahkeena Creek on a wooden bridge. As of March 2007 this bridge had been demolished by a falling tree and was somewhat difficult to cross. Hopefully it will have been repaired by the time you read this. Below the bridge the route

Take a few minutes to walk the short distance to Lemmons Viewpoint and admire the view before continuing your downward hike. Lemmons Viewpoint is named for Keith Lemmons, a firefighter who lost his life fighting a fire in August 1983.

closely parallels the creek down through a very narrow section of canyon. In a bit over 0.1 mile, the tread recrosses the creek on another wooden bridge.

Another 0.1 mile brings you to the junction with the now closed Monument Viewpoint Trail, which was to the right. A few steps farther and to the left is the Lemmons Viewpoint Trail. At this junction you have descended to 620 feet elevation.

Below the Lemmons Viewpoint Trail junction, the now paved Wahkeena Trail makes ten more switchbacks before reaching the junction with the now "closed to public use" Perdition Trail 421. The once-popular Perdition Trail led east for 1.2 miles to join the Larch Mountain Trail above Multnomah Falls. Bear left at the junction and hike on down the Wahkeena Trail. In a little under 0.2 mile, the trail crosses a concrete bridge at the base of beautiful Wahkeena Falls. One more switchback and another 0.2 mile brings you to the Wahkeena Falls Trailhead at 80 feet elevation and 6.4 miles from the Angels Rest Trailhead.

MILES AND DIRECTIONS

0.0 Begin at the Angels Rest Trailhead. GPS 45 33.616N 122 10.370W.

0.6 Arrive at Coopey Falls.

2.2 Turn right at the path to Angels Rest summit. GPS 45 33.814N 122 09.086W.

2.4 Bear left at the first junction with the Foxglove Trail. GPS 45 33.788N 122 08.941W.

3.4 Bear left again at the second junction with the Foxglove Trail.

4.7 Arrive at Wahkeena Springs.

4.8 Turn left at the junction with the Wahkeena Trail. GPS 45 34.138N 122 07.392W.

5.2 Turn left at the junction with the Vista Point Trail.

5.6 Turn right at the junction with the trail to Lemmons Viewpoint.

6.4 Finish at the Wahkeena Falls Trailhead. GPS 45 34.535N 122 07.656W.

Options: If you would like to lengthen this shuttle hike by 1.4 miles, turn right (east) at the junction of the Angels Rest and Wahkeena Trails. Follow the Wahkeena Trail for 1.2 miles to the junction with the Larch Mountain Trail. Turn left on the Larch Mountain Trail and follow it downhill for 1.8 miles to the Multnomah Falls Lodge and Trailhead. Making this slightly longer descent would also require a car shuttle to the Multnomah Falls Lodge, which is slightly less than 1 mile east of the Wahkeena Falls Trailhead along the Columbia Gorge Scenic Highway or following the Return Trail back to the Wahkeena Falls Trailhead.

27

Larch Mountain Trail 441

Climb from near sea level at the Multnomah Falls Lodge to nearly 4,000 feet elevation atop Larch Mountain. In the first 2 miles, this route passes three major waterfalls.

Start: Multnomah Falls Lodge and Trailhead
Distance/type of hike: 13.6-mile out-and-back day hike or backpack, with shuttle option
Approximate hiking time: 6 hours
Difficulty: Moderate. The trail surface is generally good, but there is a lot of elevation gain.
Best season: Mid-May through October
Canine compatibility and other trail users: Hikers and restrained dogs only up to Multnomah Creek Way, 4.8 miles from the trailhead. Above that point mountain bikes are also allowed.
Fees and permits: None if parked at Multnomah Falls Lodge and Trailhead, but if this is to be a shuttle hike, a Northwest Forest Pass is required at the Larch Mountain Picnic Area and Trailhead.
Maps: USGS 7½-min. *Multnomah Falls* quad; Geo-Graphics *Trails of the Columbia River Gorge;* National Geographic Oregon topo on CD-ROM Disk 4; DeLorme's *Oregon Atlas and Gazetteer,* p. 67, D8
Trail contacts: Columbia River Gorge National Scenic Area, Waucoma Center, 902 Wasco Avenue, Hood River, OR 97031; www.fs.fed.us/r6/columbia/forest
Special considerations: The first 1.5 miles of this hike are on the most heavily used section of trail in the Columbia River Gorge. You can expect to have company on the trail here any day of the year; on spring and summer weekends, it is often very crowded. After you get about 1.5 miles up the trail, the crowds really thin out. As with all of the Columbia Gorge Trailheads, be sure to lock your car and don't leave valuables inside.

Finding the trailhead:
From Portland, drive east on Interstate 84 to exit 31 (31 miles from Interstate 5). This is a left exit off the freeway and the parking area is between the east- and westbound lanes. Multnomah Falls Lodge and Trailhead are covered on DeLorme's *Oregon Atlas and Gazetteer.*

The Multnomah Falls Lodge and Trailhead can also be reached by leaving the freeway at exit 28. Drive southeast a short distance to the junction with the Columbia Gorge Scenic Highway. Turn left and follow the Columbia Gorge Scenic Highway east for approximately 3 miles.

There is plenty of parking at the freeway exit, but the parking is limited on the scenic highway next to the lodge. A restaurant, gift shop, and restrooms are available at the lodge.

THE HIKE

The broad paved track starts on the east side of the Multnomah Falls Lodge at 60 feet elevation. After making the first five switchbacks, the route crosses the Benson footbridge almost directly above the lower falls, 0.2 mile after leaving the lodge.

You climb moderately but steadily after crossing the bridge, passing the junction with the Gorge Trail 400. The route makes eleven more switchbacks in the 0.7 mile to the top of the ridgeline, at 810 feet elevation. Then you descend slightly, making one more switchback, and reach the junction with the trail to the viewpoint atop Multnomah Falls, and the end of the pavement. The short side trail to the right, leading to the viewpoint, is well worth taking.

The Benson footbridge was named for Simon Benson, a renowned lumberman in the early part of the twentieth century. The bridge offers a great view of Multnomah Falls, and on summer weekends there's often "standing-room only" on the bridge.

The Larch Mountain Trail quickly crosses a bridge over Multnomah Creek after passing the junction with the viewpoint trail. Just after crossing the bridge is the junction with the now closed Perdition Trail. About 0.2 mile farther along, the trail passes beneath a rock overhang as it ascends along frothing Multnomah Creek. Shortly the track makes a switchback to the right about 75 yards from the base of Twanklaskie Falls (a falls in Multnomah Creek). The tread climbs three more switchbacks, passes the top of Twanklaskie Falls, and in a short distance more reaches Ecola Falls, also in Multnomah Creek, 1.6 miles from the Multnomah Falls Lodge.

The Wahkeena Trail 420 turns to the left a little more than 0.2 mile after passing Ecola Falls. The Wahkeena Trail leads 2.8 miles northwest to the Wahkeena Trailhead. Bear left, staying on the Larch Mountain Trail, and cross a metal bridge over Multnomah Creek 2.0 miles from the trailhead.

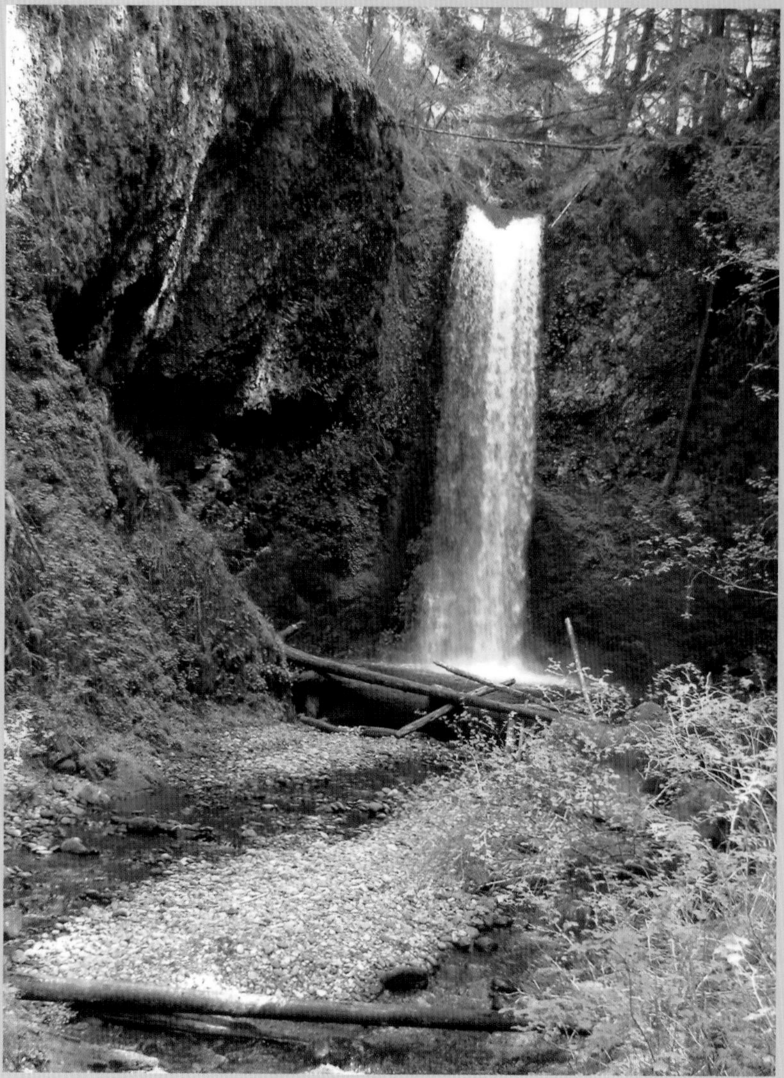

Falls in Multnomah Creek

You will cross a side stream with a waterfall above and to your left 0.5 mile farther along. Shortly after crossing the stream, there will be a steep path to the left. This is a high-water trail; just ahead the Larch Mountain Trail is chipped from a rock face very close to creek level. During times of high water, this short (0.1-mile) section of the trail may not be passable. At these times the high-water trail

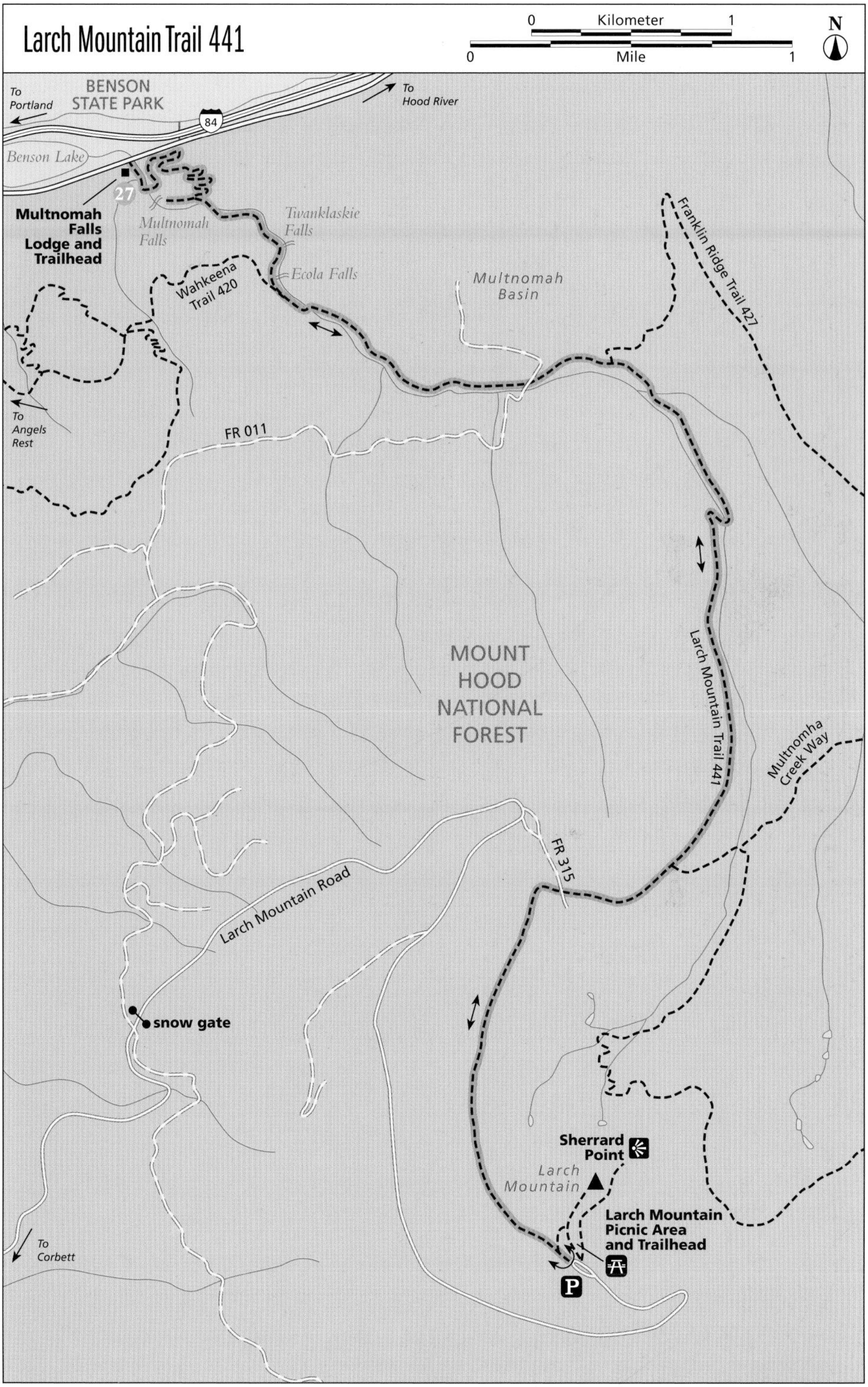

Larch Mountain Trail 441
0 Kilometer 1
0 Mile 1
N
To Portland
BENSON STATE PARK
To Hood River
84
Benson Lake
27
Multnomah Falls Lodge and Trailhead
Multnomah Falls
Twanklaskie Falls
Ecola Falls
Wahkeena Trail 420
Multnomah Basin
Franklin Ridge Trail 427
To Angels Rest
FR 011
MOUNT HOOD NATIONAL FOREST
Larch Mountain Trail 441
Multnomha Creek Way
FR 315
Larch Mountain Road
snow gate
Sherrard Point
Larch Mountain
Larch Mountain Picnic Area and Trailhead
P
To Corbett

allows passage around this short section of the Larch Mountain Trail. Shortly you will reach the junction with the other end of the high-water trail.

The Larch Mountain Trail angles across the Multnomah Basin Road FR 011, 2.8 miles from the Multnomah Falls Lodge Trailhead. By the time you reach FR 011, you have climbed to a little over 1,600 feet elevation. Another 0.2 mile of hiking brings you to the junction with the Franklin Ridge Trail 427. Hike straight ahead (east-southeast) at the junction, staying on the Larch Mountain Trail.

The route crosses a single log bridge with a cable handrail, 0.1 mile after passing the junction with the Franklin Ridge Trail, then climbs two switchbacks and continues to ascend to the southeast along a small ridgeline between the two streams.

The course crosses another single log bridge over Multnomah Creek, 0.5 mile farther along. You then climb another switchback and soon cross a talus slope. Above the talus the track continues to climb, gaining about 600 feet of elevation in the 0.9 mile to the junction with the Multnomah Creek Way 444. This junction is 4.8 miles from the Multnomah Falls Lodge and Trailhead at 2,900 feet elevation. Mountain bikes as well as hikers are allowed above this junction on the Larch Mountain Trail as well as on the Multnomah Creek Way.

The tread reaches the junction with Forest Road 315 0.5 mile from the junction with the Multnomah Creek Way. After crossing the primitive road, the track continues to climb through the forest for the last 1.5 miles to the Larch Mountain Picnic Area and Trailhead at 3,900 feet elevation. The picnic area is to your left as you approach the parking area. If you haven't arranged for a car shuttle, return to Multnomah Falls as you came. See the options below for driving directions to the Larch Mountain Picnic Area and Trailhead.

Green Tip:

If at all possible, camp in established sites. If there are none, then camp in an unobtrusive area at least 200 feet (70 paces) from the nearest water source.

MILES AND DIRECTIONS

0.0 Begin at Multnomah Falls Lodge and Trailhead. GPS 45 34.660N 122 07.030W.

1.0 Bear left at the junction with the trail to the viewpoint atop Multnomah Falls.

1.8 Bear left at the junction with the Wahkeena Trail 420.

2.8 Cross FR 011 to Multnomah Basin. Bear left, then right.

3.0 Bear right at the junction with the Franklin Ridge Trail 427. GPS 45 34.120N 122 05.154W.

4.8 Bear right at the junction with Multnomah Creek Way Trail 444.

5.3 Cross FR 315. GPS 54 32.724N 122 05.332W.

6.8 Turn around at the Larch Mountain Picnic Area and Trailhead. GPS 45 31.772N 122 05.330W.

13.6 Return to Multnomah Falls Lodge and Trailhead. GPS 45 34.660N 122 07.030W.

Options: To make this a one-way shuttle hike, have someone take a car to the Larch Mountain Picnic Area and Trailhead. To reach the Larch Mountain Picnic Area by car from the Multnomah Falls Lodge and Trailhead, head back to the west on I-84 to the Corbett exit 22. Follow the signs up Corbett Hill to the junction with the Crown Point Highway near Corbett (about 2 miles). Turn left (east) on the Crown Point Highway and drive about 2 miles to the junction with the Larch Mountain Road. Turn right onto the Larch Mountain Road and follow it for 14.3 miles to the Larch Mountain Picnic Area and Trailhead.

Whether you drive or hike to the top of Larch Mountain, take the time to hike the quarter-mile paved trail to 4,056-foot-high Sherrard Point, and take in the view of five Cascade mountain peaks.

28

Eagle Creek Trail 440 to Tunnel Falls

The Eagle Creek Trail is arguably the most beautiful route in the Columbia Gorge. Waterfall after waterfall awaits the hiker as he or she traverses the steep hillsides and cliffs of the Eagle Creek Canyon. The lower 6 miles of the Eagle Creek Trail described below pass most of the waterfalls and steep moss-covered gorges making it the most spectacular part of this 13.3-mile-long trail.

Start: Eagle Creek Trailhead.
Distance/type of hike: 12-mile out-and-back day hike or backpack
Approximate hiking time: 5 hours
Difficulty: Moderate. The trail surface is generally good and the grades are gentle, but there are a few somewhat exposed spots along the trail.
Best season: Eagle Creek Trail up to Tunnel Falls is generally free of snow most of the year. However, during periods of below-freezing weather, ice can make this route very difficult and dangerous.
Canine compatibility and other trail users: Dogs on a leash. Closed to stock and bicycles.
Fees and permits: Northwest Forest Pass and Mark O. Hatfield Wilderness permit
Maps: *Trails of the Columbia Gorge* by Geo-Graphics; National Geographic Oregon topo on CD-ROM Disk 4; DeLorme's *Oregon Atlas and Gazetteer,* p. 68, C1
Trail contacts: Columbia River Gorge National Scenic Area, Waucoma Center, 902 Wasco Avenue, Hood River, OR 97031; www.fs.fed.us/r6/columbia/forest
Special considerations: Many sections of the Eagle Creek Trail are carved out of cliff faces and/or follow relatively narrow ledges. Watch your step in these places, as it would be very easy to fall from the trail, possibly with disastrous consequences. Camping is not allowed along Eagle Creek for the first 3.3 miles from the trailhead. As with all of the Columbia Gorge Trailheads, be sure to lock your car and don't leave valuables inside.

Finding the trailhead:
Drive east from Portland on Interstate 84 to exit 41. After leaving the freeway, head south past the fish hatchery for 0.3 mile to the Eagle Creek Trailhead. There is no exit for Eagle Creek if you're coming from the east on I-84, so you must continue west on the freeway to exit 40 and turn around.

There is lots of parking at the trailhead, but at times it may be full. More parking is located 0.1 mile back toward I-84 along the road to the trailhead. Restrooms and a campground are also located close by.

THE HIKE

Douglas firs and bigleaf maples shade the route as you leave the Eagle Creek Trailhead and head southeast along the Eagle Creek Trail. Soon the tread climbs a few feet to follow a ledge cut from the rock cliffs. These cliffs are part of the Eagle Creek formation, which is some of the oldest rock that is exposed in the Columbia Gorge.

Petrified Finds

The Eagle Creek formation is composed of ancient mudflows made up of volcanic rock and ash. Heavy rains falling onto weak volcanic slopes probably caused these mudflows. The Eagle Creek formation underlies the layers of Columbia River Basalt, which form most of the cliffs in the gorge. Considerable petrified material has been found in the Eagle Creek formation.

A tiny waterfall (sometimes dry in summer) falls onto the left side of the trail, and its stream crosses the track 0.7 mile from the trailhead. A short distance farther along, the trail passes beneath another of these tiny falls. The path to the Metlako Falls viewpoint turns to the right 1.5 miles from the trailhead. Take the side route, which rejoins the main trail in a short distance, and view the beautiful waterfall. The actual viewpoint is a few yards off the side path. There is a cable rail between the viewpoint and the cliffs below. This is a spot where it is very important to stay behind the cable. The cliff below is absolutely vertical and a fall from it would likely be fatal. Be sure to keep children and dogs behind the cable also. There are plenty of cliffs one could fall over along the Eagle Creek Trail, but this spot, which is often misused, is one of the most spooky.

The route crosses Sorenson Creek on round concrete stepping stones 0.2 mile after passing the path to the Metlako Falls viewpoint. Just past Sorenson Creek is the junction with the Lower Punchbowl Trail. To the right the Lower Punchbowl Trail descends about 160 vertical feet to creek level then, continues a short distance onto a gravel bar where there is a view of Punchbowl Falls. The

Punchbowl Falls

quarter-mile side trip to the end of the Lower Punchbowl Trail is well worth the time and effort.

Back on the main Eagle Creek Trail, another quarter mile of hiking brings you to a fine viewpoint overlooking Punchbowl Falls. A short distance past the viewpoint, the route crosses a steel bridge in a side canyon. Directly below the bridge Tish Creek drops to form a waterfall. There will be a view ahead of Loowit Falls, 0.5 mile after crossing the bridge over Tish Creek. The outlet stream from Dublin Lake enters Eagle Creek next to Loowit Falls.

A short distance farther along and 3.3 miles from the trailhead, the trail crosses High Bridge. High Bridge spans a narrow gorge with the sparkling clear waters of Eagle Creek some 80 feet below. A short path to the right leads to Tenas Camp, slightly over 0.3 mile after crossing High Bridge. To the left of the trail at nearly the same spot, another short path leads to a viewpoint of a falls in Eagle Creek. The course crosses 4½ Mile Bridge (4.5 miles from the Columbia River Highway, not the trailhead) over Eagle Creek in a little more than another 0.3 mile. At the far end of the bridge, the trail appears to "T." The path to the left goes only a short distance along a ledge above the creek.

Shortly after crossing 4½ Mile Bridge, look across Eagle Creek for a side-by-side double waterfall. A little farther along, large, steep, and frothing Opal Creek joins Eagle Creek from the far side. The tread passes a sign with facts about the

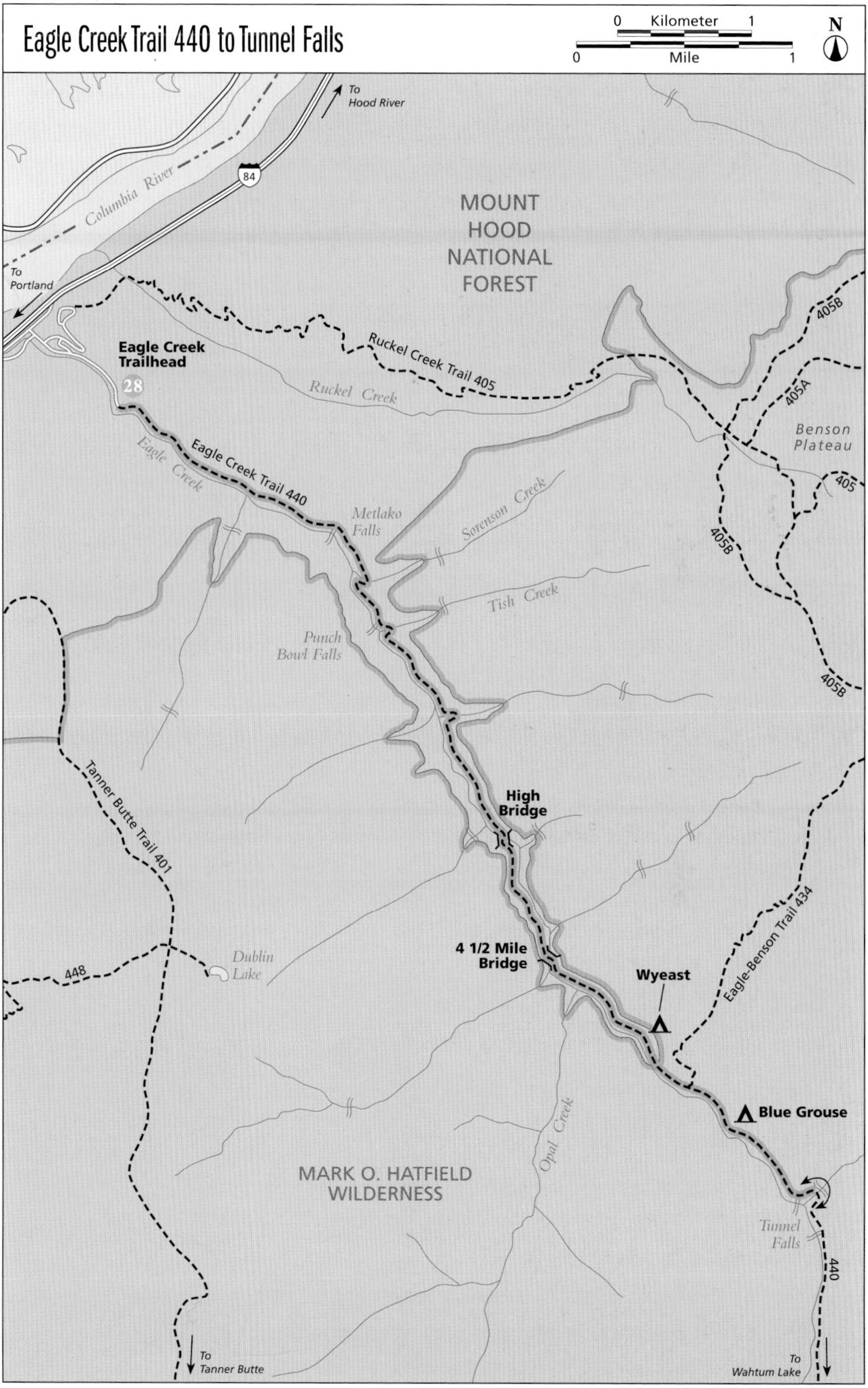
Eagle Creek Trail 440 to Tunnel Falls
0 Kilometer 1
0 Mile 1
N
To Hood River
84
Columbia River
MOUNT HOOD NATIONAL FOREST
To Portland
Eagle Creek Trailhead
28
Ruckel Creek Trail 405
Ruckel Creek
405B
405A
Benson Plateau
405
Eagle Creek
Eagle Creek Trail 440
Metlako Falls
Sorenson Creek
Tish Creek
Punch Bowl Falls
405B
405B
High Bridge
Tanner Butte Trail 401
4 1/2 Mile Bridge
Wyeast
Eagle-Benson Trail 434
Dublin Lake
448
Blue Grouse
Opal Creek
MARK O. HATFIELD WILDERNESS
Tunnel Falls
440
To Tanner Butte
To Wahtum Lake

1902 forest fire that burned this area 0.2 mile farther along. You may have noticed that most of the large Douglas firs along the trail show very old fire scars.

The track crosses a wooden bridge over sometimes-dry Wyeast Creek and reaches Wyeast Camp 4.8 miles from the trailhead. There are several campsites available at Wyeast Camp.

A little over 0.1 mile after passing Wyeast Camp, the trail enters the Mark O. Hatfield Wilderness. There is a wilderness registration box here where you can obtain a wilderness permit. Just after entering the wilderness, the route crosses a stream without the benefit of a bridge. The junction with the Eagle-Benson Trail 434 is reached 0.2 mile after crossing the stream. This junction is 5.1 miles from Eagle Creek Trailhead, at 960 feet elevation. The steep Eagle-Benson Trail climbs to the northeast (left) to join the Pacific Crest National Scenic Trail (PCT) in 3 miles.

The campsites of Blue Grouse Camp will be to the right of the trail 0.2 mile after passing the junction with the Eagle-Benson Trail. The route follows a ledge chipped from the cliff 0.5 mile after passing the Blue Grouse Camp. Here you walk on the tops of the basalt columns that form these cliffs. Below to the right, Eagle Creek drops over a waterfall.

Slightly over 0.1 mile ahead and tucked back in the side canyon of the East Fork of Eagle Creek is Tunnel Falls. The trail tunnels through the solid basalt rock behind the beautiful waterfall. Well below the trail Tunnel Falls crashes into a clear pool. The elevation at Tunnel Falls is 1,200 feet and you are 6 miles from the Eagle Creek Trailhead. If this is a day hike, this is the spot where you turn around. For an overnight backpack or shuttle trip, see the options below.

MILES AND DIRECTIONS

0.0 Begin at the Eagle Creek Trailhead. GPS 45 38.228N 121 55.187W.

1.5 Bear left at the path to Metlako Falls.

1.7 Bear left at the junction with Lower Punchbowl Trail.

3.3 Cross High Bridge.

4.8 Arrive at Wyeast Camp.

5.1 Bear right at the junction with the Eagle-Benson Trail. GPS 45 35.470N 121 51.782W.

5.3 Arrive at Blue Grouse Camp.

6.0 Turn around at Tunnel Falls.

12.0 Return to the Eagle Creek Trailhead. GPS 45 38.228N 121 55.187W.

Options: Continuing along the Eagle Creek Trail to Wahtum Lake makes a wonderful overnight backpack or one-way shuttle hike to the Wahtum Lake Trailhead. From Tunnel Falls, continue southeast on the Eagle Creek Trail for 1.6 miles to the junction with the Eagle-Tanner Trail 433. At the junction make a left turn, staying on the Eagle Creek Trail. After climbing for another 2.2 miles, you will reach the junction with the Indian Springs Trail 435. Bear left at the junction, staying on the Eagle Creek Trail, and climb another 3.5 miles to Wahtum Lake. The Wahtum Lake Trailhead is about 0.2 mile south of and 200 feet higher than Wahtum Lake.

To reach the Wahtum Lake Trailhead from the Eagle Creek Trailhead, first drive back to I-84 and head east for 23 miles to exit 64 at Hood River, then head south on Oregon Route 35 for 6 miles to the Odell turnoff. Turn right and go to Odell. Turn right as you enter the town and follow Odell Highway 1.5 miles north to Summit Road. Turn left on Summit Road and follow it 2 miles to Dee Highway. Turn left on Dee Highway and follow it 4.2 miles to Dee Mill and the junction with Lost Lake Road. Turn right on Lost Lake Road and follow it 5 miles, then turn right on the unmarked Forest Road 13. Follow FR 13 4.4 miles to the junction with FR 1310. Turn right on FR 1310 and follow it 5.9 miles to Wahtum Lake Trailhead at the end of the pavement.

Green Tip:

For rest stops, go off-trail so others won't have to get around you. Head for resilient surfaces without vegetation.

Mount Hood and Salmon-Huckleberry Wilderness Region

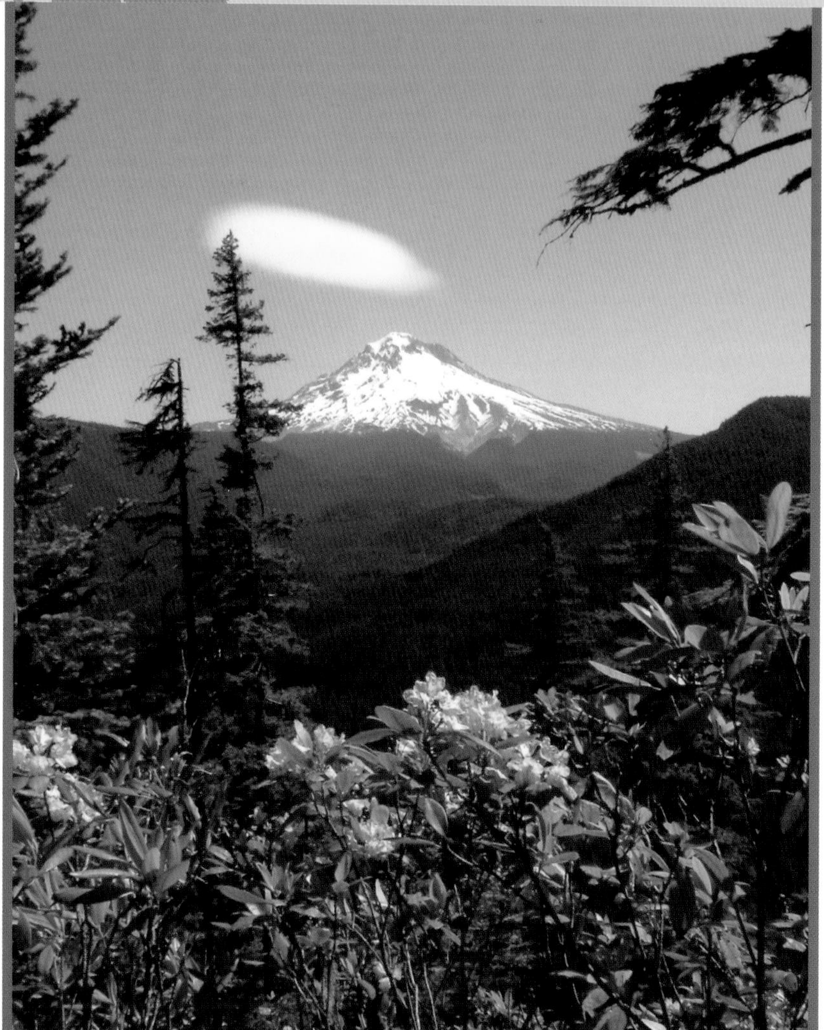

Mount Hood with lenticular cloud above

This region includes parts of the Mount Hood and the Salmon-Huckleberry Wilderness Areas east of Portland. All of these hikes are accessed from U.S. Highway 26. Hikes 29, 30, 31, and 34 are located on Zigzag Mountain, a long southwestern spur of Mount Hood. The open country atop Zigzag Mountain shows the hiker panoramic views as well as marvelous wildflowers. Hikes 32 and 36 reach the flowered covered alpine country on the slopes of Mount Hood itself. Hikes 38 and 41 reach ridgetops with superb views of Mount Hood as well as other Cascade peaks. Hike 35 passes a spectacular waterfall, and Hike 38 follows a section of an alternate route for the Old Oregon Trail.

Many of these hikes are highlighted with spectacular views of the ice-clad, craggy summit of Mount Hood.

Honeysuckle

29

Zigzag Mountain Trails 798, 2000, 778, and 775

Hike, mostly downhill, from high on the south slope of Mount Hood near Timberline Lodge to a trailhead deep in the densely forested Zigzag Canyon. The total elevation gain for this hike is about 2,600 feet and the elevation loss is approximately 6,200 feet.

Start: Timberline Lodge.
Distance/type of hike: 17.9-mile shuttle day hike or backpack
Approximate hiking time: 7.5 hours
Difficulty: Moderate in the direction described below, strenuous in the opposite direction
Best season: Late July through September
Canine compatibility and other trail users: Dogs are allowed on this trail but must be controlled when close to stock and wildlife. This trail is open to stock as well as hikers but not to mountain bikes.
Fees and permits: Mount Hood Wilderness Permit. A Northwest Forest Pass is required if parking at the Zigzag Mountain Trailhead.
Maps: *Mount Hood South, Government Camp,* and *Rhododendron* USGS 7½-min. quads; USDA Forest Service *Zigzag Ranger District;* Adventure Maps Inc. *Mt. Hood/NW Oregon Trail Map;* National Geographic Oregon topo on CD-ROM Disk 4; DeLorme's *Oregon Atlas and Gazetteer,* p. 62, B3
Trail contacts: USDA Forest Service, Zigzag Ranger District, 70220 East Highway 26, Zigzag, OR 97049; (503) 622-3191; www.fs.fed.us/r6/mthood
Special considerations: If the Zigzag River is high because of recent rains or major snowmelt, the ford 3 miles from Timberline Lodge can be difficult and possibly dangerous.

Finding the trailhead:
Drive east from Portland on U.S. Highway 26 to the junction with Timberline Road, just east of Government Camp. Turn left (north) onto Timberline Road and follow it 5.2 miles to the large parking area just east of Wyeast Day Lodge. Wyeast Day Lodge offers restrooms, food service, and a gift shop. A short distance away is Timberline Lodge, which has overnight accommodations.

To reach the Zigzag Mountain Trailhead, where this hike ends, turn north off US 26 42 miles east of Portland at the tiny town of Zigzag on East Lolo Pass Road. Follow East Lolo Pass Road for 0.3 mile, then turn east (right) on East

Mountain Drive (Forest Road 1819). Follow FR 1819 for 0.5 mile to the trailhead. GPS signals are very hard to get at this trailhead. There is room to park several cars at the Zigzag Mountain Trailhead, but there are no other facilities.

THE HIKE

Before starting your hike, get your Mount Hood Wilderness permit at the east entrance of the Wyeast Day Lodge. This hike begins on the Mountaineer Trail 798. From the parking area east of Wyeast Day Lodge, walk west up the road a short distance to the much smaller overnight parking area for Timberline Lodge. From the west end of the Timberline Lodge parking lot, continue west on a service road. In a few yards you will pass beneath the Magic Mile Ski Lift, where you'll bear left through a small gravel parking area and pick up the Mountaineer Trail, heading west. The route passes beneath the Storm'n Norman Ski Lift about 0.4 mile after leaving the Timberline Lodge Parking Area. You then climb gently for a little

Mount Hood lily

over 0.3 mile, reaching 5,930 feet elevation, at the junction with the Pacific Crest National Scenic Trail 2000 (PCT).

At the junction turn left on the PCT and descend gently. The course crosses the Little Zigzag River, enters the Mount Hood Wilderness, and reaches the junction with the Hidden Lake Trail 779, 0.6 mile after leaving the junction with the Mountaineer Trail. Hidden Lake is 3 miles to the southwest along the Hidden Lake Trail. Bear right, staying on the PCT to the rim of Zigzag Canyon. Along the rim the route descends to the west, then makes three switchbacks as it works its way down to the ford of the Zigzag River, at 4,680 feet elevation. This crossing is generally easy but at times could be difficult and dangerous. Once across the river the tread climbs for about 0.5 mile to the junction with the Paradise Park Loop 757. Bear left at the junction and continue northwest on the PCT for another 0.4 mile to the junction with the Paradise Park Trail 778. This junction is 3.9 miles from Timberline Lodge at 5,350 feet elevation.

Turn left at the junction on the Paradise Park Trail, and descend for 0.2 mile to the junction with the Zigzag Mountain Trail 775 at 5,050 feet elevation. Turn right on the Zigzag Mountain Trail and begin your hike along the crest of Zigzag Mountain.

Green Tip:

Before you start for home, have you left the wilderness as you'd want to see it?

The Zigzag Mountain Trail heads north from its junction with Paradise Park Trail. The trail climbs slightly for the first 0.3 mile, crossing a couple small streams along the way. Then the course turns westerly and begins to descend through woods and huckleberry bushes. After descending for about 0.8 mile and losing 500 feet of elevation, rhododendrons start to show up along the trail.

The track then levels out along the ridgeline and even climbs a little. In late July large and beautiful Mount Hood lilies (*Lilium washingtonianum*), bloom along this ridge. The route generally follows the ridgeline along the top of Zigzag Mountain for the next 1.9 miles, to the junction with the Burnt Lake Trail North 772. To the right (north) along this semi-open ridge, Mount Adams is in view through openings in the vegetation.

The junction with the Burnt Lake North Trail is reached at a low spot in the ridgeline, at 4,580 feet elevation, 3.1 miles from the junction with the Paradise Park Trail. To the right (north) on Trail 772, Burnt Lake is 0.9 mile farther. Once past the junction the Zigzag Mountain Trail climbs along the ridgeline for 0.3 mile to the

Zigzag Mountain Trails 798, 2000, 778, and 775

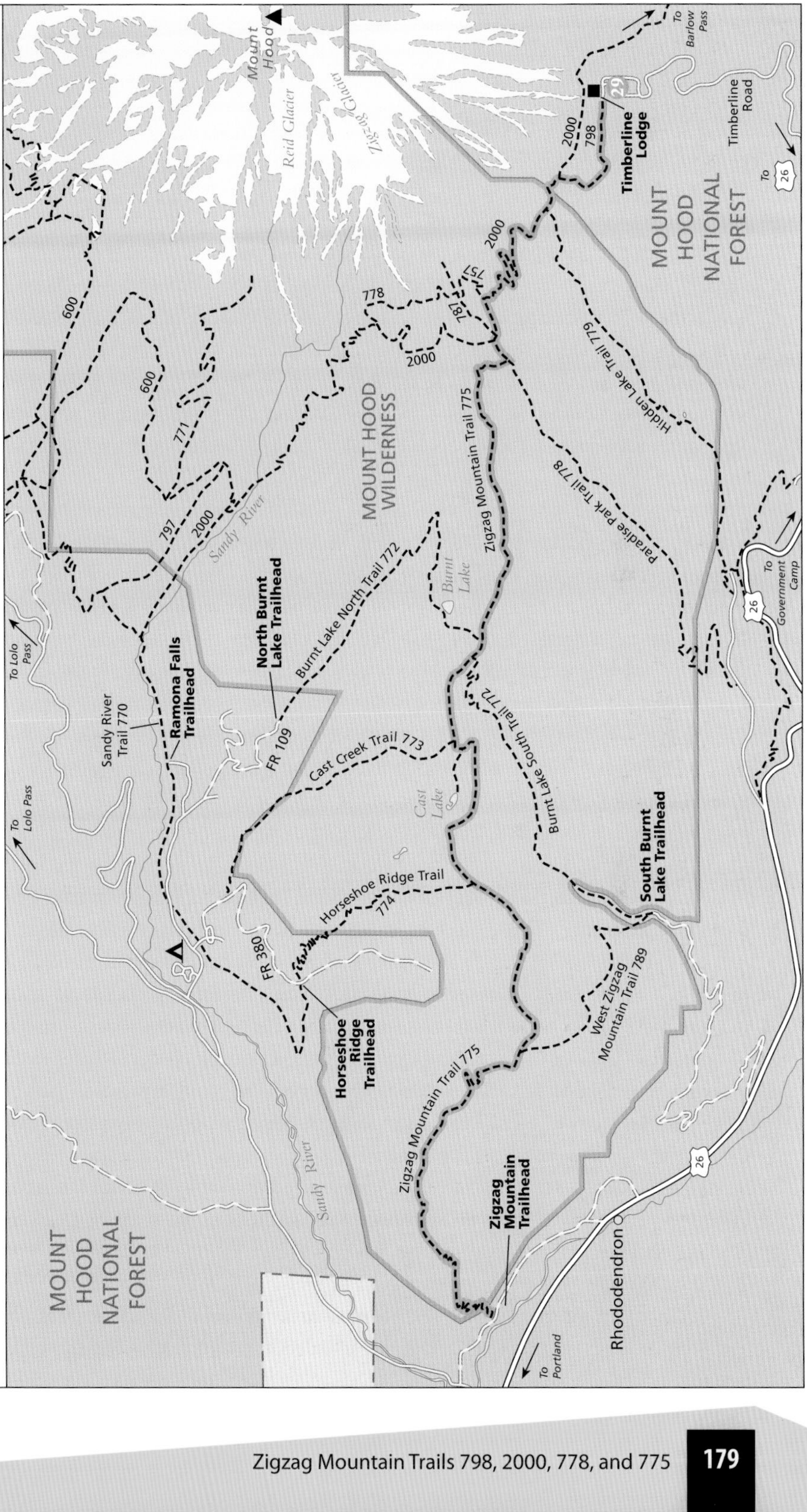

junction with Burnt Lake South Trail (also number 772), at 4,750 feet elevation. Burnt Lake South Trail turns left (south) at the junction and descends for 3.7 miles to the South Burnt Lake Trailhead.

Passing this junction the Zigzag Mountain Trail climbs the open ridge to the northwest. After climbing steeply for 0.1 mile, the tread bears slightly left of the ridge and traverses around the highest point. The route quickly regains the ridgeline, where a path heads back to the east, for a short distance, to the high point.

The steep rocky trail then descends the ridgeline and soon enters the woods. A quarter mile down the ridge, at 4,500 feet elevation, is the junction with the Cast Creek Trail 773. At the junction the Cast Creek Trail goes straight ahead and the Zigzag Mountain Trail turns to the left. Turn left and descend gently for 0.2 mile to the junction with the Cast Lake Trail 796. Cast Lake, which is only about 0.5 mile to the northwest, makes a good campsite if you're backpacking along Zigzag Mountain.

Leaving the junction with the Cast Lake Trail, the Zigzag Mountain Trail continues south for another 0.1 mile, dropping slightly to the junction with the Devil's Tie Trail 767, at 4,350 feet elevation. At the junction the Zigzag Mountain Trail turns to the right (west) and soon begins to climb. After climbing for 0.6 mile, the trail flattens out to traverse a brushy slope, where Cast Lake can be seen far below to the right. Mount Hood, Mount Adams, and Mount St. Helens are also in view, as is Mount Rainier if the air is clear enough. After traversing the slope the trail follows a ridge, then climbs steeply, making a couple of tiny switchbacks to the top of a rise. The junction with the Horseshoe Ridge Trail 774 is reached after descending for 0.2 mile past the top of the rise. The elevation at the junction is 4,720 feet and it's 1.7 miles from the junction with the Devil's Tie. In the open ridge top area around the junction, beargrass, lupine, and Mount Hood lilies often nearly cover the ground.

From the junction with the Horseshoe Ridge Trail, you continue to follow the ridge, first southwest then west, for 2 miles to the junction with the West Zigzag Mountain Trail 789. The route may be a bit overgrown and rough in places between these junctions. There are a couple of spots with short, steep switchbacks and places where the trail is a little faint. At the junction, elevation 4,460 feet, the West Zigzag Mountain Trail turns to the left (southeast) and descends for 2.3 miles to South Burnt Lake Trailhead.

There is a viewpoint to the left of the trail at 0.2 mile after passing the junction. The remains of an old lookout are visible at the viewpoint, which overlooks the town of Rhododendron. At the viewpoint the trail turns to the right and climbs a short distance to the top of a rise. It soon leaves the ridgeline, descends slightly, and makes a couple of switchbacks. The course then passes beneath a rock outcropping before climbing back to the ridge. The track follows the right side of the ridge for a short distance, then descends, making five switchbacks.

The route soon regains the ridgeline, makes an ascending traverse around the right side of a high point, and then shortly begins its 3.8-mile descent into Zigzag Canyon and the Zigzag Mountain Trailhead. The trailhead, at 1,590 feet elevation, is 5.7 miles from the junction with the West Zigzag Mountain Trail and 17.9 miles from where you started at Timberline Lodge.

MILES AND DIRECTIONS

0.0 Begin at Timberline Lodge. GPS 45 19.858N 121 42.679W.

0.7 Turn left at the junction with the Pacific Crest Trail 2000. GPS 45 20.168N 121 43.312W.

1.3 Continue straight ahead at the junction with Hidden Lake Trail 779. GPS 45 20.322N 121 44.029W.

3.9 Turn left at the junction with Paradise Park Trail 778. GPS 45 20.649N 121 45.263 W.

4.1 Turn right at the junction with Zigzag Mountain Trail 775. GPS 45 20.594N 121 45.517W.

7.5 Continue straight ahead at the junction with Burnt Lake South Trail 772. GPS 45 20.906N 121 48.764W.

8.4 Continue straight ahead at the junction with Cast Lake Trail 796.

10.2 Continue straight ahead at the junction with Horseshoe Ridge Trail 774. GPS 45 20.871N 121 51.102W.

12.2 Continue straight ahead at the junction with West Zigzag Mountain Trail 789. GPS 45 20.507N 121 52.934W.

17.9 End your hike at the Zigzag Mountain Trailhead.

Options: Access Zigzag Mountain Trail via the Paradise Park Trail, or make a loop via Burnt Lake South Trail and West Zigzag Mountain Trail.

30

West Zigzag Mountain Trail 789

Hike from South Burnt Lake Trailhead to the top of Zigzag Mountain and the junction with the Zigzag Mountain Trail. This is one of the easiest access routes to the top of Zigzag Mountain.

Start: South Burnt Lake Trailhead
Distance/type of hike: 4.6-mile out-and-back day hike or backpack
Approximate hiking time: 2.5 hours
Difficulty: Moderate
Best season: Mid-June through September
Canine compatibility and other trail users: The West Zigzag Mountain Trail is open to stock as well as hikers. Because most of this route is within the Mount Hood Wilderness, mountain bikes are prohibited. Dogs are allowed but must be controlled when close to stock and wildlife.
Fees and permits: Mount Hood Wilderness Permit and Northwest Forest Pass
Maps: USDA Forest Service *Zigzag Ranger District* or *Government Camp* and *Rhododendron* 7½-min. USGS quads; Adventure Maps Inc. *Mt. Hood/NW Oregon Trail Map;* National Geographic Oregon topo on CD-ROM Disk 4; DeLorme's *Oregon Atlas and Gazetteer,* p. 62, B2
Trail contacts: USDA Forest Service, Zigzag Ranger District, 70220 East Highway 26, Zigzag, OR 97049; (503) 622-3191; www.fs.fed.us/r6/mthood

Finding the trailhead:
From Portland, head east on U.S. Highway 26 for 46 miles. Then turn left (north) onto "Road 27." (The junction with Road 27 is just before reaching Milepost 46.) Follow the paved Road 27 for 0.6 mile to the end of the pavement. Then turn left on Zigzag Mountain Road (Forest Road 207). There is a sign at this junction that points to the trailheads. Follow FR 207 for 4.5 miles to its end at the South Burnt Lake Trailhead. The last couple of miles of FR 207 may be very rough, rocky, and eroded. A high-clearance vehicle may be necessary. The trailhead for West Zigzag Mountain Trail is 100 yards south of South Burnt Lake Trailhead on FR 207 at 3,300 feet elevation.

DeLorme's *Oregon Atlas and Gazetteer* covers the area, but the trailhead is not labeled on this map. The National Geographic Oregon CD-ROM topo covers the trailhead area and shows the trail correctly; however, the trailhead is not labeled on this map.

There is parking for several cars at the trailhead but no other facilities.

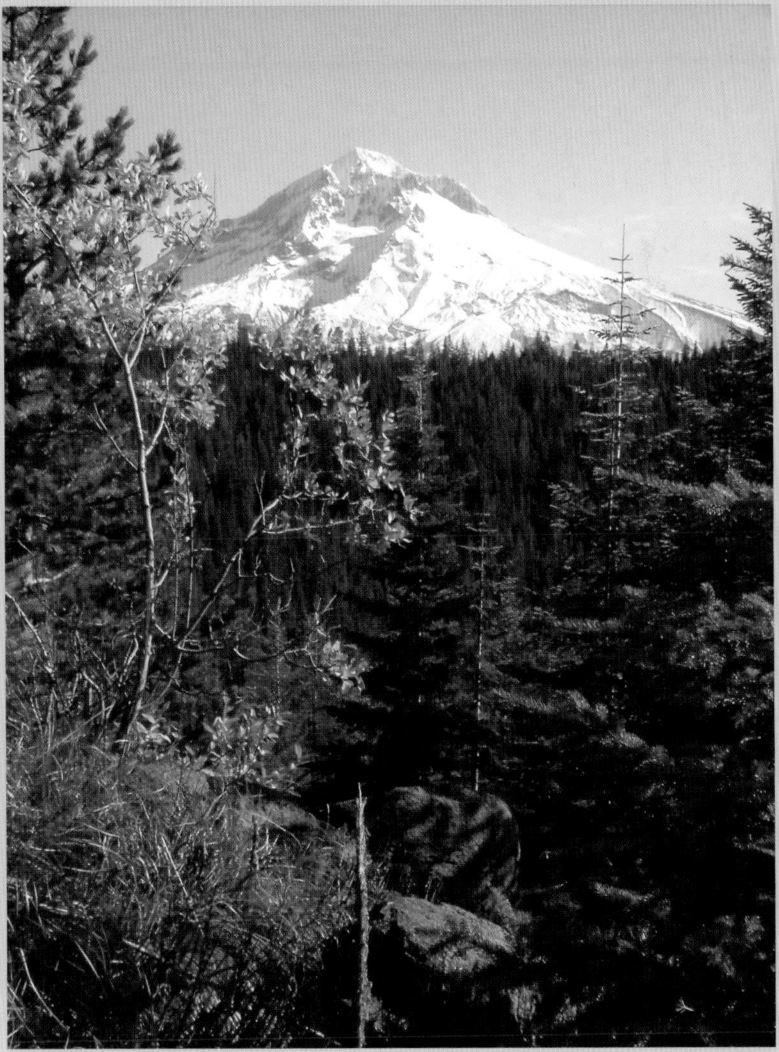

Mount Hood over Zigzag Mountain

West Zigzag Mountain Trail 789

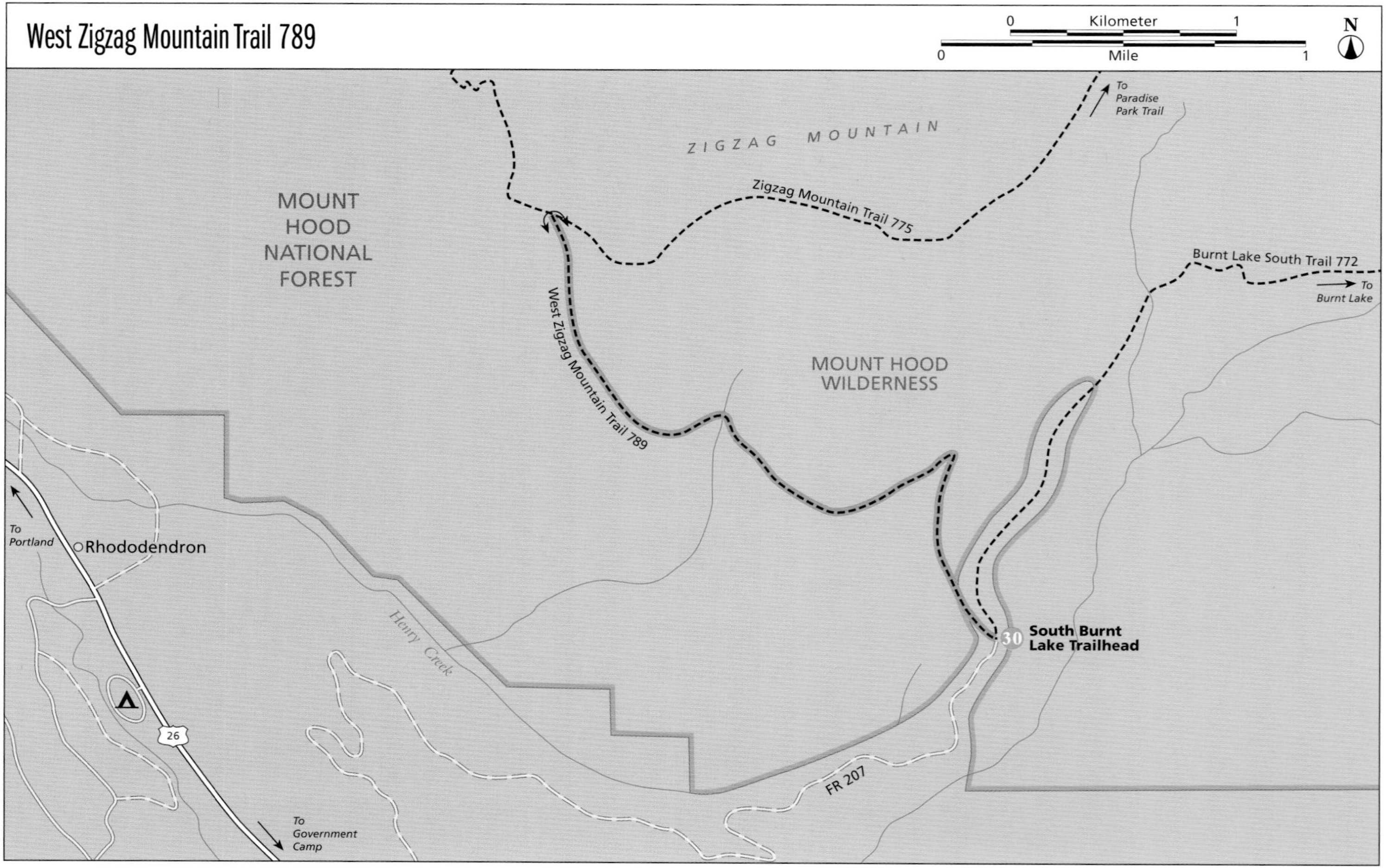

THE HIKE

First walk 100 yards west (back the way you came) along FR 207, then turn right (northwest) on the West Zigzag Mountain Trail. The Mount Hood Wilderness boundary sign and the wilderness registration box, where you can fill out your wilderness permit, are reached about 15 yards into the hike. At first the West Zigzag Mountain Trail descends gently through the western hemlock and western red cedar forest with an understory of rhododendrons.

In about 300 yards the route crosses a creek, then begins to climb rather steeply. The track climbs for 0.6 mile before making a switchback to the left, at 3,840 feet elevation. After passing the switchback the grade moderates and you traverse a slope covered with rhododendrons, vine maple, western hemlock, Douglas fir, western red cedar, and beargrass. The tread climbs gently to 3,960 feet elevation, then descends 160 feet to another creek crossing 0.7 mile past the switchback. Once across this stream the path climbs steadily for another 0.8 mile to the junction with the Zigzag Mountain Trail 775 at 4,460 feet elevation, on the ridgeline of Zigzag Mountain. Return to the trailhead by retracing your steps or for a longer alternate return hike that fortunately does not require a car shuttle.

MILES AND DIRECTIONS

0.0 Begin at the South Burnt Lake Trailhead. GPS 45 19.490N 121 51.432W.

2.3 Turn around at the junction with Zigzag Mountain Trail 775. GPS 45 20.507N 121 52.934W.

4.6 Return to the South Burnt Lake Trailhead. GPS 45 19.490N 121 51.432W.

Options: A 9-mile loop hike can be made by combining the West Zigzag Mountain Trail with a section of the Zigzag Mountain Trail 775, the Devil's Tie 767, and the Burnt Lake South Trail 772. To make this loop, turn right (east) on the Zigzag Mountain Trail and follow it for 3.7 miles to the junction with the Devils Tie (trail). Turn right on the Devils Tie and hike 0.4 mile to the junction with the Burnt Lake South Trail. Turn right on the Burnt Lake South Trail and hike 2.6 miles to the South Burnt Lake Trailhead.

31

Burnt Lake South Trail 772

Hike from South Burnt Lake Trailhead over the top of Zigzag Mountain, with its spectacular view of the southwest side of Mount Hood. Then descend to Burnt Lake in a timbered pocket on the northern slope of Zigzag Mountain.

Start: South Burnt Lake Trailhead
Distance/type of hike: 9.8-mile out-and-back day hike or backpack
Approximate hiking time: 5 hours
Difficulty: Moderate. The trail has a few rough and rocky spots.
Best season: Mid-June through September
Canine compatibility and other trail users: This trail is open to stock as well as hikers. Dogs are allowed on this trail but must be controlled when close to stock and wildlife.
Fees and permits: Northwest Forest Pass and Mount Hood Wilderness Permit
Maps: USDA Forest Service *Zigzag Ranger District, Government Camp* 7½-min. USGS quad; Adventure Maps Inc. *Mt. Hood/NW Oregon Trail Map;* National Geographic Oregon topo on CD-ROM Disk 4; DeLorme's *Oregon Atlas and Gazetteer,* p. 62, B2
Trail contacts: USDA Forest Service, Zigzag Ranger District, 70220 East Highway 26, Zigzag, OR 97049; (503) 622-3191; www.fs.fed.us/r6/mthood
Special considerations: If this is an early-season trip, before July 1, the last 0.9 mile of the trail to Burnt Lake may be under snow and hard to follow.

Finding the trailhead:
Drive east from Portland on U.S. Highway 26 to Rhododendron. Continue east from Rhododendron on US 26 for another 1.5 miles to the junction with Road 27. The junction with Road 27 is just before reaching Milepost 46 (46 miles from Portland). Turn left (north) on Road 27 and follow it for 0.6 mile to the end of the pavement. Then turn left on Zigzag Mountain Road (Forest Road 207). There is a sign at this junction that points to the trailheads. Follow FR 207 for 4.5 miles to its end at the trailhead. The last couple of miles of FR 207 may be very rough, rocky, and eroded and may require a high-clearance vehicle. There is presently no sign marking this trailhead, which is at 3,310 feet elevation.

DeLorme's *Oregon Atlas and Gazetteer* covers the area, but the trailhead is not labeled on this map. The National Geographic Oregon CD-ROM topo covers the trailhead area and shows most of the trail correctly; however, the trailhead is neither shown correctly nor labeled on this map.

There is parking for several cars at the trailhead but no other facilities.

THE HIKE

The Burnt Lake South Trail leads north from the South Burnt Lake Trailhead. The route, which is actually an abandoned roadbed at this point, climbs gradually through a mixed forest of Douglas fir, western red cedar, and western hemlock, with an understory of rhododendrons. The Mount Hood Wilderness Boundary and wilderness registration box is reached 0.4 mile after leaving the trailhead. Get your wilderness permit here and continue your hike up the abandoned roadbed.

Pika

Burnt Lake South Trail 772

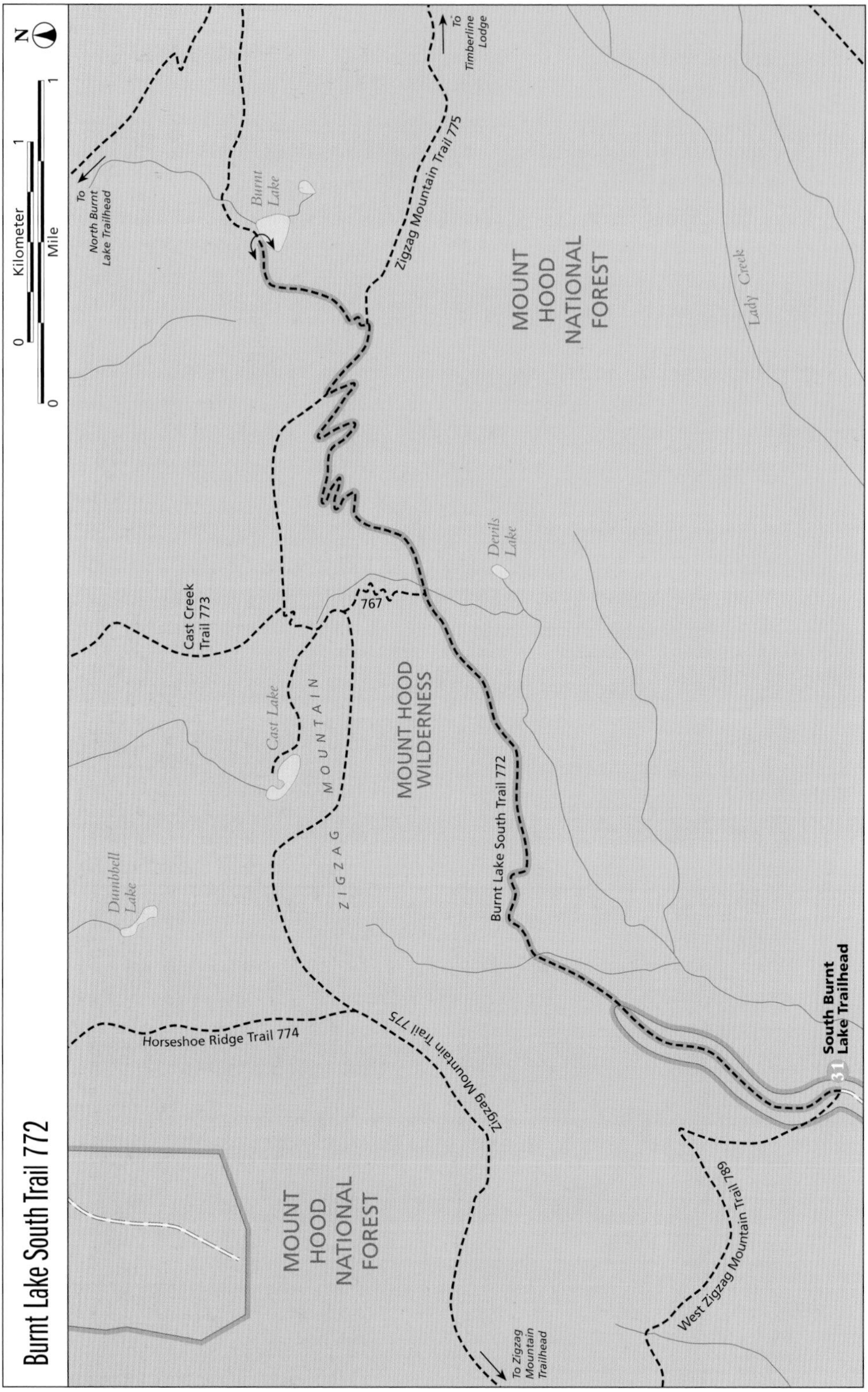

Rhododendron

Several tiny streams cross the trail as it continues to climb gently through the woods. The course enters an open area 1.1 miles after passing the wilderness boundary. When I hiked this trail, I saw a bear along the edge of this opening. The shiny black animal quickly left at my approach. Shortly you will reach the junction with the path to Devil's Meadow. Bear left at the junction, staying on Trail 772. At this point Burnt Lake South Trail leaves the now vague abandoned roadbed.

After passing the junction with the Devil's Meadow Trail, the Burnt Lake South Trail climbs a bit more steeply. The route reaches the junction with the Devil's Tie 767 0.6 mile farther along. Bear right (east-northeast) at the junction with the Devil's Tie and quickly cross a creek. The track then climbs through a brushy area, where the trail is deeply eroded in spots. Past the brushy area the course makes several switchbacks and crosses a couple of small streams as it climbs to the top of Zigzag Mountain. On the ridgeline of Zigzag Mountain is the junction with the Zigzag Mountain Trail 775. The open ridgeline at the junction affords a close-up view of Mount Hood and Burnt Lake. This junction, at 4,750 feet elevation, is 3.7 miles from South Burnt Lake Trailhead. To the right along the Zigzag Mountain Trail and the Pacific Crest National Scenic Trail 2000 (PCT), it's 7.5 miles to Timberline Lodge, and to the left it's 10.4 miles to the Zigzag Mountain Trailhead.

To continue to Burnt Lake, turn right (southeast) on Zigzag Mountain Trail and follow it for 0.3 mile, descending slightly, to the junction with the Burnt Lake North Trail (also number 772). Turn left on Trail 772 and head down, losing 500 feet of elevation in the 0.9 mile to Burnt Lake. You will cross a stream a short distance before reaching the lake. The section of trail from the Zigzag Mountain Trail to the lake may be snow-covered and hard to follow until late June.

The eight-acre lake, at 4,060 feet elevation, has several campsites around its timbered shoreline. For the fisherman, Burnt Lake contains a good population of brook trout (*Savelinus fontinalis*), mostly in the 8-to-10-inch size range. Occasionally these brightly colored fish get up to 14 inches here but don't count on it. Return as you came or see the options below.

Green Tip:
When choosing trail snacks, opt for homemade goodies that aren't packaged.

MILES AND DIRECTIONS

0.0 Begin at the South Burnt Lake Trailhead. GPS 45 19.490N 121 51.432W.

2.6 Bear right (east-northeast) at the junction with the Devil's Tie 767.

3.7 Turn right at the junction with the Zigzag Mountain Trail 775. GPS 45 20.906N 121 48.764W.

4.0 Turn left at the junction with Burnt Lake North Trail.

4.9 Turn around at Burnt Lake. GPS 45 21.091N 121 48.167W.

9.8 Return to the South Burnt Lake Trailhead. GPS 45 19.490N 121 51.432W.

Options: There are many possibilities for one-way and loop trips on Zigzag Mountain. Look at your map to see which one may be right for your party.

If a car shuttle can be arranged, you might want to descend from Burnt Lake via the Burnt Lake North Trail, for 3.3 miles, to North Burnt Lake Trailhead. To reach the North Burnt Lake Trailhead by car, backtrack to US 26 and turn right (west). Follow US 26 for about 4 miles to the junction with East Lolo Pass Road (Forest Road 18) at the tiny town of Zigzag. Turn right (north) on East Lolo Pass Road and follow it for 4.2 miles to the junction with FR 1825. Turn right on FR 1825 and follow it for 2.5 miles to Lost Creek Campground. Don't enter the campground; go straight ahead on what becomes FR 109 for 1.7 more miles, where the road ends at the trailhead (elevation 2,650 feet).

Paradise Park Trail 778

Hike via the Paradise Park Trail from the Paradise Park Trailhead to one of the best flower gardens on Mount Hood in Paradise Park.

Start: Paradise Park Trailhead
Distance/type of hike: 12.2-mile out-and-back day hike or backpack
Approximate hiking time: 7 hours
Difficulty: Moderate to strenuous. The trail surface is generally good, but this hike involves considerable elevation gain.
Best season: Late July through September. Flowers are best in August.
Canine compatibility and other trail users: Dogs are allowed on this trail but must be controlled when close to stock and wildlife. This trail is open to stock as well as hikers but not to mountain bikes.
Fees and permits: Northwest Forest Pass and Mount Hood Wilderness Permit
Maps: USDA Forest Service *Zigzag Ranger District;* Adventure Maps Inc. *Mt. Hood/NW Oregon Trail Map* or *Government Camp* 7½-min. USGS quad; National Geographic Oregon topo on CD-ROM Disk 4; DeLorme's *Oregon Atlas and Gazetteer,* p. 62, B2
Trail contacts: USDA Forest Service, Zigzag Ranger District, 70220 East Highway 26, Zigzag, OR 97049; (503) 622-3191; www.fs.fed.us/r6/mthood

Finding the trailhead:
From Portland, head east on U.S. Highway 26 for 48 miles. Turn north off US 26 0.7 mile east of Milepost 48 on Forest Road 2639. FR 2639 (Kiwanis Camp Road) is marked "Road 39" as you turn off the highway. Follow FR 2639 for 1.3 miles, then turn left onto a side road marked to "Paradise Park Trailhead." Follow the side road 0.1 mile, crossing a bridge, to the trailhead and a small primitive campground. The trail is on the left side of the road shortly after crossing the bridge, at 2,840 feet elevation.

DeLorme's *Oregon Atlas and Gazetteer* covers the area and shows this trail, but the trailhead is not labeled on this map. The National Geographic Oregon CD-ROM topo on Disk 4 covers the trailhead area and shows most of the trail correctly. However the trailhead is neither shown correctly nor labeled on this map.

There is parking for several cars near the trailhead.

THE HIKE

As you leave the trailhead, the route makes a couple of short switchbacks. It then heads northeast, with the campground to the right, to the wilderness registration box. Stop and get your wilderness permit here, then continue to climb very gently through the forest of Douglas fir, western hemlock, and western red cedar, and a few scattered lodgepole pines, and rhododendrons.

Western Red Cedar (*Thuja plicata*)

The western red cedar (*Thuja plicata;* pronounced *thoo*-yah ply-*cate*-ah) is the larger and most common of the two species of cedars that are native to the Mount Hood area. These trees may reach a height of 200 feet or more when mature. Their trunks are huge, often with a very pronounced and deeply fluted butt swell.

The thin bark of the western red cedar is a cinnamon color and appears stringy. This fibrous bark was often peeled from the trees by Native Americans and used to weave fabric for cloths. Because of its thin bark, the western red cedar is very susceptible to fire damage. The western red cedar's small, scale-like leaves are shiny and a yellow-green color. The cones are only about 0.5 inch long and light brown in color. Each cone produces six seeds that don't seem to be an important food source for small forest dwellers.

The heavy rainfall and mild, humid climate in the canyon bottoms around Mount Hood provide nearly perfect growing conditions for western red cedars. They are usually found along stream banks or around wetlands, where their feet (roots) can be wet most of the year. Because they live in these wet areas and have no need to reach deep into the ground for water, the roots of the western red cedar are shallow. These shallow roots make even large mature trees very susceptible to wind-throw. When mature, the highest parts of the western red cedar trees often die, leaving a naked, spiked top.

After about 0.5 mile the route makes a switchback to the left and begins to climb a little more steeply. The trail climbs moderately for 1.3 miles, then becomes nearly flat. In another 0.5 mile it reaches a ridgeline at 3,700 feet elevation.

The course bears slightly left to climb along the ridgeline, where you will pass several viewpoints. These viewpoints, overlooking the Zigzag Canyon, are a few feet to the right of the trail. The tread ascends along the ridge for 0.9 mile to where the ridge broadens out. Here the route bears off the right side of the ridgeline. Soon the trail makes a switchback to the left and climbs to regain the ridgeline. Above here the ridge is very broad and poorly defined.

Avalanche lily

In another 0.5 mile the trail comes alongside a small stream. This stream, which is to the left of the trail, is usually the only water along this route. There is a campsite on the left side of the trail 0.4 mile farther along. No water is located at the campsite, but there is a small stream 100 yards to the northwest, through the brush, that

Paradise Park Trail 778

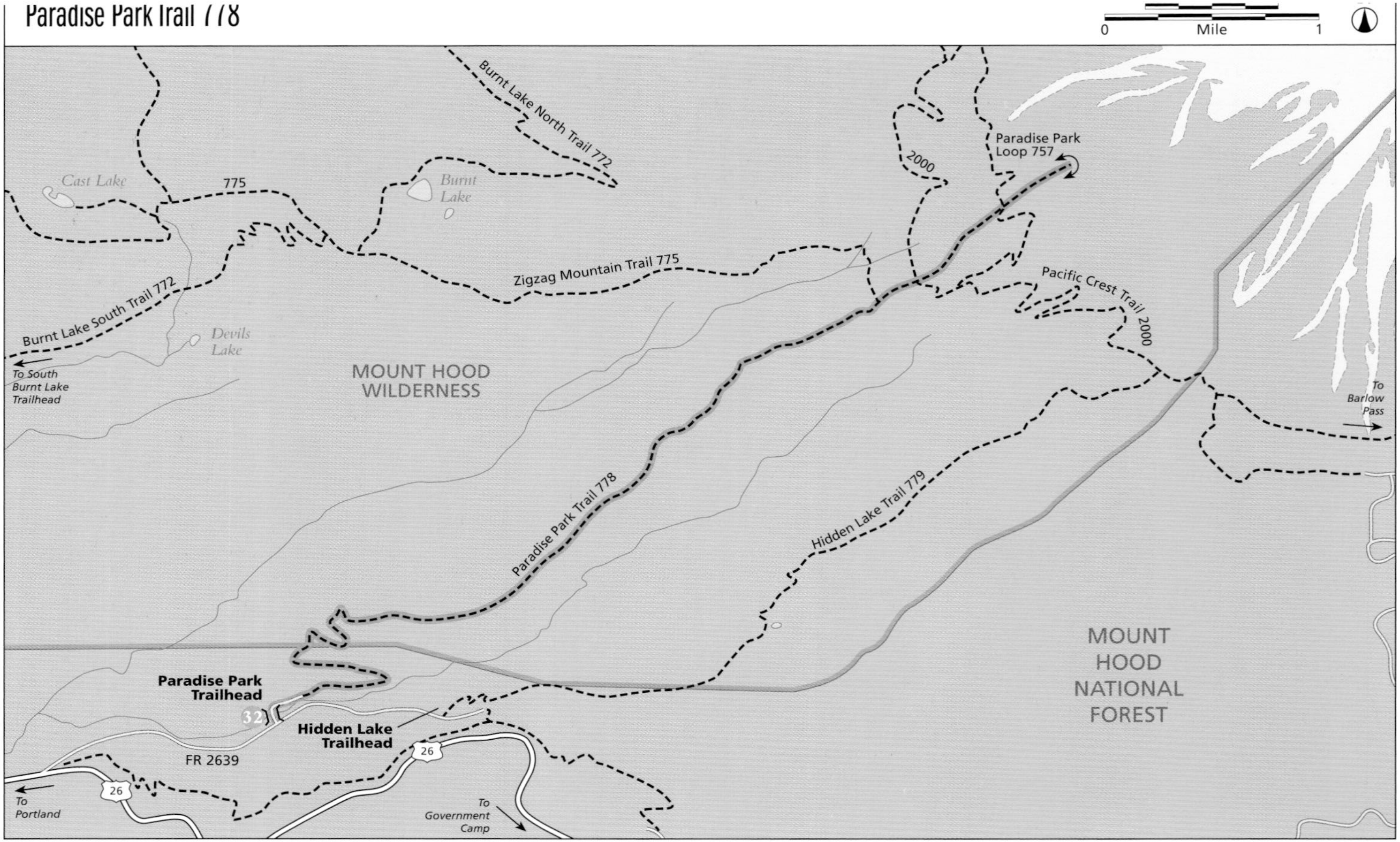

can be used as a water source. This stream may dry up at times so it would pay to check it before setting up camp. The elevation at the campsite is 4,710 feet.

You will reach the junction with the Zigzag Mountain Trail 775, at 5,050 feet elevation, 0.4 mile after passing the campsite. At the junction the Zigzag Mountain Trail turns to the left, heading north at first, then leading westerly along the crest of Zigzag Mountain. Past the junction with the Zigzag Mountain Trail, the Paradise Park Trail continues to climb for another 0.2 mile to the junction with the Pacific Crest National Scenic Trail 2000 (PCT). Avalanche lilies are often abundant along this section of trail.

The Paradise Park Trail crosses the PCT and continues on up through open woods and small sloping meadows. In another 0.6 mile you will reach the junction with the Paradise Park Loop Trail 757, at 5,750 feet elevation. The campsites in Paradise Park are to the left along the loop trail. This is the official end of Paradise Park Trail.

From the junction, a well defined but unmaintained path climbs on up through the meadows and islands of timber. The path climbs northeast, soon leaving the timber behind, to a large rock cairn on a ridge. Here the path fades out at 6,220 feet elevation. The view at the cairn is well worth the climb. The dark imposing cliffs of Mississippi Head are close by, and above them looms the ice-clad, craggy summit of Mount Hood. Some of the best displays of flowers to be found anywhere are in the Paradise Park area in August. Return the way you came or check the options below for an alternate return hike.

Brook trout

MILES AND DIRECTIONS

0.0 Begin at the Paradise Park Trailhead. GPS 45 18.868N 121 48.943W.

5.0 Bear right at the junction with Zigzag Mountain Trail 775. GPS 45 20.594N 121 45.517W.

5.2 Continue straight ahead at the junction with Pacific Crest National Scenic Trail 2000. GPS 45 20.649N 121 45.263 W.

5.8 Continue straight ahead at the junction with Paradise Park Loop Trail 757.

6.1 Turn around at the end of the path.

12.2 Return to the Paradise Park Trailhead. GPS 45 18.868N 121 48.943W.

Options: A 13.6-mile loop hike can be made by turning right (south) on the Paradise Park Loop Trail 757 and descending it to the PCT. Turn left (east) on the PCT and follow it for 2.3 miles to the Hidden Lake Trail 779. Turn right (southwest) on the Hidden Lake Trail and descend it for 5 miles to the Hidden Lake Trailhead on FR 2639. This would require a short, 0.7-mile car shuttle or walk between the Paradise Park and Hidden Lake Trailheads.

Green Tip:

When hiking in a group, walk single file on established trails to avoid widening them. Don't create new trails where there were none before.

Hidden Lake Trail 779

Make the 2-mile hike to the rhododendron-lined shore of Hidden Lake to camp and fish, or continue another 3 miles to a junction with the Pacific Crest National Scenic Trail 2000 (PCT). This trail is not particularly scenic but does have the advantage of going by a lake. The Hidden Lake Trail is often used as an access or return route for hikes along this part of the PCT.

Start: Hidden Lake Trailhead
Distance/type of hike: 10-mile out-and-back day hike to the junction with the PCT or 4-mile backpack to Hidden Lake
Approximate hiking time: 5 hours
Difficulty: Moderate to strenuous. The trail surface is generally good, but the grade is steep in places.
Best season: Mid-June to mid-October up to Hidden Lake, mid-July through September above Hidden Lake
Canine compatibility and other trail users: Dogs are allowed on this trail but must be controlled when close to stock and wildlife. The Hidden Lake Trail is open to stock as well as hikers. Because most of this route is within the Mount Hood Wilderness, mountain bikes are prohibited.
Fees and permits: Northwest Forest Pass and Mount Hood Wilderness Permit
Maps: Adventure Maps Inc. *Mt. Hood/NW Oregon Trail Map;* USDA Forest Service *Zigzag Ranger District or Government Camp and Mount Hood South* 7½-min. USGS quad; National Geographic Oregon topo on CD-ROM Disk 4; DeLorme's *Oregon Atlas and Gazetteer,* p. 62, B2
Trail contacts: USDA Forest Service, Zigzag Ranger District, 70220 East Highway 26, Zigzag, OR 97049; (503) 622-3191; www.fs.fed.us/r6/mthood.
Special considerations: Mosquitoes can be very bad in early season.

Finding the trailhead:
From Portland, head east on U.S. Highway 26 for 48 miles. Turn north (left) off US 26, 0.7 mile east of Milepost 48 onto Forest Road 2639. FR

2639 (Kiwanis Camp Road) is marked "Road 39" as you turn off the highway. Follow FR 2639 for 2 miles to the Hidden Lake Trailhead at 3,060 feet elevation. The DeLorme's *Oregon Atlas and Gazetteer* covers the area and shows this trail, but the trailhead is not labeled on this map. The National Geographic Oregon CD-ROM topo shows the trail correctly, but the trailhead is not labeled on this map. There is parking for several cars at the trailhead but no other facilities.

THE HIKE

The route climbs as you leave the Hidden Lake Trailhead. In a few yards you will reach a picnic table and the wilderness registration box. Get your wilderness permit here before continuing your hike. The track makes three switchbacks, then climbs a bit more before flattening out. Look for a viewpoint to the right just before the route levels. The flat spot in the trail doesn't last long as the trail soon climbs steeply again, making a couple more switchbacks. The grade moderates 1.1 miles from the trailhead. From here the course climbs gently through forest with

Hidden Lake

a rhododendron understory, for another 0.9 mile, to the junction with the path to Hidden Lake. This path turns to the right and follows the outlet stream for a few yards to the lake. The Hidden Lake Trail crosses the stream and soon reaches a junction with another path to the right, which also goes to Hidden Lake.

Both of these side paths lead to campsites next to the lake. Hidden Lake contains a sizable population of trout in the 6-to-8-inch size range. The elevation of Hidden Lake is 3,840 feet. Much of the lake's shoreline is covered with rhododendrons, which bloom in late June.

After passing Hidden Lake, the Hidden Lake Trail climbs gently and crosses a creek before starting up a series of switchbacks. Half a mile above Hidden Lake, the grade moderates as the course continues to climb through the Douglas fir and western hemlock forest.

Washington's State Tree

The stately western hemlock (*Tsuga heterophylla*), the state tree of Washington, grows best in cool, wet areas at lower to middle elevations. Mature trees here can attain a height of 170 to 200 feet and live for more than 500 years. The western hemlock is a very shade-tolerant species and prefers sites where the soil is high in humus content.

The drooping central leader (at the very top of the tree) is the easiest way to identify a hemlock from a distance. Western hemlock needles are short and uneven in length, varying from 0.3 to 0.7 inch long and yellow-green in color. The needles are irregularly spaced along the twigs. The cones are very small, 0.7 to 1.3 inches long, and brown in color. After maturing and spreading their seeds, the cones drop to the ground intact. These cones may be thick on the forest floor beneath a mature tree. Western hemlock bark is rough, scaly, and brown. On old trees it becomes thick and furrowed. The bark is high in tannin and can be used for tanning purposes. Bark slivers from the western hemlock can be inflammatory and should be quickly removed. When cut, mature western hemlock trees are often hollow and in some cases may be nearly filled with water. When wet, hemlock wood is very heavy and may not even float in water.

As you get higher there are more openings in the woods, where beargrass and other flowers bloom to add color. Nearly 2,000 vertical feet and 3 miles after passing Hidden Lake, you will reach the junction with the Pacific Crest National Scenic Trail 2000 (PCT). This junction is at approximately 5,800 feet elevation, and there may be patches of snow along the upper mile of this trail into late July. Return the way you came or see the options below for an alternate return hike.

Hidden Lake Trail 779

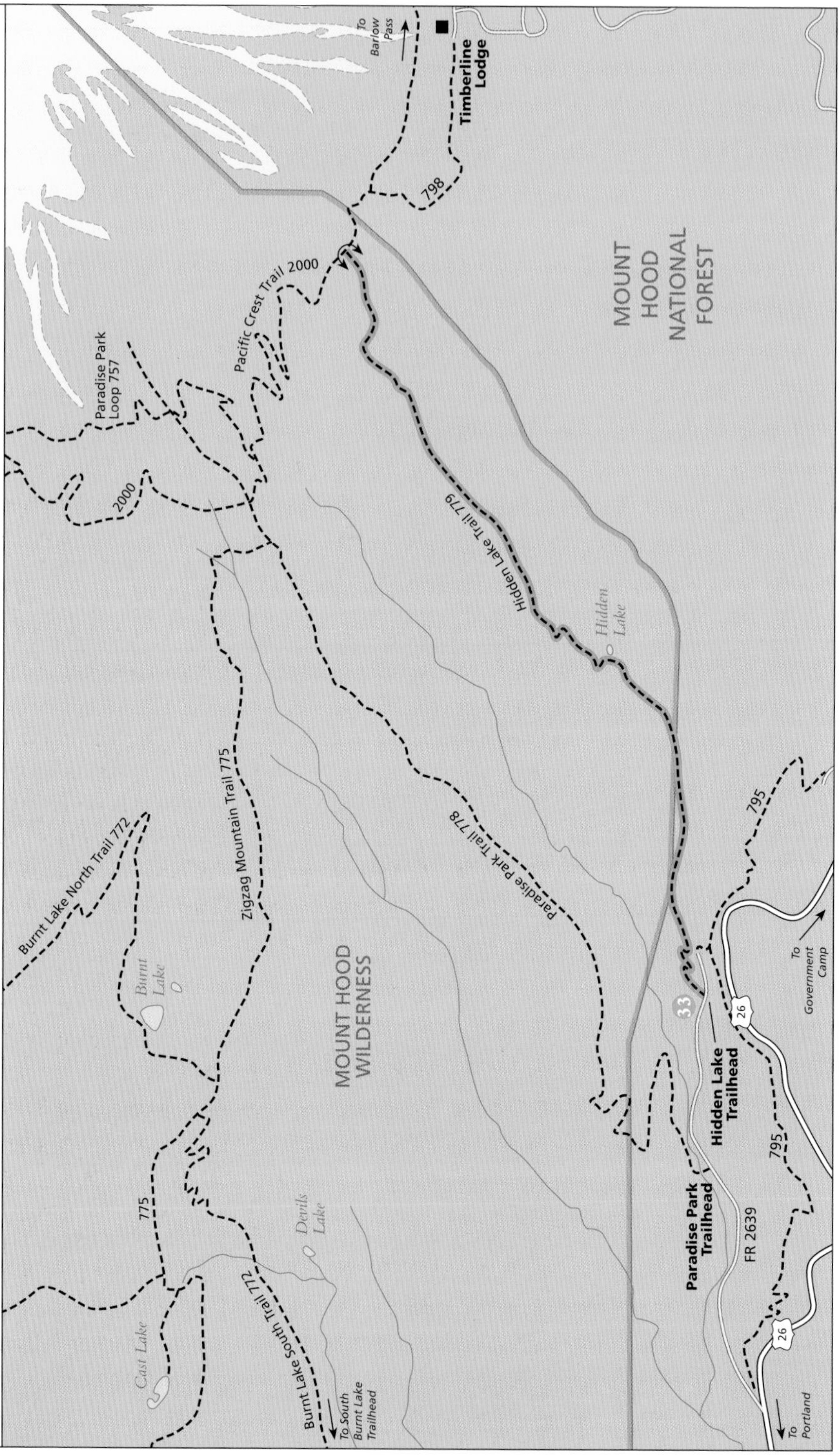

MILES AND DIRECTIONS

0.0 Begin at the Hidden Lake Trailhead. GPS 45 18.808N 121 47.977W.

2.0 Continue straight ahead at the second path to Hidden Lake. GPS 45 19.205N 121 46.182W.

5.0 Turn around at the junction with Pacific Crest Trail 2000. GPS 45 20.322N 121 44.029W.

10.0 Return to the Hidden Lake Trailhead. GPS 45 18.808N 121 47.977W.

Options: An alternate return hike can be made by turning left on the PCT and following it for 2.3 miles to the Paradise Park Trail 778, then turning left again and descending the Paradise Park Trail to the Paradise Park Trailhead on FR 2639. The Paradise Park Trailhead and the Hidden Lake Trailhead are only 0.7 mile apart along the road.

One can also make a one-way trip from Timberline Lodge by taking PCT west from the lodge for 1.3 miles, then turning left and descending the Hidden Lake Trail. Hiking down from Timberline Lodge requires a car shuttle between the lodge and the Hidden Lake Trailhead.

To reach Timberline Lodge by car, follow US 26 to the east end of Government Camp, then turn left (north) on Timberline Road and follow it 5.2 miles to the large parking area just east of Wyeast Day Lodge. The Mountaineer Trail 798 is used here to access the PCT. From the parking area east of Wyeast Day Lodge, walk west up the road a short distance to the much smaller overnight parking area for Timberline Lodge. From the west end of the Timberline Lodge parking lot, continue west on a service road. In a few yards you will pass beneath the Magic Mile Ski Lift. Bear left through a small gravel parking area and pick up the Mountaineer Trail, heading west. The route passes beneath the Storm'n Norman Ski Lift about 0.4 mile after leaving the Timberline Lodge parking area. You then climb gently, reaching 5,930 feet elevation, at the junction with the PCT in a little over 0.3 mile.

Turn left on the PCT, descend gently, and soon cross the Little Zigzag River. The route reaches the junction with the Hidden Lake Trail 779, 0.6 mile after leaving the junction with the Mountaineer Trail. Turn left on the Hidden Lake Trail and descend for 5 miles to the Hidden Lake Trailhead.

34

Horseshoe Ridge Trail 774

Hike up Horseshoe Ridge to the flower-covered crest of Zigzag Mountain and the junction with the Zigzag Mountain Trail. This route offers spectacular views of the volcanic peaks of the northern Oregon and southern Washington Cascades, as well as exquisite wildflower displays.

Start: Horseshoe Ridge Trailhead
Distance/type of hike: 6-mile out-and-back day hike or backpack
Approximate hiking time: 3.5 hours
Difficulty: Moderate
Best season: Mid-June through September
Canine compatibility and other trail users: Dogs are allowed on this trail but must be controlled when close to stock and wildlife. This trail is open to stock as well as hikers but not mountain bikes.
Fees and permits: Northwest Forest Pass and Mount Hood Wilderness Permit
Maps: *Government Camp* USGS 7½-min. quad; USDA Forest Service *Zigzag Ranger District;* Adventure Maps Inc. *Mt. Hood/NW Oregon Trail Map;* National Geographic Oregon topo on CD-ROM Disk 4; DeLorme's *Oregon Atlas and Gazetteer,* p. 62, B2
Trail contacts: USDA Forest Service, Zigzag Ranger District, 70220 East Highway 26, Zigzag, OR 97049; (503) 622-3191; www.fs.fed.us/r6/mthood

Finding the trailhead:
From Portland, drive 42 miles east on U.S. Highway 26 to the junction with East Lolo Pass Road (Forest Road 18) at Zigzag. Turn left and head north on East Lolo Pass Road for 4.2 miles to the junction with Forest Road 1825. Turn right on FR 1825 and follow it 1.2 miles to the junction with Forest Road 380. Turn right on FR 380 and follow it for 2.1 miles to Horseshoe Ridge Trailhead, at 2,760 feet elevation. DeLorme's *Oregon Atlas and*

Gazetteer covers the area and shows the trail, but the trailhead is not shown or labeled on this map. There is parking for three or four cars at the trailhead but no other facilities.

THE HIKE

Leaving the trailhead, the Horseshoe Ridge Trail first climbs to the east, through a dense stand of rhododendrons. After making a switchback the route reaches a signboard, with a trail map. Past the map the course continues to climb, making five more switchbacks before reaching Forest Road 388, at 3,100 feet elevation, 0.4 mile from the trailhead. The point where the Horseshoe Ridge Trail crosses FR 388 can be reached by four-wheel-drive vehicle by continuing on FR 380 approximately 0.7 mile, then turning left on FR 388 and driving another 0.7 mile to the point where the trail crosses the road. There is a gate on FR 388, but it hasn't been closed for years.

Washington's State Flower

The Pacific rhododendron (*Rhododendron macrophyllum*) is the state flower of Washington. The evergreen shrubs can grow up to 20 feet tall in some locations but are usually only 5 to 10 feet. The rhododendron's large pink flowers bloom from May to July, depending on elevation, and may nearly cover the shrubs. The leathery leaves resemble these of the laurel and were often mistakenly identified as such by early settlers. Laurel Hill, just west of Government Camp, was so named because of this mistaken identity.

Turn right on the roadbed and walk a few feet before bearing left onto the trail. After crossing FR 388, the tread continues climbing. After several more switchbacks, the course passes the Mount Hood Wilderness boundary at 3,560 feet elevation. The route reaches a saddle on the ridge shortly after entering the wilderness. From here the trail generally climbs up the ridgeline for about 1.6 miles. Then you begin an ascending traverse on an open slope at 4,660 feet elevation. Just before reaching the open slope, Mount St. Helens and Mount Adams come into view to the north and Mount Hood rises high above, nearby to the east.

Along the traverse, Mount Jefferson comes into view far to the south. The open slope along the traverse is mostly covered with beargrass and huckleberry bushes, with many other colorful flowers sprouting between them. After traversing the

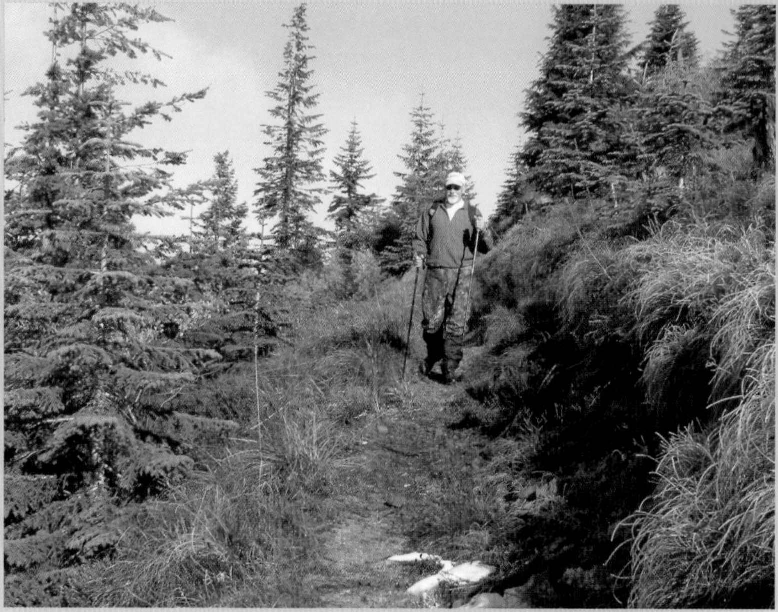

Horseshoe Ridge Trail

open slope for 0.3 mile, you will reach the Zigzag Mountain Trail 775, on the ridgeline of Zigzag Mountain at 4,720 feet elevation. Return the way you came or check the options below for an alternate descent route.

Green Tip:
Hiking and snowshoeing are great carbon-free winter activities!

MILES AND DIRECTIONS

0.0 Begin at Horseshoe Ridge Trailhead. GPS 45 22.182N 121 52.153W.

0.4 The trail crosses FR 388. GPS 45 22.141N 121 51.886W.

1.0 Arrive at the Mount Hood Wilderness boundary.

Horseshoe Ridge Trail 774

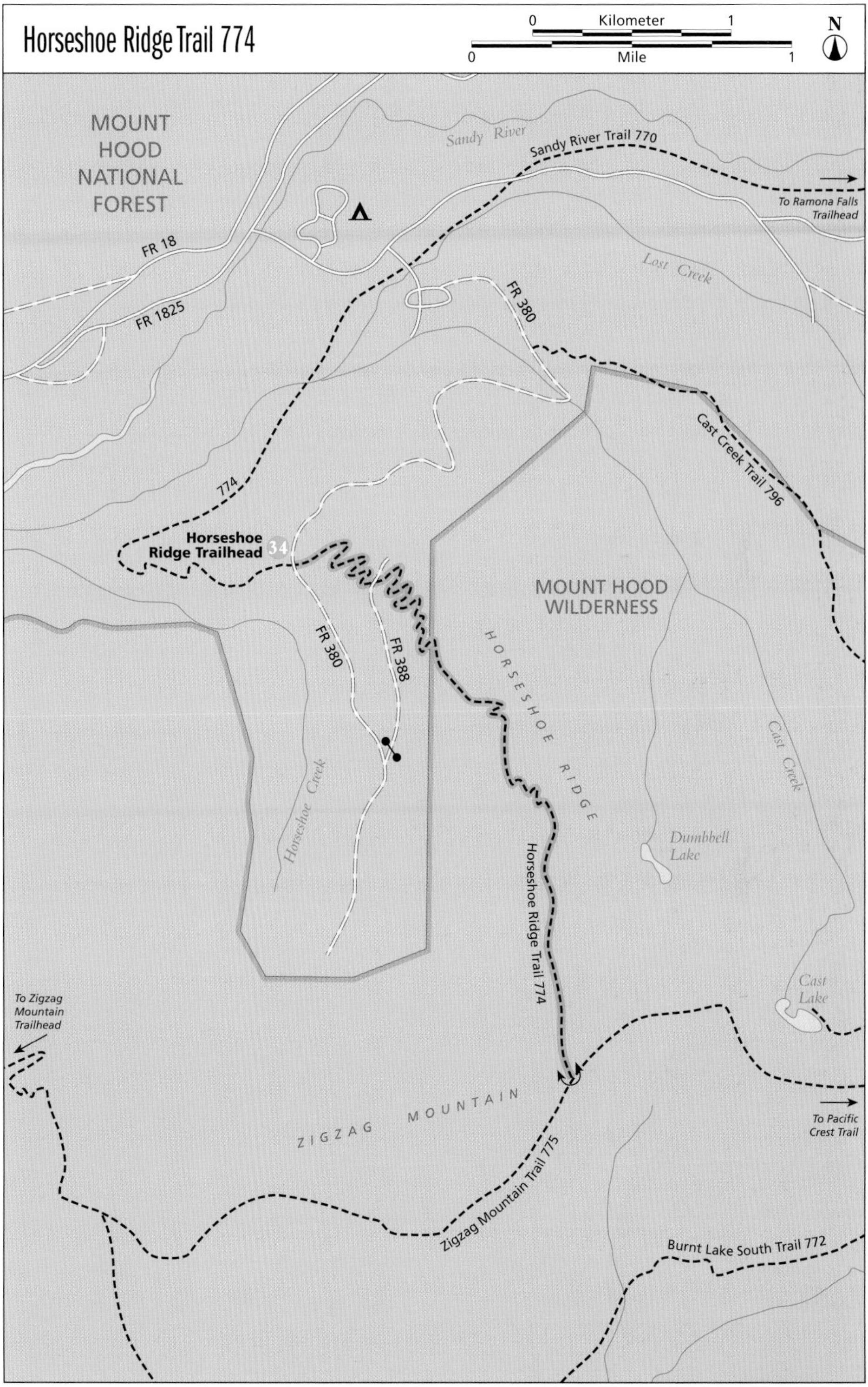

2.7 The trail begins to traverse on the open slope.

3.0 Turn around at the junction with Zigzag Mountain Trail 775. GPS 45 20.871N 121 51.102W.

6.0 Return to Horseshoe Ridge Trailhead. GPS 45 22.182N 121 52.153W.

Options: There are several possible ways to descend from Zigzag Mountain. All of them, except returning via the same route, require a car shuttle or a walk on a road to complete.

One of the better alternate descent routes is via the Burnt Lake North Trail 772. To descend this route, turn left (east) on the Zigzag Mountain Trail and hike 3 miles along the ridgeline of Zigzag Mountain to the second junction with Trail 772. At the junction, turn left on Burnt Lake North Trail and descend for 0.9 mile to Burnt Lake. Past the lake continue your descent for another 3.3 miles to North Burnt Lake Trailhead.

To reach the North Burnt Lake Trailhead from the Horseshoe Ridge Trailhead by car, first backtrack on FR 380 for 2.1 miles to the junction with FR 1825. Turn right on FR 1825 and follow it for 1.3 miles to Lost Creek Campground. Don't enter the campground; go straight ahead on what becomes FR 109 for 1.7 more miles where the road ends at the trailhead (elevation 2,650 feet). There is parking for several cars at the trailhead but no other facilities.

Ramona Falls Loop Trails 770 and 797

Hike the Sandy River Trail from the Ramona Falls Trailhead to the Ramona Falls Loop. Then follow the very scenic 4.5-mile loop to beautiful Ramona Falls and back. This trail is used as an access route to the Pacific Crest National Scenic Trail 2000 and the Yocum Ridge Trail 771.

Start: Ramona Falls Trailhead
Distance/type of hike: 7.3-mile lollipop-loop day hike
Approximate hiking time: 3.5 hours
Difficulty: Easy
Best season: Late May through October
Canine compatibility and other trail users: Dogs are allowed on this trail but must be controlled when close to stock and wildlife. Mountain bikes are prohibited and stock is only allowed on part of this route.
Fees and permits: Mount Hood Wilderness Permit and Northwest Forest Pass
Maps: USDA *Forest Service Zigzag Ranger District;* Adventure Maps Inc. *Mt. Hood/NW Oregon Trail Map;* National Geographic Oregon topo on CD-ROM Disk 4; DeLorme's *Oregon Atlas and Gazetteer,* p. 62, A1
Trail contacts: USDA Forest Service, Zigzag Ranger District, 70220 East Highway 26, Zigzag, OR 97049; (503) 622-3191; www.fs.fed.us/r6/mthood

Finding the trailhead:
Drive 42 miles east from Portland on U.S. Highway 26 to the tiny town of Zigzag. Turn left (north) off US 26 on East Lolo Pass Road (Forest Road 18). Follow FR 18 for 4.2 miles to the junction with Forest Road 1825. Turn right (east) on FR 1825 and follow it 2.3 miles to the junction with Forest Road 100. Turn left (east) on FR 100 and follow it 0.3 mile to the point where a concrete barrier blocks the road. A few feet before reaching the barrier, turn left on Forest Road 24 and follow it 0.2 mile to the large parking area

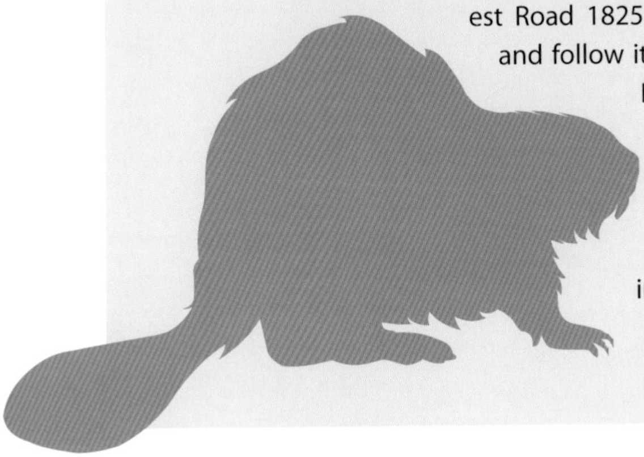

35

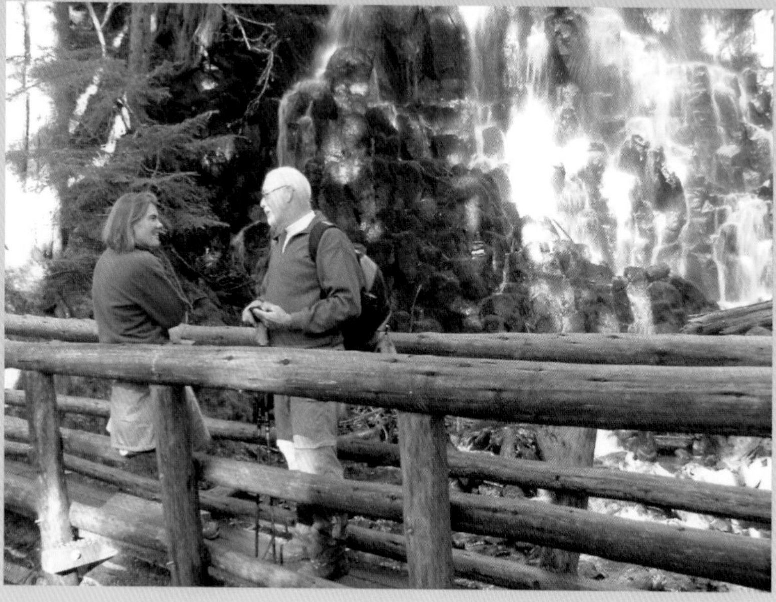

Bridge below Ramona Falls

and trailhead. There are signs along the way pointing to Ramona Falls Trail. DeLorme's *Oregon Atlas and Gazetteer* covers the area, but the trailhead is not marked and part of the trail is shown as a road.

THE HIKE

Leaving the large parking at 2,450 feet elevation, the route heads east to join the Sandy River Trail 0.2 mile from the trailhead. The course climbs gently through the forest of alder, western hemlock, Douglas fir, and lodgepole pine.

Parts of the first mile of the trail were washed out in the November 2006 flood, and the trail has been rerouted in several places.

Slightly over 1 mile from the trailhead, the tread crosses the Sandy River. A new bridge is scheduled to be installed here. The junction with the Ramona Falls Loop Trail 797 and the Pacific Crest National Scenic Trail 2000 (PCT) is reached 1.4 miles from the trailhead.

Turn right (east-southeast) at the junction to begin the Ramona Falls Loop. Leaving the junction the trace climbs gently to the east, passing the wilderness registration box, where you can secure your Mount Hood Wilderness Permit. After climbing for 0.5 mile and getting some distance above the Sandy River, the course enters the Mount Hood Wilderness. The second junction with the PCT is reached at 3,290 feet elevation, 1.1 miles after passing the wilderness boundary. Turn left at the junction and continue to climb toward Ramona Falls.

Lodgepole Pine (*Pinus contorta*)

Lodgepole pine is the only native two-needle pine in this area. That means that its needles come out of the twigs in bundles of two rather than three or five as is true with some other pines. The bark of a lodgepole is usually gray, scaly, and thin. Lodgepole pine cones are small, usually less than 2 inches long. These cones may remain on the tree and hold their seeds for several years after maturing. Many of these cones, even though they are mature, won't release their seeds unless a forest fire heats them. A few days after the fire has passed, the cones open, dispersing the seeds into the burned over area. For this reason, lodgepoles are often the first trees to regrow after a forest fire. It's a good thing that lodgepoles are able to do this because their thin bark makes them especially susceptible to being killed by fire.

The tread passes through a wooden fence designed to prevent horses from reaching Ramona Falls, 0.6 mile after leaving the junction. A short distance past the fence is the bridge, just below beautiful Ramona Falls. A few yards past the bridge is the junction with the Timberline Trail 600. See the options below if you would like to extend your hike from here to high on Yocum Ridge.

To continue on the Ramona Falls Loop, bear to the left at the junction, and descend crossing a couple of footbridges. The first bridge is over a side stream and the second over Ramona Falls Creek. After crossing the creek, the trail veers slightly away from it and winds down through the hemlocks and rhododendrons for 0.3 mile before getting close to the creek again. Rock cliffs rise above the creek on the opposite side of the trail for the next 0.5 mile as you head downstream. Then the route crosses the creek on another wooden footbridge. Near the footbridge the cliffs quickly diminish. The trail crosses a small stream a couple hundred yards farther along, then bears away to the right of Ramona Falls Creek.

The junction with a hikers' alternate for the PCT is reached 0.5 mile farther along, and the main PCT is another 0.1 mile farther. Bear left at both of these junctions. The trail then heads to the southwest for another 0.6 mile to the junction with the Sandy River Trail 770, completing the loop. Turn right at the junction, cross the Sandy River, and retrace your steps to the Ramona Falls Trailhead.

Ramona Falls Loop Trails 770 and 797

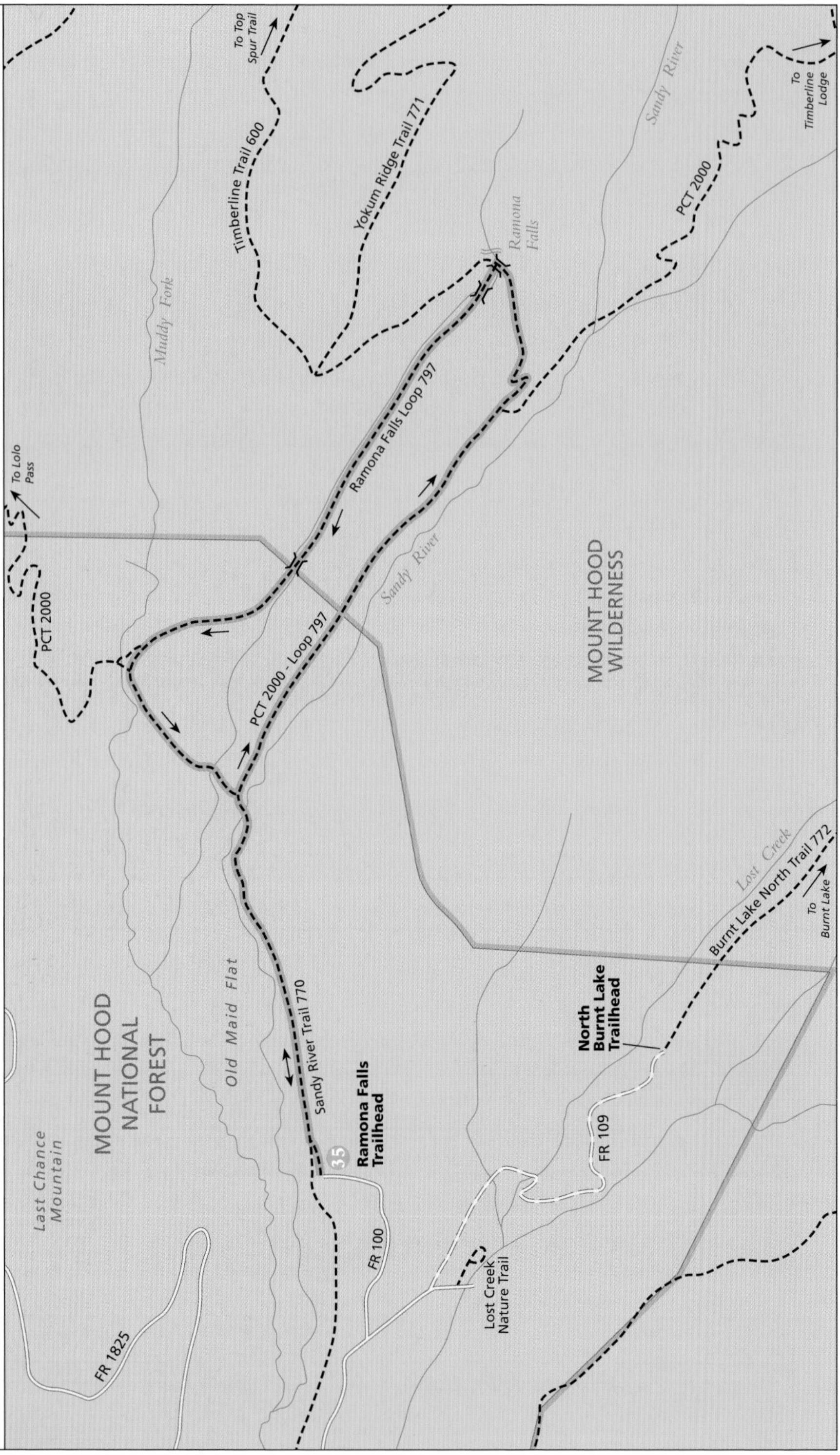

MILES AND DIRECTIONS

0.0 Begin at the Ramona Falls Trailhead. GPS 45 23.206N 121 49.909W.

1.4 Bear right at the junction with the PCT and the Ramona Falls Loop 797. GPS 45 23.466N 121 48.486W.

3.0 Turn left at the second junction with the PCT. GPS 45 22.791N 121 47.052W.

3.5 Bear left at Ramona Falls and the junction with Timberline Trail 600. GPS 45 22.805N 121 46.599W.

5.3 Turn left at the third junction with the PCT. GPS 45 23.729N 121 48.048W.

5.9 Turn right at the junction with Sandy River Trail 770. GPS 45 23.466N 121 48.486W.

7.3 Return to the Ramona Falls Trailhead. GPS 45 23.206N 121 49.909W.

Options: To make the strenuous but very rewarding side trip to Yocum Ridge, high on the western slope of Mount Hood, turn right (northwest) on the Timberline Trail 600 a few yards after crossing the bridge over Ramona Falls Creek just below Ramona Falls. Follow the Timberline Trail for 0.6 mile to the junction with the Yocum Ridge Trail 771.

Turn right and climb east-southeast on the Yocum Ridge Trail. In slightly less than 5 miles, the Yocum Ridge Trail ends at a primitive campsite at 6,320 feet elevation high on Yocum Ridge. This campsite is situated on some of the best-view property in the West. Unless you are planning to climb to the summit of Mount Hood via Yocum Ridge, this campsite is the place to turn around. The Yocum Ridge Route to the summit is one of the most difficult and dangerous routes on the mountain.

36 McNeil Point Shelter Trails 784A, 2000, 600, and 600M

Climb the Top Spur Trail through old-growth forest to the junction with the Timberline Trail. Traverse through forest and meadows to the challenging McNeil Point Trail. Then make an even higher loop, through the flower-covered alpine terrain, to the McNeil Point Shelter.

Start: Top Spur Trailhead
Distance/type of hike: 8.3-mile lollipop-loop day hike or backpack
Approximate hiking time: 4.5 hours
Difficulty: Strenuous due to Trail 600M being very rough and steep
Best season: August through September
Canine compatibility and other trail users: Dogs are allowed on these trails but must be controlled when close to stock and wildlife. This route is open to stock as well as hikers but not mountain bikes.
Fees and permits: Northwest Forest Pass and Mount Hood Wilderness Permit
Maps: Geo-Graphics *Mount Hood Wilderness;* Adventure Maps Inc. *Mt. Hood/NW Oregon Trail Map;* National Geographic Oregon topo on CD-ROM Disk 4; USDA Forest Service *Zigzag Ranger District;* DeLorme's *Oregon Atlas and Gazetteer,* p. 62, A2
Trail contacts: USDA Forest Service, Zigzag Ranger District, 70220 East Highway 26, Zigzag, OR 97049; (503) 622-3191; www.fs.fed.us/r6/mthood
Special considerations: The route west from the McNeil Point Shelter down to the Timberline Trail is very steep and rough.

Finding the trailhead:
From Portland, drive 42 miles east on U.S. Highway 26 to the junction with East Lolo Pass Road (Forest Road 18) at Zigzag. Turn left on East Lolo Pass Road, across the highway from the Zigzag Ranger Station. Follow FR 18 on the pavement for 10.6 miles to Lolo Pass. At the pass turn right on Forest Road 1825 and follow it 3 miles to a junction signed to Top Spur Trailhead. Turn left at the junction and go another 1.6 miles to the trailhead. The National Geographic Oregon CD-ROM topo and USDA Forest Service *Zigzag Ranger District* maps cover the area but don't show Trail 600M. There is parking for several cars at the trailhead and usually a portable restroom.

THE HIKE

Leaving the trailhead at 3,960 feet elevation, the trail climbs to the north, quickly entering beautiful old-growth forest. The trail winds its way on up, crossing a couple of small streams along the way, to the junction with Pacific Crest National Scenic Trail 2000 (PCT), at 4,280 feet elevation. Turn right on the PCT and walk 120 yards to the four-way junction with the Timberline Trail 600.

At the junction turn left (east) on the Timberline Trail. The tread traverses the heavily forested north slope of Bald Mountain for 0.5 mile to the junction with the McGee Creek Trail 627. Bear right and continue on the Timberline Trail. The route enters the Mount Hood Wilderness 0.3 mile after passing the junction with the McGee Creek Trail and shortly reaches a ridgeline.

The route climbs along the ridge through the forest for 0.8 mile, then enters an open area on the ridgetop at just over 5,000 feet elevation. The view of the west face of Mount Hood is breathtaking from here. The Muddy Fork of the Sandy River flows in the canyon bottom 1,200 feet below to the right. Water streams from the terminus of Sandy Glacier and drops over rock walls to charge the rushing Muddy

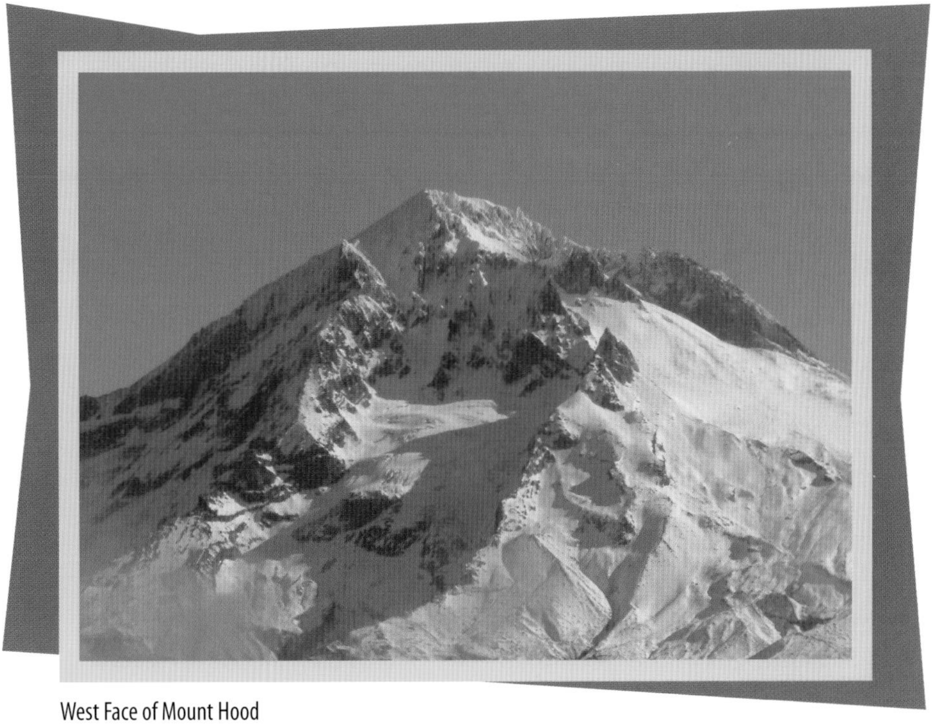

West Face of Mount Hood

Fork. Unfortunately this semi-open area lasts only a couple hundred yards before you reenter the timber.

Past the open area the tread descends slightly, then climbs a bit to traverse on the left side of the ridgeline. The course then winds its way up to the first unmarked junction with the McNeil Point Trail 600M, at 5,370 feet elevation. Bear left, staying on the Timberline Trail, cross several small streams, and pass beneath a talus slope. Watch and listen for pikas in the talus slope. The route then climbs, making a couple of switchbacks and passing between two melt ponds, before reaching the junction with the Mazama Trail 625. The junction with Mazama Trail, at 5,580 feet elevation, is 3.6 miles from the trailhead. The unmarked junction with the east end of the McNeil Point Trail 600M is reached 0.2 mile past the junction with the Mazama Trail, just before crossing a small stream.

Turn right (southeast) on the McNeil Point Trail, quickly cross the small stream, and head south up a little, open, flower-covered valley. The tread ascends moderately along the stream, crossing it a couple more times in the next 0.3 mile. Then you bear to the left and climb steeply for a short distance to a ridgeline. On the ridge the trail turns right and ascends a few feet up the ridge. Here it meets a section of the Timberline Trail that was abandoned long ago. Bear right on the abandoned section of the Timberline Trail, which has now become the McNeil Point Trail, and traverse the slopes above the head of McGee Creek to another ridgeline. On this ridgeline a path goes a few yards to the right to a viewpoint.

The McNeil Point Trail bears left, traverses a gentler slope, and soon crosses a fork of McGee Creek. The track then climbs a steep open slope. On the upper part of this ascent the trail crosses a steep rocky side hill. This short section can be a little tedious to cross, especially early or late in the season when it can get very icy.

Past the steep slope the terrain moderates and the route bears to the right off the abandoned section of the Timberline Trail to head westerly. The trail is braided in this area; try to stay on the main trail to minimize the disturbance to this fragile environment. Soon McNeil Point Shelter comes into view at 6,070 feet elevation.

The McNeil Point Shelter

The McNeil Point Shelter was built in the 1930s for use as a campsite along the Timberline Trail. However, because of routing problems, the Timberline Trail was constructed at an elevation several hundred feet lower in this area. The McNeil Point Shelter was named for Fred McNeil, a journalist and author. Strangely, it seems that McNeil much preferred wooden shelters to the rock ones like the one that is named after him.

McNeil Point Shelter Trails 784A, 2000, 600, and 600M

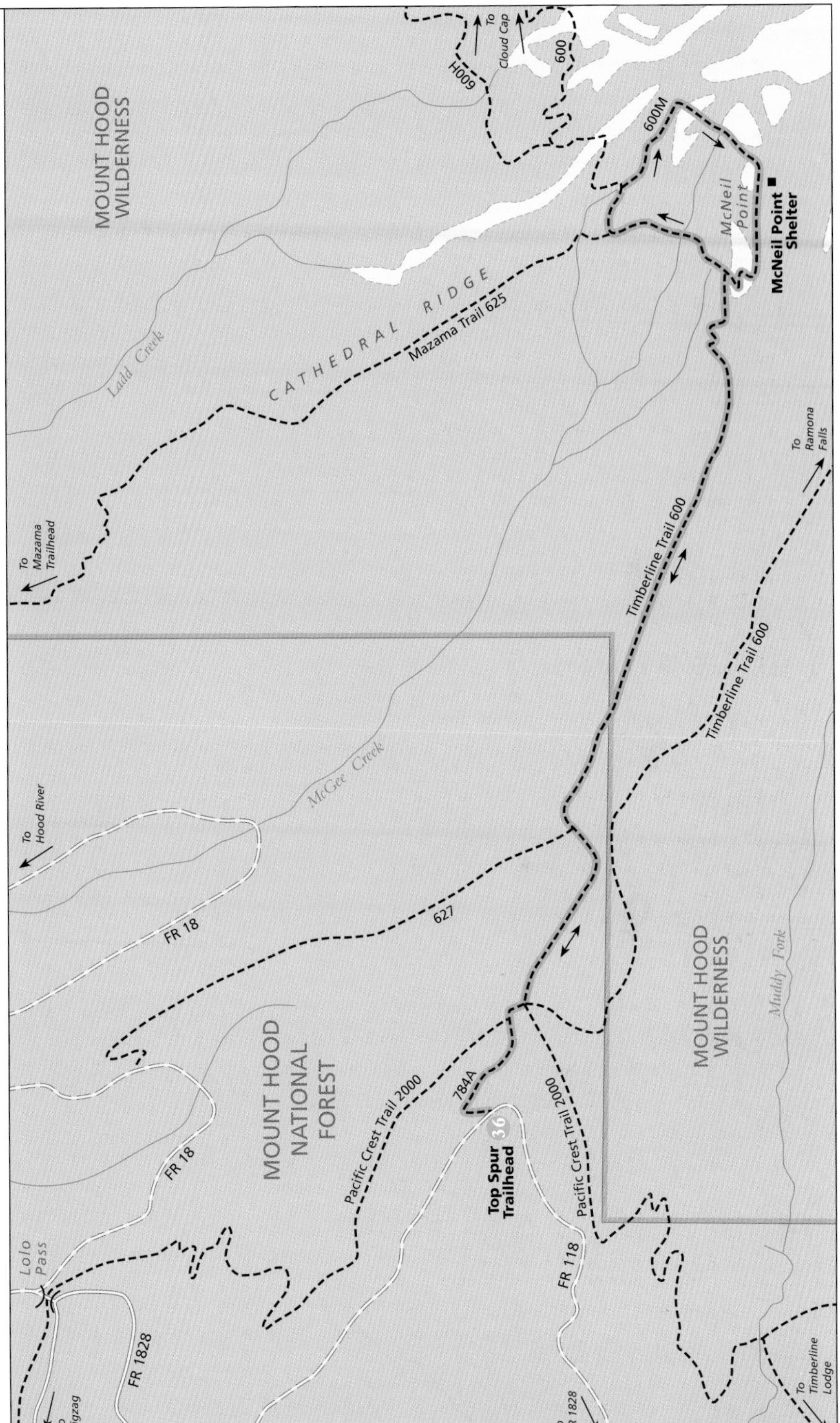

Leaving McNeil Point Shelter the trail quickly begins to descend steeply to the west. From here down to the Timberline Trail, the route is very steep and rough. It is generally necessary to use your hands for balance in spots. If your party wishes not to make this descent, turn around and retrace your steps from here to the Timberline Trail and back to the Top Spur Trailhead. The trail, if it can be called that, works its way down the rocky ridgeline for 0.5 mile, then turns right and descends a sloping meadow the last 0.1 mile to the Timberline Trail. Turn left and retrace your steps to the Top Spur Trailhead.

MILES AND DIRECTIONS

0.0 Begin at the Top Spur Trailhead. GPS 45 24.462N 121 47.152W.

0.5 Turn right at the junction with the Pacific Crest Trail 2000.

0.6 Turn left at the junction with the Timberline Trail 600 and the Bald Mountain Trail 784. GPS 45 24.318N 121 46.703W.

1.1 Bear right at the junction with the McGee Creek Trail 627.

2.9 Bear left at the first junction with the McNeil Point Trail 600m.

3.6 Bear right at the junction with the Mazama Trail 625. GPS 45 24.129N 121 43.970W.

3.8 Turn right at the second junction with the McNeil Point Trail 600M.

4.8 Arrive at McNeil Point Shelter.

5.4 Turn left at the junction with the Timberline Trail 600.

8.3 Return to the Top Spur Trailhead. GPS 45 24.462N 121 47.152W.

Options: With a short car shuttle back to Lolo Pass, you can descend the PCT northwest to there rather than hiking back down to the Top Spur Trailhead. This would add about 2.2 miles to your hike.

Pioneer Bridle Trail 795

The Pioneer Bridle Trail generally follows a section of the historic Barlow Road. In places the historic route is marked with signs, but in others one can only guess at its exact route. The fact is that there may have been several variations in the route as it descended the difficult Laurel Hill section. Laurel Hill was named for the rhododendrons that cover large parts of it.

Start: Glacier View Trailhead
Distance/type of hike: 4.4-mile shuttle day hike
Approximate hiking time: 2.5 hours
Difficulty: Easy in the direction described, moderate heading uphill
Best season: June through October
Canine compatibility and other trail users: This trail is open to stock and mountain bikes as well as hikers and skiers in the winter. Dogs are okay as long as they are under control
Fees and permits: Northwest Forest Pass
Maps: USGS *Government Camp* 7½-min. quad; Geo-Graphics *Mount Hood Wilderness* and *Columbia Gorge/Mount Hood Recreation Map;* USDA Forest Service *Zigzag Ranger District;* Adventure Maps Inc. *Mt. Hood/NW Oregon Trail Map;* National Geographic Oregon topo on CD-ROM Disk 4; DeLorme's *Oregon Atlas and Gazetteer,* p. 62, B2
Trail contacts: USDA Forest Service, Zigzag Ranger District, 70220 East Highway 26, Zigzag, OR 97049; (503) 622-3191; www.fs.fed.us/r6/mthood
Special considerations: Much of this trail is within earshot of U.S. Highway 26, so traffic noise may bother some hikers.

Finding the trailhead:
Drive east from Portland on US 26 for slightly over 52 miles. Turn left (north) on Forest Road 522, which is just across the highway from the western entrance to Ski Bowl. Drive to the point where the road is blocked with a gate, about 0.1 mile. The trail leaves from the right side of the road. The elevation at the trailhead is 3,620 feet.

THE HIKE

Western hemlocks, western red cedars, Douglas firs, and noble firs form a dense forest canopy as the Pioneer Bridle Trail leaves the Glacier View Sno-park and Trailhead. A reader board close to the trailhead maps out the winter ski trails. After checking the reader board, backtrack a few steps to a sign pointing out the Pioneer Bridle Trail and head west-northwest. In a little over 0.1 mile, the wide, smooth trail intersects the route of the historic Barlow Road.

The Barlow Road

The Barlow Road was an alternate route to the Willamette Valley from the Dalles, at the western end of the Oregon Trail. The normal river route from the Dalles west through the Columbia Gorge entailed loading the wagons on boats and floating them down the river. There was often a waiting list to get on these boats and they were expensive. The Barlow Road was constructed in 1846. Tolls were charged for passage but they were much more affordable than the passage down the Columbia River.

Soon the course begins to descend. After hiking another 0.3 mile and losing about 100 feet of elevation, you will cross a wooden bridge and shortly reach the junction with the Enid Lake Ski Trail. The ski trail turns right; bear left, staying on the Pioneer Bridle Trail. Past the junction the route crosses another bridge and in 0.2 mile reaches a junction with another ski trail. Bear right here.

The trail becomes a little rocky as you descend from the junction, between the tall rhododendrons, and cross beneath a power line. Now the route is close to US 26 and you can hear the constant traffic. The trail soon forks again. Bear right—the trail to the left is a steep shortcut.

One mile from the junction with the Enid Lake Ski Trail and 1.4 miles from the Glacier View Trailhead, there will be a trail sign and a path to the right. This path shortly reaches a paved but abandoned road. See the options below for a description of the route from here to Little Zigzag Falls. To continue on the Pioneer Bridle Trail, bear left and descend. In a few yards the route passes through a high but narrow tunnel, beneath the paved roadbed.

There will be another trail junction 0.1 mile from the junction with the route to Little Zigzag Falls. There are no signs at this junction. Bear left (nearly straight ahead) to continue on the Pioneer Bridle Trail. The trail comes very close to, but below, Highway 26, 0.1 mile farther along. The rock fill to your left here, supporting the highway, has a colony of pikas living in it. Just past the rock fill, there will

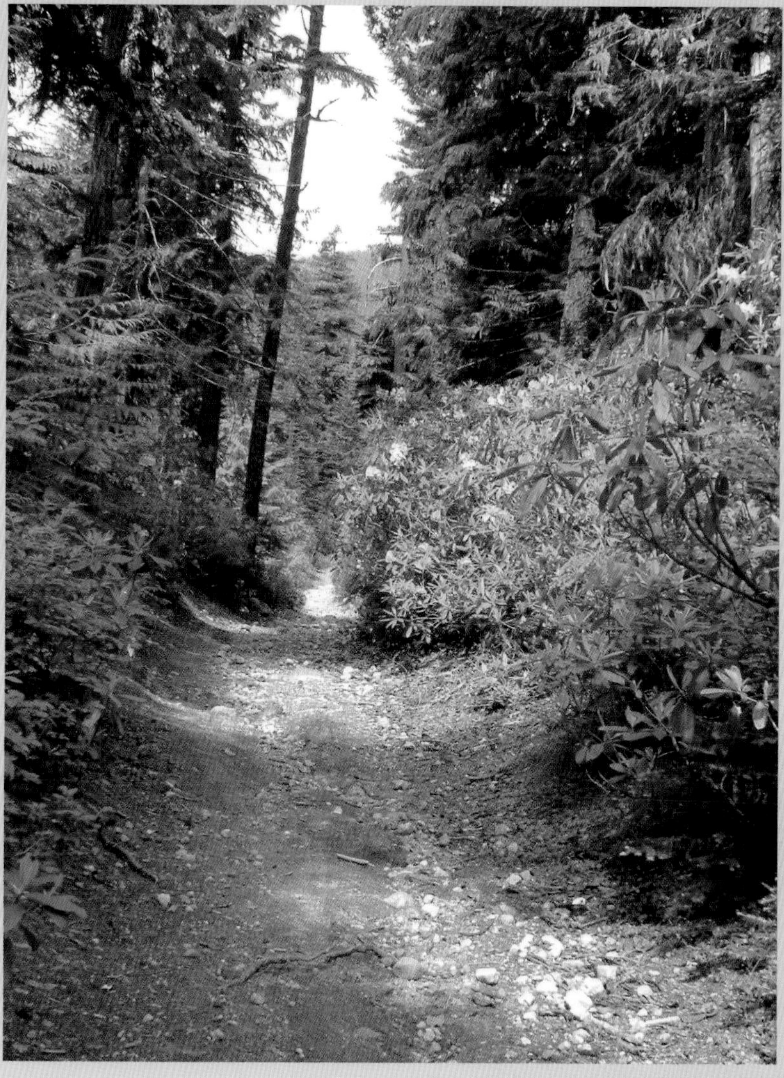

Pioneer Bridle Trail through the rhododendrons

be another unmarked trail junction. Bear right, staying on the main trail, and start to climb.

The route climbs for a short distance, then flattens as you pass an abandoned vertical mine shaft, surrounded by a rail fence. As you traverse the rocky trail, along the bottom of a talus slope 0.1 mile past the mine shaft, watch and listen for another colony of pikas. Soon the trail climbs again, gaining a little over 100 vertical feet to

Pioneer Bridle Trail 795

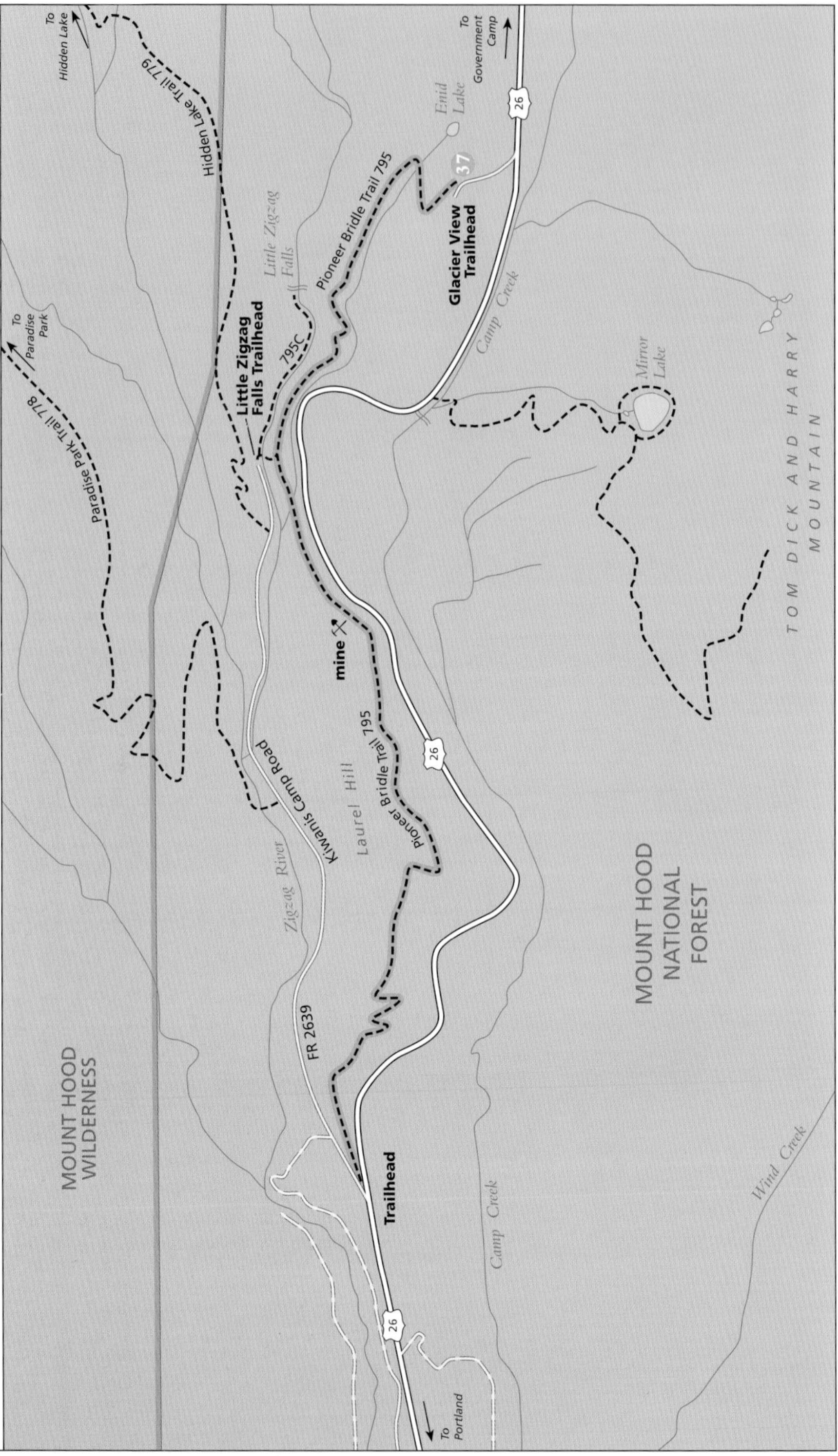

reach the top of the infamous Laurel Hill. Pioneers who followed the Barlow Road dreaded the steep descent of Laurel Hill.

After following the top of Laurel Hill for a little more than 0.3 mile, the trail begins to descend off the hills western end. Fortunately the Pioneer Bridle Trail doesn't follow the exact route of the Barlow Road here. The trail makes four switchbacks as you head down the west end of Laurel Hill. The Barlow Road, which the trail follows only in spots, went nearly straight down. The Barlow Road was so steep here that logs were often dragged behind the wagons to slow their descent.

After losing about 600 feet of elevation, the route flattens at the bottom of Laurel Hill. You pass a path to the right leading to "Road 39," 0.3 mile from the last switchback. Another few yards of walking brings you to a trailhead along US 26 and the end of this hike.

MILES AND DIRECTIONS

0.0 Begin at the Glacier View Trailhead. GPS 45 18.315N 121 46.772W.

0.4 Go straight ahead at the junction with Enid Lake Ski Trail.

1.4 Bear left at the junction with the road to the Little Zigzag Falls Trail.

1.9 Pass the mine tunnel.

4.4 Finish at the trailhead on US 26. GPS 45 18.611N 121 50.214W.

Options: A side trip to Little Zigzag Falls is a great addition to the easy hike along the Pioneer Bridle Trail. To reach the falls, turn right at the junction 1.4 miles from the Glacier View Trailhead. In a short distance you will reach the paved but abandoned roadbed of the continuation of "Road 39," which is also the old highway to Government Camp. Turn right on the roadbed and follow it for 0.1 mile to the Little Zigzag Falls Trailhead, at the end of the open part of Road 39, GPS 45 18.839N 121 47.754W. From the trailhead parking area, head east on Little Zigzag Falls Trail 795C, along the left (north) side of the Little Zigzag River. After hiking along this sparkling little river for 0.3 mile, the trail ends at a viewpoint just below the falls.

If you would like to reach the Little Zigzag Falls Trailhead by car, turn north off US 26 0.7 mile east of Milepost 48 (mileposts indicate the mileage from Portland), on FR 2639 (signed as ROAD 39). Follow FR 2639 for 2.2 miles to the parking area and trailhead.

38

Devils Peak Lookout via Cool Creek Trail 794

Climb along steep but scenic Cool Creek Trail to the top of Hunchback Mountain and the Devils Peak Lookout, where you can spend the night if you are so inclined and brought your sleeping bag.

Start: Cool Creek Trailhead
Distance/type of hike: 8.2-mile out-and-back day hike or overnighter
Approximate hiking time: 5 hours round-trip
Difficulty: Strenuous, due to the steep trail and sometimes rough trail surface
Best season: Mid-June through September
Canine compatibility and other trail users: Dogs are okay on this trail as long as they are under control. This route is not well suited for horse traffic.
Fees and permits: None
Maps: USGS *Rhododendron and Government Camp* 7½ minute quads; Adventure Maps Inc. *Mt. Hood/NW Oregon Trail Map;* USDA Forest Service *Zigzag Ranger District;* National Geographic Oregon topo on CD-ROM Disk 4; DeLorme's *Oregon Atlas and Gazetteer,* p. 62, B1 and B2
Trail contacts: USDA Forest Service, Zigzag Ranger District, 70220 East Highway 26, Zigzag, OR 97049; (503) 622-3191; www.fs.fed.us/r6/mthood
Special considerations: No regular trail maintenance; so logs may obstruct this trail at any given time. But this is usually not a major problem.

Finding the trailhead:
Drive east from Portland on U.S. Highway 26 for 43.7 miles (0.7 mile east of Milepost 43) to the junction with Still Creek Road. Turn right (southeast) on Still Creek Road and follow it for 3.4 miles to the easy-to-miss Cool Creek Trailhead. The trailhead is on the right side of the road, approximately 0.5 mile

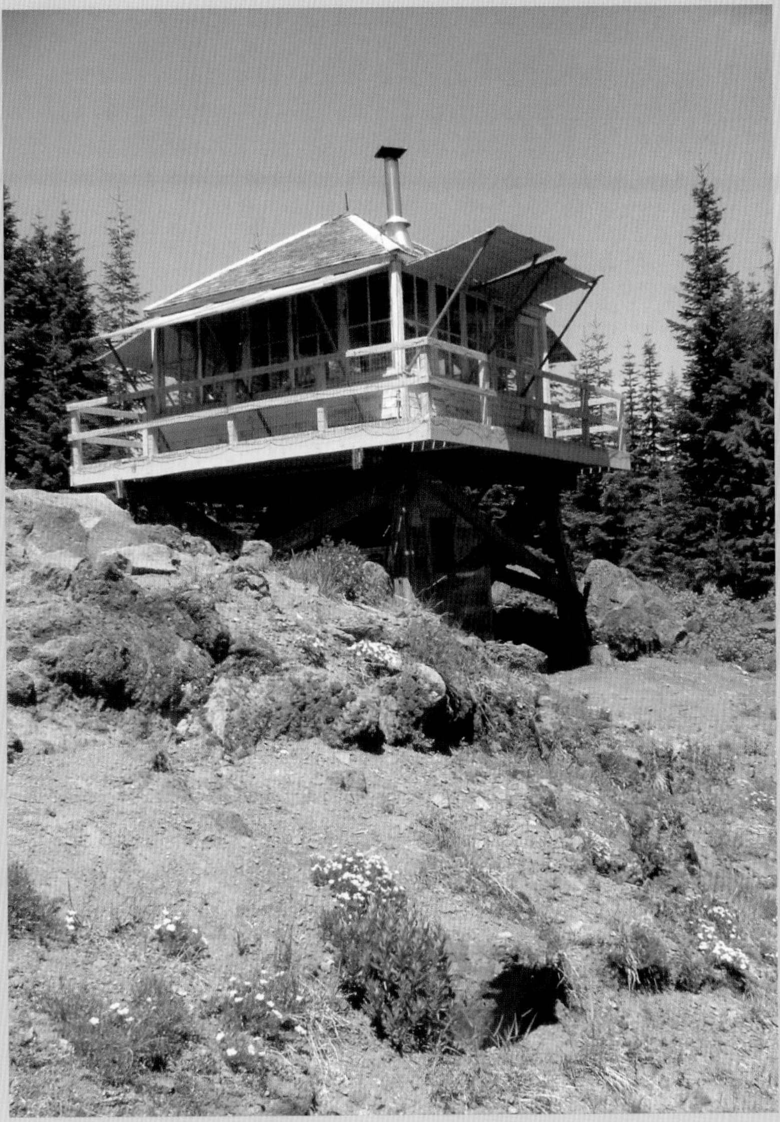

Devils Peak Lookout

after the pavement ends. There is parking for three or four cars on the left side of the road a few yards before the trailhead is reached. The elevation at the trailhead is 1,870 feet.

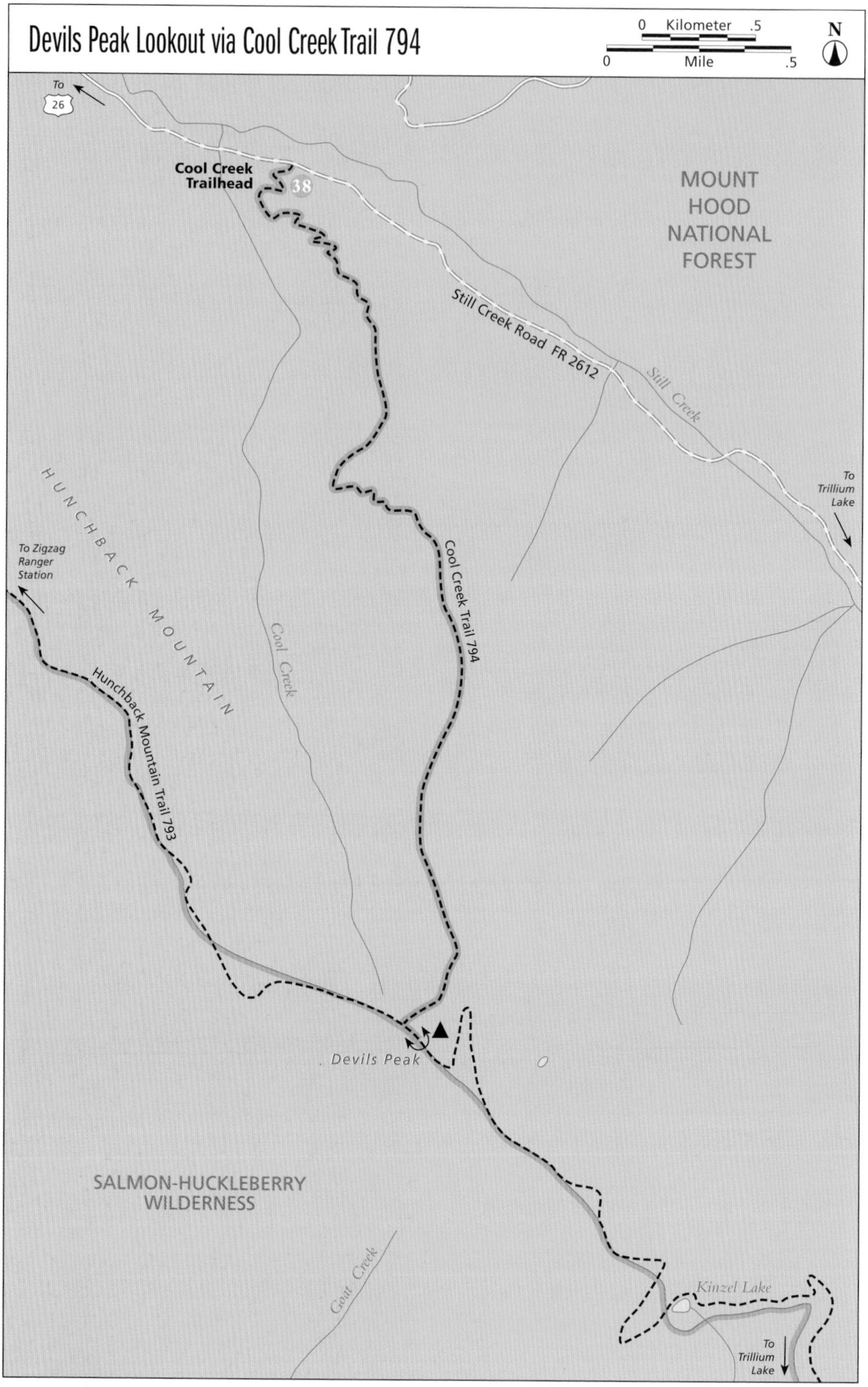
Devils Peak Lookout via Cool Creek Trail 794
0 Kilometer .5
0 Mile .5
N
To
26
Cool Creek
Trailhead
38
MOUNT
HOOD
NATIONAL
FOREST
Still Creek Road FR 2612
Still Creek
To
Trillium
Lake
HUNCHBACK MOUNTAIN
To Zigzag
Ranger
Station
Cool Creek
Cool Creek Trail 794
Hunchback Mountain Trail 793
Devils Peak
SALMON-HUCKLEBERRY
WILDERNESS
Goat Creek
Kinzel Lake
To
Trillium
Lake

THE HIKE

The Cool Creek Trail begins to climb immediately as you leave the poorly marked trailhead. The track ascends through dense forest, reaching the first of many switchbacks in 250 yards. Soon you'll see tall rhododendrons, which bloom in June, lining the sides of the trail. There will be a steep path to the right at a switchback 0.6 mile from the trailhead. The purpose of this path is not evident as it fades out quickly and is somewhat exposed. It's best not to explore this short path.

About 0.1 mile after passing the path, Mount Hood comes into view ahead and to the left. Along this section of the route, watch for large showy Mount Hood lilies (*Lilium washingtonianum*), growing at the trailside. Another side path leads to the left 0.7 mile farther along. This path leads a few feet to a viewpoint at 3,050 feet elevation, where Mount Hood can be seen through the trees.

You will climb steeply, staying close to the ridgeline for a short distance, then bear left, leaving the ridge and crossing a couple of tiny streams, which may be dry. The route climbs numerous switchbacks in the next 1.1 miles to reach the top of a poorly defined ridgeline at 4,140 feet elevation.

The trail climbs along this indistinct ridgeline for slightly over 0.6 mile, where another path to the left leads to a rocky outcrop and viewpoint. A couple tenths of a mile farther along, there is another viewpoint to the left at 4,680 feet elevation. Shortly the tread crosses a steep, rocky, open slope, which may be covered with blooming larkspur, phlox, and paintbrush in late June. At the upper end of this opening, look behind you for a view of Mount St. Helens, Mount Rainier, and Mount Adams.

The route reaches its end at the junction with the Hunchback Trail 793, 0.3 mile after crossing the open slope and 4 miles from the Cool Creek Trailhead. To continue on to the Devils Peak Lookout, turn right on the Hunchback Trail and follow it for a short distance to another junction, this one without the benefit of a sign. Turn left at this junction and quickly ascend the last few yards to the Devils Peak Lookout.

The lookout, at 5,045 feet elevation, is 4.1 miles from the Cool Creek Trailhead, and by the time you reach it, you will have climbed nearly 3,200 feet. The open rocky ridgetop surrounding the lookout blooms with larkspur, phlox, and cat's ear lilies (*Calochortus subalpinus*) in late June. The lookout was built in 1949 and used until 1974. Because of the tree growth around it, it would be of only marginal use as a fire lookout now. The lookout is left unlocked for public use; please respect it and if necessary clean up after those who haven't.

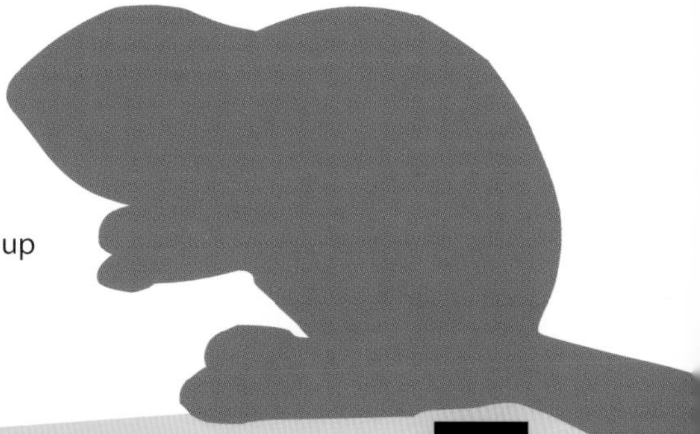

This is not the closest way to reach the Devils Peak Lookout. It can be reached via a much shorter route with far less climbing from Kenzel Lake. However, the road to Kenzel Lake is very rough and may be impassable.

MILES AND DIRECTIONS

0.0 Begin at the Cool Creek Trailhead. GPS 45 17.854N 121 53.056W.

4.0 Bear right at the junction with the Hunchback Trail 793. GPS 45 15.900N 121 52.527W.

4.1 Turn around at Devils Peak Lookout. GPS 45 15.850N 121 52.540W.

8.2 Return to the Cool Creek Trailhead. GPS 45 17.854N 121 53.056W.

Options: For a longer return hike, you may wish to follow the Hunchback Trail 793 for 8 miles to the northwest to the Zigzag Ranger Station in Zigzag. Returning this way requires a car shuttle to the Zigzag Ranger Station. To make this shuttle, return as you came along Still Creek Road for 3.7 miles to the junction with US 26. Turn left on US 26 and follow it west for 1.7 miles to the ranger station, which will be on your left.

Green Canyon Way Trail 793A

Climb through mostly second-growth forest from deep in the Salmon River Canyon to the ridgeline of Hunchback Mountain. Along the way a couple of small open slopes bloom profusely with wildflowers in June and offer views of the Salmon River Canyon far below. Close to the unmarked junction with the Hunchback Mountain Trail, glimpses of Mount Hood can be seen through the noble fir timber.

Start: Green Canyon Trailhead
Distance/type of hike: 7.4-mile out-and-back day hike
Approximate hiking time: 4 hours round-trip
Difficulty: Strenuous, due to the steep trail and limited maintenance
Best season: Early June through September
Canine compatibility and other trail users: Hikers only; dogs are allowed but horses and other stock prohibited
Fees and permits: Northwest Forest Pass
Maps: *Rhododendron* USGS 7½-min. quad; USDA Forest Service *Zigzag Ranger District* or *Salmon-Huckleberry Wilderness;* Adventure Maps Inc. *Mt. Hood/NW Oregon Trail Map;* National Geographic Oregon topo on CD-ROM Disk 4; DeLorme's *Oregon Atlas and Gazetteer,* p. 62, B1
Trail contacts: USDA Forest Service, Zigzag Ranger District, 70220 East Highway 26, Zigzag, OR 97049; (503) 622-3191; www.fs.fed.us/r6/mthood
Special considerations: No water along this trail

Finding the trailhead:
From Portland, drive east on U.S. Highway 26 for 41.9 miles (0.9 mile past Milepost 41), then turn right (south) on the Salmon River Road (Forest Road 2618). Follow the Salmon River Road approximately 5 miles to the Green Canyon Campground entrance. The Green Canyon Trailhead is on the left side of the road, directly across from the campground entrance, at 1,600 feet elevation.

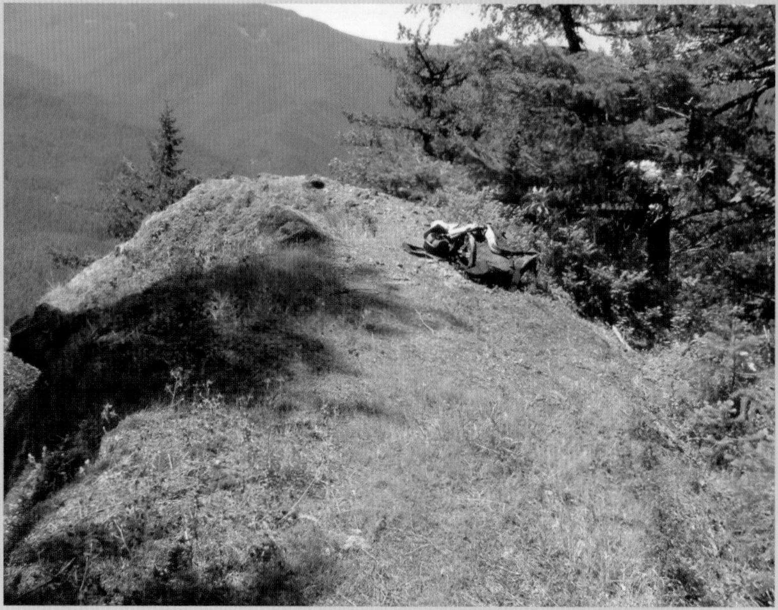

Flower-covered viewpoint along Green Canyon Way

THE HIKE

Head east as you leave the Green Canyon Trailhead. In a few yards the route reaches a signboard, where you bear right to head southeast. The track crosses the canyon bottom, through the mixed age forest of western hemlock, Douglas fir and bigleaf maple, for a short distance then begins its climb. A few large old-growth Douglas fir trees mix in here with the younger, medium-size timber. Oxalis, maidenhair fern, and Oregon grape cover the forest floor beside the course.

The trail makes its first switchback as it enters the Salmon-Huckleberry Wilderness a quarter mile from the trailhead. The route is fairly steep in places as you climb toward the top of Hunchback Mountain. In the next 1.9 miles, the track makes thirteen more switchbacks as you climb to a ridge crossing at about 3,250 feet elevation. As the trail crosses this ridge, the forest opens up, allowing for views of the Salmon River Canyon below and to the east.

The route continues its climb, generally following the ridgeline to the northeast, then descends slightly to a small saddle. Soon the track begins another series of eight switchbacks. Watch for fairy slipper orchids at the trailside as you climb. At

Green Canyon Way Trail 793A

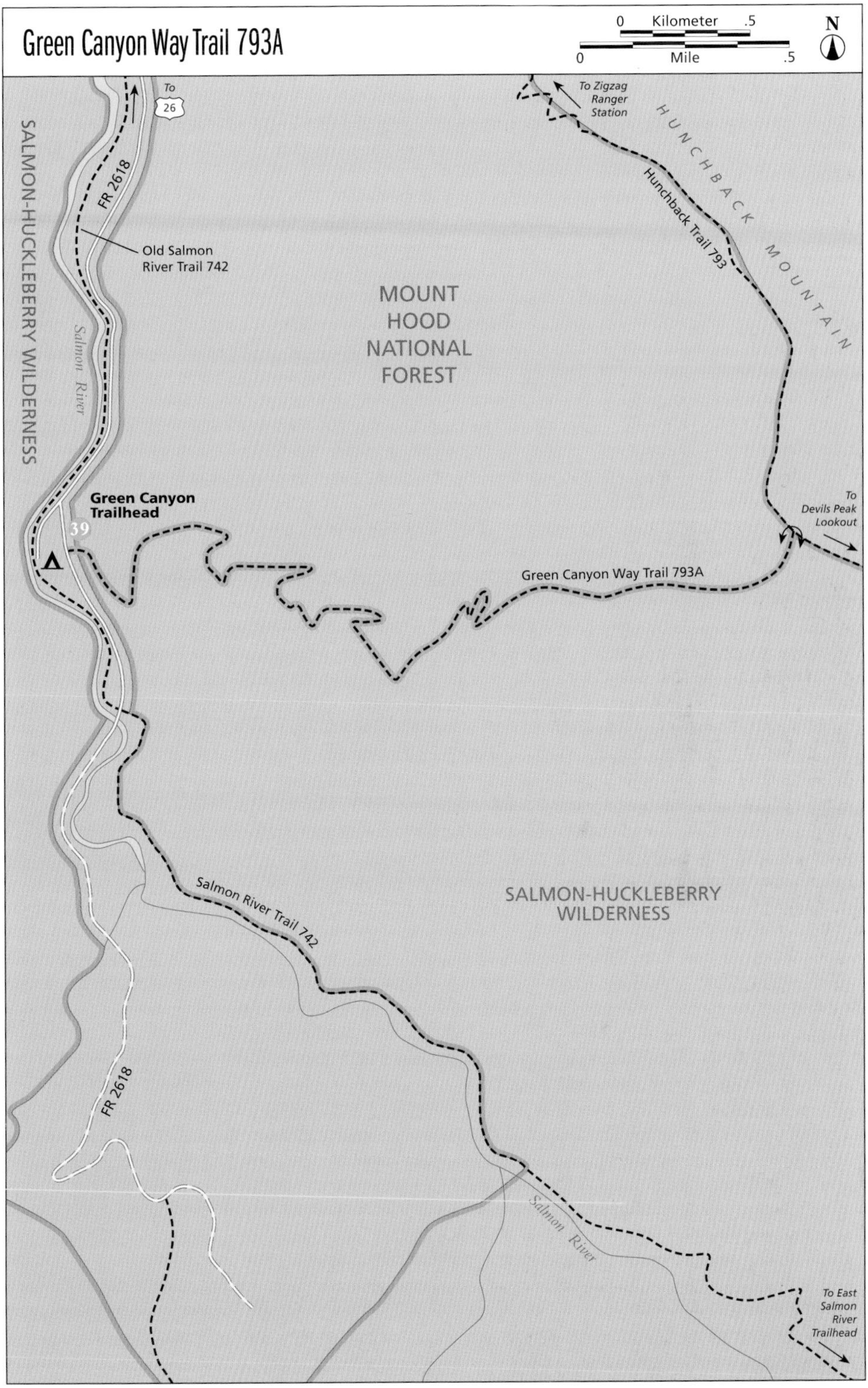

the eighth switchback, 2.9 miles from the trailhead at 3,650 feet elevation, there is an uphill side path to the right. This path leads 50 yards to a viewpoint atop a rocky outcropping. In early June this outcropping is a kaleidoscope of blooming penstemon, larkspur, rhododendron, and paintbrush. There are even a couple of wild rose bushes here that bloom at about the same time.

Above the path to the viewpoint, the main trail soon passes a patch of devil's club.

Devil's Club (*Oplopanax horridum*)

If you ever somehow end up in a patch of devil's club, you will understand how it got its common name. Devil's club can grow up to 15 feet tall, but it is usually less than 10. Its half-inch-long spines that cover the stems easily identify it. The stems don't branch heavily but are often crooked and tangled. Devil's club leaves resemble those of a maple on the top, but beneath they also have spines. The bright red shiny berries are eaten with gusto by bears; however, they are not considered edible for humans.

Devil's club was a plant of many uses to Native Americans. It was used medically to treat diverse ailments from arthritis and rheumatism to ulcers. Charcoal from burning devil's club was used for making face paint and tattoos. The wood was carved into special fishing lures.

Then the course continues its climb to the east, generally staying close to the ridgeline for 0.7 mile to the junction with the Hunchback Trail 793, atop Hunchback Mountain. There is no sign marking this junction at present.

This junction at 4,020 feet elevation, 3.7 miles from the trailhead, is the end of Green Canyon Way. To the left along the Hunchback Mountain Trail, it's about 5.5

Green Tip:

Minimize the use and impact of fires. Use designated fire spots or existing fire rings (if permitted). When building fires, use small sticks (less than 1.5 inches in diameter) that you find on the ground. Keep your fire small, burn it to ash, put it out completely, and scatter the cool ashes. If you can, it's best to avoid making a fire at all.

miles to the Zigzag Ranger Station in the town of Zigzag. To the right it's 2.5 miles to the Devils Peak Lookout and the junction with the Cool Creek Trail. Return as you came or see the options below for a one-way shuttle hike.

MILES AND DIRECTIONS

0.0 Begin at the Green Canyon Trailhead. GPS 45 16.975N 121 56.504W.

2.9 Arrive at the side path to a viewpoint.

3.7 Turn around at the junction with the Hunchback Trail 793. GPS 45 17.039N 121 54.400W.

7.4 Return to the Green Canyon Trailhead. GPS 45 16.975N 121 56.504W.

Options: If you can arrange a car shuttle, you could descend via the Hunchback Mountain Trail to the Zigzag Ranger Station. To reach the ranger station by car, first go back the way you came to the junction with US 26. Turn right on US 26 and go a short distance to the ranger station, which will be on the right.

40

Salmon River Trail 742

Hike into the heart of the Salmon-Huckleberry Wilderness along the forested slope of the Salmon River Canyon. Old-growth forest, flowers, and scattered viewpoints greet the hiker walking along this generally easy route.

Start: West Salmon River Trailhead
Distance/type of hike: 9.6-mile out-and-back day hike or backpack
Approximate hiking time: 4.5 hours
Difficulty: Easy to moderate. Most of the trail is smooth but there are a few steep grades and rocky spots.
Best season: April through November
Canine compatibility and other trail users: Hikers only; restrained dogs
Fees and permits: Northwest Forest Pass. A Salmon-Huckleberry Wilderness Permit is required between May 15 and October 15.
Maps: *Rhododendron* and *High Rock* USGS 7½ minute quads; USDA Forest Service *Zigzag Ranger District;* Adventure Maps Inc. *Mt. Hood/NW Oregon Trail Map;* National Geographic Oregon topo on CD-ROM Disk 4; DeLorme's *Oregon Atlas and Gazetteer,* p. 62, B1
Trail contacts: USDA Forest Service, Zigzag Ranger District, 70220 East Highway 26, Zigzag, OR 97049; (503) 622-3191; www.fs.fed.us/r6/mthood

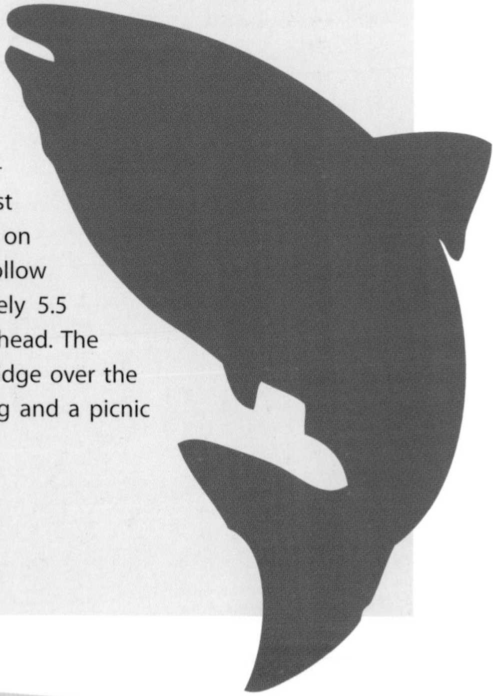

Finding the trailhead:
From Portland, drive east on U.S. Highway 26 for 41.9 miles (0.9 mile past Milepost 41), then turn right (south) on the Salmon River Road (FR 2618). Follow the Salmon River Road approximately 5.5 miles to the West Salmon River Trailhead. The trailhead is just before crossing a bridge over the Salmon River. There is ample parking and a picnic table at the trailhead.

THE HIKE

From the trailhead at 1,600 feet elevation, the Salmon River Trail 742 leads southeasterly. The track heads upstream along the cold, clear Salmon River through a forest of red alder, western red cedar, Douglas fir, and vine maple, with a few rose bushes to add a splash of pink. Paintbrush and rhododendron crowd the trailside and stonecrop sprouts from the rocky outcrops.

The course goes through a rock notch a quarter mile from the trailhead. A path to the right leads to a campsite 0.6 mile from the trailhead, as the trail passes through beautiful old-growth forest. At 1.1 miles the route crosses a small wooden footbridge and in another 0.3 mile it crosses another footbridge, this one with a handrail. Between the bridges another path to the right leads to a campsite next to the river.

Shortly there will be a nice campsite below the trail to the right, next to the river. A sign here points to the left, to a "toilet area." The route passes a couple more campsites then crosses a single log bridge with a handrail on one side. Shortly after crossing the bridge, the track reaches the wilderness registration box, where you can obtain your wilderness permit. Just past the registration box, 2 miles from the

Vine maple

Salmon River Trail 742

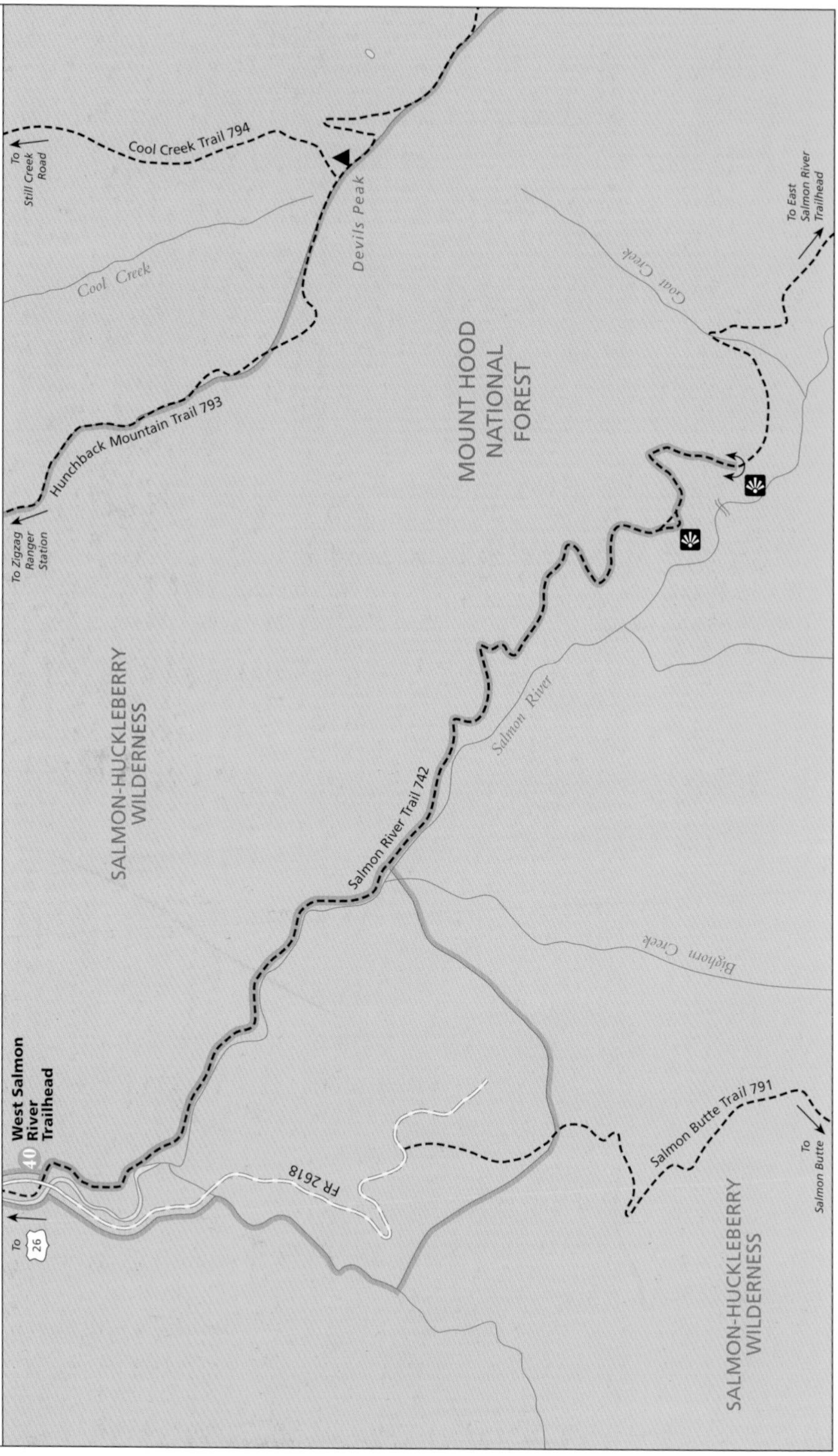

trailhead, you will enter the Salmon-Huckleberry Wilderness. The elevation at the wilderness boundary is 1,760 feet.

In the wilderness the route passes a couple more campsites, then begins to climb gently. The trail flattens again at slightly over 1,900 feet elevation, 0.7 mile after passing the wilderness boundary. You are now well above the river. The tread soon climbs gently again, after crossing a small stream in a side draw. The trail forks 1.6 miles past the wilderness boundary, at the edge of an open slope. The trail to the left stays in the woods, crosses a small ridge, and rejoins the right fork in about a quarter mile. If you don't like traversing a fairly steep open slope, take the trail to the left. But if you would like a better view, the right fork is the one to take. A few yards ahead on the right fork, there is a viewpoint overlooking Final Falls.

Past the viewpoint the route traverses the open slope, then reenters the woods, makes a switchback, and rejoins the path that crosses the small ridge. There will be another path to the right 0.2 mile farther along. This path leads 30 yards to a viewpoint with a limited view but within earshot of the falls in the river below. Past the path the trail cuts far back into a side draw and crosses a creek. The route emerges from the side draw in another 0.3 mile, where there is a path to the right to another viewpoint. At the junction with this path, there is a possible dry campsite, at 2,420 feet elevation. This viewpoint, 4.8 miles from the trailhead, makes a

Final Falls

good turnaround point. There are no trails leading down to any of the falls. To continue on the Salmon River Trail see the options below.

MILES AND DIRECTIONS

0.0 Begin at the West Salmon River Trailhead. GPS 45 16.672N 121 56.383W.

2.0 Arrive at the wilderness boundary. GPS 45 15.732N 121 55.165W.

3.7 Arrive at the viewpoint overlooking Final Falls.

4.8 Turn around at the viewpoint. GPS 45 14.785N 121 53.730W.

9.6 Return to the West Salmon River Trailhead. GPS 45 16.672N 121 56.383W.

Options: If you have arranged a car shuttle and time and energy permit, you can continue another 9.5 miles to the East Salmon River Trailhead, making this a 14.3-mile one-way hike. The USDA Forest Service *Zigzag Ranger District* map covers the car shuttle route, as does the National Geographic Oregon topo on CD-ROM Disk 4. The GPS coordinates at the East Salmon River Trailhead are 45 13.590N 121 46.408W. The roads to the East Trailhead may not be snow-free until mid-June some years.

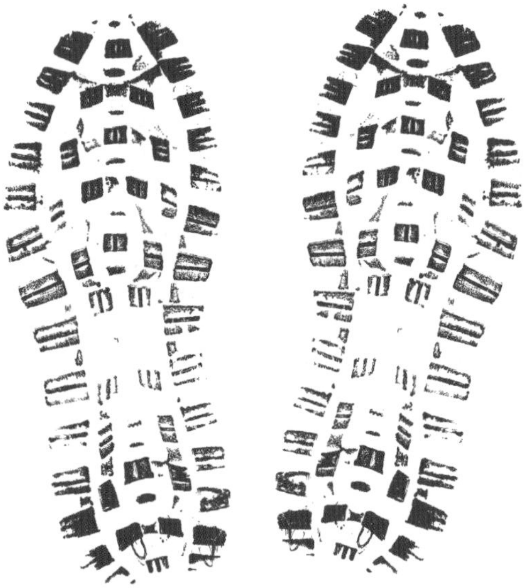

41

Mirror Lake—
Tom Dick and Harry Mountain Trail 664

Hike to Mirror Lake and possibly camp overnight. Then you can follow the often rhododendron-lined route to the summit of Tom Dick and Harry Mountain, and arguably the best view of the south side of Mount Hood. Once on the summit, be sure to allow plenty of time for enjoying the view and taking photos. Mounts Jefferson, Adams, Rainier and St. Helens are also in view from the summit on clear days.

Start: Mirror Lake Trailhead
Distance/type of hike: 6.6-mile out-and-back day hike or backpack
Approximate hiking time: 4 hours
Difficulty: Moderate
Best season: Late June through September
Canine compatibility and other trail users: Restrained dogs; no other stock or mountain bikes
Fees and permits: Northwest Forest Pass
Maps: USGS *Government Camp* 7½-min. quad; Adventure Maps Inc. *Mt. Hood/NW Oregon Trail Map;* USDA Forest Service *Zigzag Ranger District;* National Geographic Oregon CD-ROM Disk 4; DeLorme's *Oregon Atlas and Gazetteer,* p. 62, B2.
Trail contacts: USDA Forest Service, Zigzag Ranger District, 70220 East Highway 26, Zigzag, OR 97049; (503) 622-3191; www.fs.fed.us/r6/mthood
Special considerations: This trail, especially up to Mirror Lake, is very heavily used.

Finding the trailhead:
Drive east from Portland on U.S. Highway 26 for slightly over 51 miles. The Mirror Lake Trailhead and a large roadside parking area will be on your right. The elevation at the trailhead is 3,440 feet.

41

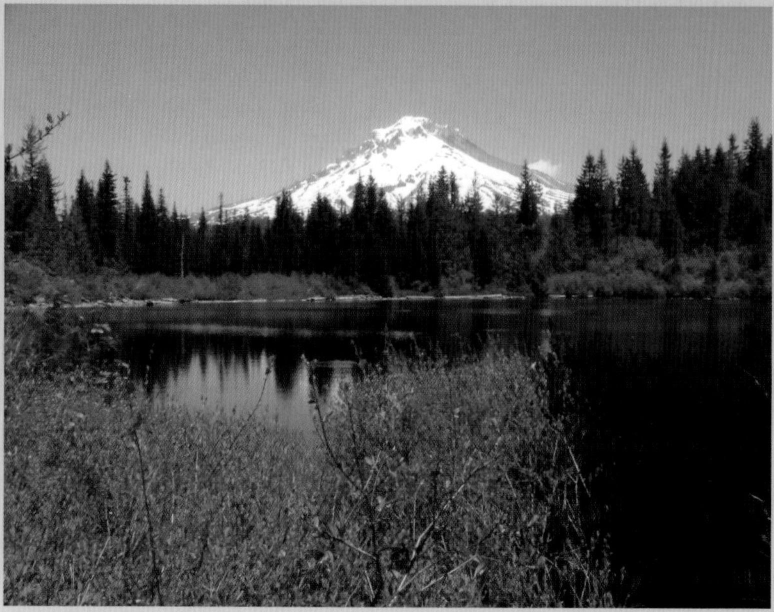

Mount Hood over Mirror Lake

THE HIKE

As you leave the trailhead, the Mirror Lake Trail crosses a footbridge, over the rhododendron and alder-lined bubbling waters of Camp Creek. As you enter the woods on the south side of the creek, the wide, smooth tread passes a signboard and a picnic table. Shortly there will be a path to the right. Bear left here, staying on the main trail, and soon cross another footbridge.

Past the second footbridge the woods soon thins out. Rhododendrons now form the woodland understory—in places it seems as though the route had been cut through a jungle of them. The track crosses a talus slope 0.5 mile from the trailhead. Watch and listen for pikas here. After crossing the talus, the course makes a switchback and recrosses the rocky slope.

At 4,100 feet elevation, 1.4 miles from the trailhead, you will reach the first junction with the Mirror Lake Loop Trail. To the left the loop trail follows the shoreline of Mirror Lake for 0.4 mile to rejoin the main trail 0.1 mile ahead. To continue toward Tom Dick and Harry Mountain, bear right at the junction. In a few yards there will be a path to the right, which leads to some campsites. Huckleberry bushes line the trail, between, the bushes, penstemon, and beargrass cover the volcanic soil, and Mirror Lake is in view to the left.

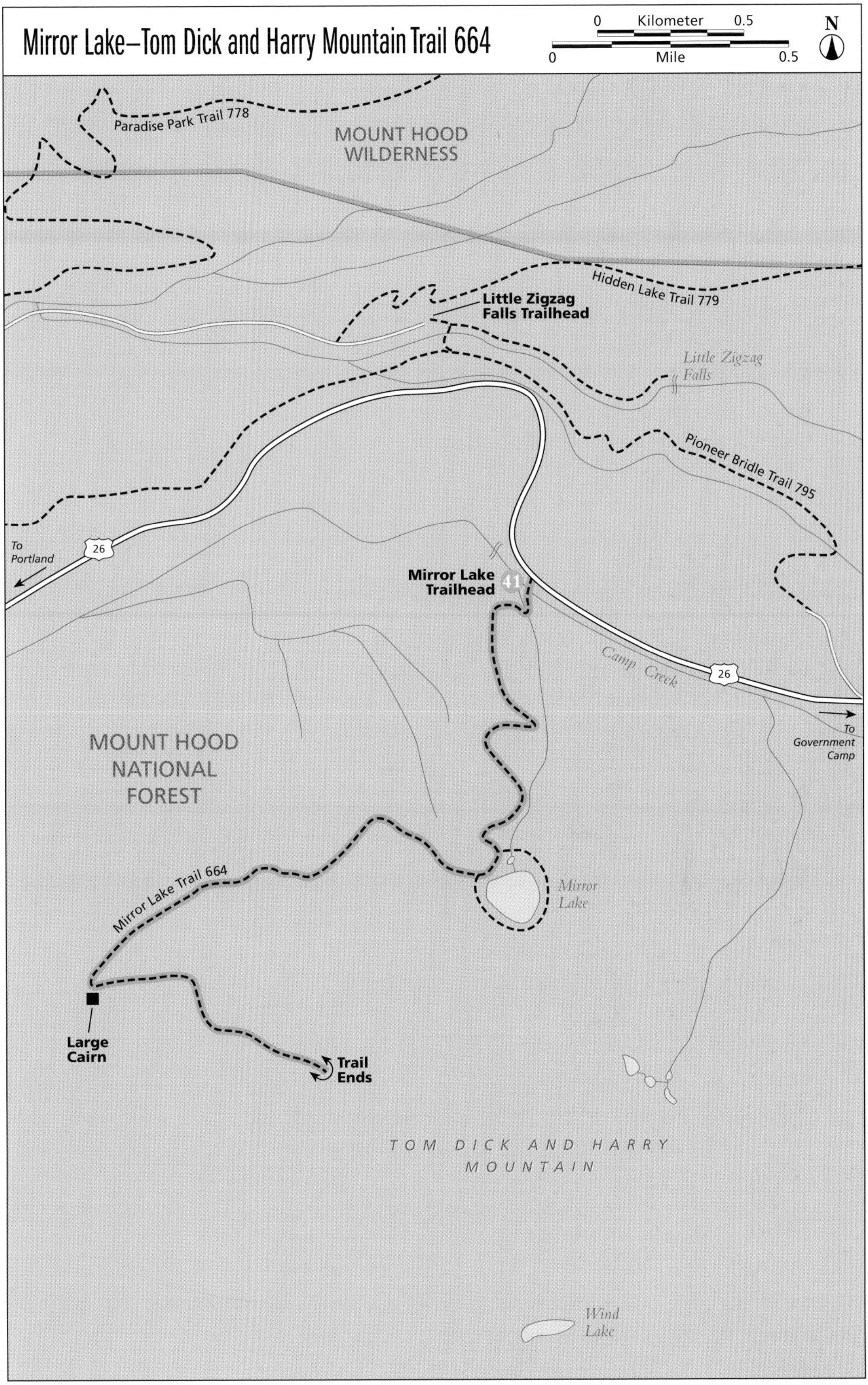
Mirror Lake–Tom Dick and Harry Mountain Trail 664
0 Kilometer 0.5
0 Mile 0.5
N
Paradise Park Trail 778
MOUNT HOOD WILDERNESS
Hidden Lake Trail 779
Little Zigzag Falls Trailhead
Little Zigzag Falls
Pioneer Bridle Trail 795
To Portland
26
Mirror Lake Trailhead
41
Camp Creek
To Government Camp
MOUNT HOOD NATIONAL FOREST
Mirror Lake Trail 664
Mirror Lake
Large Cairn
Trail Ends
TOM DICK AND HARRY MOUNTAIN
Wind Lake

At the second junction with the Mirror Lake Loop, 1.5 miles from the trailhead, bear right and begin the climb of Tom Dick and Harry Mountain. Above the lake the trail becomes narrower and somewhat rougher. Soon the ice-clad, craggy summit of Mount Hood is in view to the right through the trees. The route soon crosses a talus slope. The course reaches a ridgeline, at a little over 4,500 feet elevation, 1.1 miles from the second junction with the Mirror Lake Loop. Here the trail makes a switchback to the left next to a huge rock cairn.

On the ridgeline the trail leads east, climbing gently but steadily. Lodgepole pine (*Pinus contorta*), becomes the dominant tree along this drier ridge. The route steepens 0.4 mile after passing the large cairn. In another quarter mile the trail leaves the timber and climbs the last few feet to its end, at 4,920 feet elevation, on the rocky ridgeline of Tom Dick and Harry Mountain.

This is the place to rest and take in the 360-degree view. To the south the 10,497-foot-high pinnacle of Mount Jefferson stands high above the crest of the Cascade Range. To the northwest over the green hills is Mount St. Helens. To the right of St. Helens, far in the distance, the glacier-covered summit of 14,408-foot-high Mount Rainier floats above the lesser peaks. To the north, just to the right of Mount Rainier is the bulky form of 12,276-foot-high Mount Adams. And close by to the northeast is Mount Hood at 11,235 feet high, dominating the view over the town of Government Camp. Once you have spent the time to enjoy this fantastically beautiful spot, return to the Mirror Lake Trailhead as you came.

MILES AND DIRECTIONS

0.0 Begin at the Mirror Lake Trailhead. GPS 45 18.395N 121 47.489W.

1.4 Bear right at the first junction with the Mirror Lake Loop. GPS 45 17.912N 121 47.580W.

3.3 Turn around at the summit of Tom, Dick and Harry Mountain. GPS 45 17.570N 121 48.035 W.

6.6 Return to the Mirror Lake Trailhead. GPS 45 18.395N 121 47.489W.

Options: On the return trip take the time to circle Mirror Lake on the Mirror Lake Loop Trail. It will add only 0.3 mile to the hike.

Honorable Mentions

Cast Creek Trail 775

This is a strenuous 7.4-mile out-and-back hike on the northern side of Zigzag Mountain, to a beautiful sub-alpine lake that abounds with brook trout. To reach the trailhead, follow Oregon Route 26 east from Portland for 42 miles to Zigzag. Then turn left and head north on East Lolo Pass Road (Forest Road 18) for 4.2 miles to the junction with Forest Road 1825. Turn right on FR 1825 and follow it 1.2 miles to the junction with Forest Road 380. Turn right on FR 380 and follow it for 0.6 mile, passing Riley Horse Camp to the Cast Creek Trailhead, GPS 45 22.832N 121 51.299W.

Trail contact: USDA Forest Service, Zigzag Ranger District, 70220 East Highway 26, Zigzag, OR 97049; (503) 622-3191; www.fs.fed.us/r6/mthood

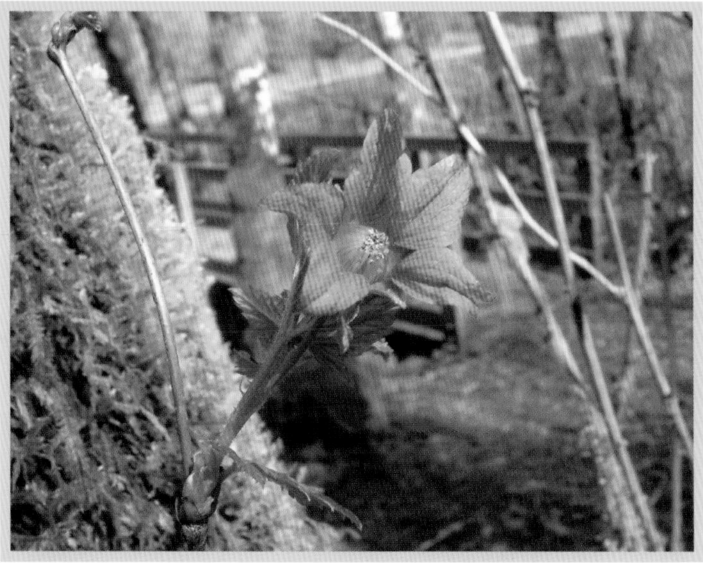

Salmonberry

Mountaineer Trail 798

The first 0.7 mile of this moderate-to-strenuous 2.8-mile loop hike to Silcox Hut and back, above Timberline Lodge, is the same as the Zigzag Mountain Trail hike. Start at Timberline Lodge and proceed 0.7 mile to the junction with the Pacific Crest Trail.

Then make the rest of the loop beneath the majestic south slope of Mount Hood, through alpine rock gardens that are often covered with flowers.

Trail contact: USDA Forest Service, Zigzag Ranger District, 70220 East Highway 26, Zigzag, OR 97049; (503) 622-3191; www.fs.fed.us/r6/mthood

Lost Creek Nature Trail

This very easy, short, paved nature trail is next to Lost Creek Campground. The trail is a good one to take with small children. Its total length is only about 0.75 mile, including a side trip to the beaver pond, and it is nearly flat. This trail is wheelchair accessible. To reach the Lost Creek Nature Trail from Zigzag, follow Lolo Pass Road north for 4.2 miles to junction with Forest Road 1825. Turn right on FR 1825 and follow it for 2.5 miles to Lost Creek Campground. Instead of entering the campground, go straight ahead on what becomes Forest Road 109 for 1.7 more miles to where the road ends at the trailhead (elevation 2,650 feet).

Trail contact: USDA Forest Service, Zigzag Ranger District, 70220 East Highway 26, Zigzag, OR 97049; (503) 622-3191; www.fs.fed.us/r6/mthood

Mazama Trail 625

This 7.6-mile round-trip hike starts at the new Mazama Trailhead and goes up Cathedral Ridge to the Timberline Trail and back. To reach the trailhead from Zigzag, follow the East Lolo Pass Road Forest Road 18 for 10.6 miles to Lolo Pass. Turn right at the pass and leave the pavement on Forest Road 1810. Follow FR 1810 for 5.4 miles then turn right on Forest Road 1811. Follow FR 1811 for 2.4 miles to the trailhead.

Trail contact: USDA Forest Service, Hood River Ranger District, 6780 Highway 35, Mount Hood–Parkdale, OR 97041; (541) 352-6002 or (503) 666-0701

Glossary

alp A mountainside meadow

avalanche A snow and/or ice slide. An avalanche may also include large amounts of other material such as rock and forest debris.

cairn A stack or pile of rocks that marks the trail or route

cirque A bowl-shaped area where a glacier has eaten its way into a mountain slope, then melted. A cirque is formed at the head of a glacier.

cornice A wind-deposited snowdrift on the lee side of a ridgeline. Cornices are often overhanging and can be very unstable. They should be avoided, both above and below, when hiking and especially when skiing.

exposure In climbing, the amount of exposure refers to the possibility of falling farther than just to the ground at your feet. In a highly exposed spot, it would be possible to fall several tens to several thousands of feet.

fire scars Charred bark, and in some cases wood, on the trunks of living trees, generally caused by a long-ago forest fire

FR Forest Road

GPS Global Positioning System

lava flow A stream of molten rock flowing from a volcano, or a stream of rock after it has cooled and hardened

mixed forest, mixed woods A forest made up of several species of trees

notch Small pass on ridgeline, often between rock outcroppings. It is smaller than a saddle.

old-growth forest Forest that has never been logged and has not been burned in a fire hot enough to kill the mature trees in the last one hundred years

OR Oregon highway or state route; used preceding the route number, for example, OR 18

pumice The solidified froth of volcanic rock. Pumice is a high-silica-content, light-colored rock that is light enough to float.

saddle A low point on a ridge, usually with a gentle slope. A saddle is larger than a notch.

second-growth forest Forest that was logged many years ago and has regrown to medium-size timber

talus, talus slope A slope covered with large rocks or boulders

true fir Genus *Abies*. For the purposes of this book: grand fir, noble fir, subalpine fir, and Pacific silver fir; does not include the Douglas fir, a completely different species

understory Shrubs and small trees growing, usually shaded, beneath the forest canopy

US United States highway

WA Washington highway or state route; used preceding the route number, for example, WA 503

Index

About the Author

A native of the Northwest, Fred Barstad has spent a large part of the last forty-five years hiking, climbing, skiing, and snowshoeing in the region's canyons, deserts, and mountains. He has climbed most of the Cascades volcanoes, including more than sixty summit climbs of Mount Hood, as well as Mount McKinley in Alaska and the Mexican volcanoes.

Growing up in the Willamette Valley, Fred became very familiar with the area covered by *Best Hikes Near Portland* at an early age. In fact, one of the hikes covered here was only a mile from his childhood home. This is Fred's tenth FalconGuide, all of them covering areas in Oregon, Washington, and Idaho. Fred lives in Enterprise, Oregon, at the base of the Wallowa Mountains, where he continues to enjoy his passion for the outdoors.

Visit the premier outdoor online community ...
FALCON GUIDES®
LOGIN | CREATE AN ACCOUNT
Search
HOME
ABOUT US
CONTACT US
BOOKS
BLOGS
PHOTOS
TRAIL FINDER
4 of 6
The Art of Cycling
Bicycling In Traffic
Part one: Beyond the Vehicular Cycling Principle
HIKING WITH KIDS
HAPPY TRAILS Hiking in the Great Outdoors is a simple gift we all can give our children, grandchildren, and young friends. Unlike playing music, writing poetry, painting pictures, or other activities that also can fill your soul, hiking does not require any special skill. All you need to do is put one foot in front of the other in the outdoors, repeatedly. And breathe deeply.
LEARN MORE
FEATURED NEW BOOK
SCAVENGER HIKE ADVENTURES: GREAT SMOKY MOUNTAINS NATIONAL PARK
A Totally New Interactive Hiking Guide
Introducing a brand new genre of hiking guide. Readers follow clues to find over 200 hidden natural and historic treasures on as many as 14 easy, moderate, and extreme hikes national parks. Follow the clues and find such things as a tree clawed open by a bear searching for food, an ancient Indian footpath, the remains of an old Model T Ford deep in the forest, and over 200 other unusual treasures.
CLICK HERE TO FIND OUT MORE
RECENT BLOG POSTS
A Dry River
Stat-mongering -- Look Out!
Lizard Man
Tropical Tip of Texas
Lions And Snakes and Bears...Oh My! "Don's PCT Update"
Bikin' in C'ville
The Red Store
Journey to Idyllwild
A Spring Quandary
Whew!! Rocky Mountain book is printed I'm going camping!!
more
EXPERT BLOGS
Arrowleaf Balsamroot—Another
By: Bert Gildart
Splitter camps #2
By: Katie Brown
Splitter camp
By: Katie Brown
Beth Rodden
Dean Potter
Jason Kehl
Josh Wharton
Steph Davis
outfit your mind
falcon.com